JUSTICE AND MERCY IN PIERS PLOWMAN:
A READING OF THE B TEXT VISIO

Justice and Mercy in Piers Plowman
A Reading of the B Text Visio

MYRA STOKES

CROOM HELM
London & Canberra

©1984 Myra Stokes
Croom Helm Ltd, Provident House, Burrell Row,
Beckenham, Kent BR3 1AT
Croom Helm Australia, PO Box 391, Manuka,
ACT 2603, Australia

British Library Cataloguing in Publication Data

Stokes, Myra
   Justice and mercy in Piers Plowman.
   1. Langland, William. Piers Plowman.
   I. Title
   821'.1   PR2015
   ISBN 0-7099-2354-6

Printed in Great Britain by Biddles Ltd, Guildford, Surrey

CONTENTS

ACKNOWLEDGEMENTS

To the labours of past and present editors of *Piers Plowman*, who have done so much to make this long and difficult poem accessible to the would-be literary critic, I naturally owe more than the foot-notes can adequately acknowledge. My greatest debt, however, is to my colleagues, Professor J.A. Burrow, Mr. I.B. Bishop, and Dr. A.J. Minnis, who have all been quite uncommonly generous with their time, ideas, and suggestions, and whose constant assistance, encouragement, and patience have been invaluable. I would also like to thank Mrs. Jan Tarling for the painstaking care and industry she devoted to the extremely exacting task of typing up the MS of this book for camera-copy.

Myra Stokes
Bristol

CHAPTER I

JUSTICE, MERCY, AND LAW

Piers Plowman and its Context: Contemporary Concepts of Justice and Law

I: *Justice*

That law, justice, government are issues frequently to the fore in *Piers Plowman* is a fact that has not gone unnoticed by critics.[1] These were matters more sacred to the medieval mind than they perhaps are today, and ones which played a more central and crucial rôle in theology. Justice, whose emblem was the scales, was thought to operate on a first principle of equal balance, exactly measured equivalence between desert and reward: equity, in fact. Underlying all law, written, unwritten, and divine, it was claimed, lay the principle of 'do as you would be done by', for as you have sown so shall you reap. This was "the golden rule" of justice, available even to pagans, not specific to particular cultures or theologies, but known innately, revealed by "resoun and moral philosophie", the God-given faculties by which human nature was capable of discerning right from wrong, unaided by written laws or the revelations of the Christian faith. It was therefore described as "the law of nature", the basis of that justice it is connatural to man to observe.[2] God being the author of nature, it had, therefore, divine sanction, and even law-givers were obliged to obey it; it is, consequently, announced by an angel in the Prologue to Langland's poem, as a principle of justice binding on the king himself and prior to the specific laws promulgated by him in his own particular kingdom: *'Qualia vis metere, talia grana sere'* (sow such grain as you hope to reap).[3]

The principle of equivalence thus conceived of as essential to justice (like for like, *quid pro quo*, 'tit for tat' in the modern parlance, 'tooth for tooth' in the ancient) entailed a corresponding emphasis on rewards and punishments: for it is by those means that good reaps good, and bad reaps bad, by which do-well has well and do-evil has evil, as Langland puts it (VII.112-3). God being justice itself would ensure that no ill and no good would remain unbalanced in His eternal scales by its answering reward or punishment. There would be,

ultimately, no ill-doing without penalty, or good
without guerdon: *non ay pecado sin pena nin bien
sin galardon* could be repeated as a by-word by the
Spanish poet Juan Ruiz.[4] Perhaps in response to
the notorious injustices committed by the courts of
this world, where Mede held sway, victimizing the
innocent and buying exemption for the guilty (she
"leteth passe prisoners and paieth for hem ofte ...
And taketh the trewe bi the top and tieth hym
faste", III.137-40), medieval piety clung tenac-
iously to the absoluteness of "the justice of God,
whose justice is an everlasting justice, and His law
is equity ... allotting to each that which belongs
to him".[5] Apparent miscarriages were temporary;
all men would eventually have exactly remeasured
unto them the well or ill they had done. It was in
this that God's justice essentially consisted: "His
ri3twisnes (is seen) in harde punischynge of synne,
His sobfastnes in trewe rewardynge of gode werkes";
He "quyte3 vchon as hys desserte", "rewardeth ryht
as men deserveth: *reddet unicuique iuxta opera
sua*"[6]. This immutable and rigorous equity is not
infrequently alluded to by Shakespeare in lines
such as "Like doth quit like, and measure still for
measure" (*Measure for Measure*, V.i.414), and
"Wrong hath but wrong, and blame the due of blame"
(*Richard III*, V.i.29). And the author of
perhaps the greatest poem of the entire Middle
Ages, *La Divina Commedia*, declared that its theme
was precisely the equity of divine retribution:
"the subject is man, as by good or ill deserts, in
the exercise of the freedom of his choice, he
becomes liable to rewarding or punishing justice".[7]

And as with the King of kings, so (ideally)
with the temporal rulers whose principle responsibility it was to uphold His justice on earth. The
king was regarded as a "likeness on earth of the
divine majesty", since he held an office "instituted by God for the punishment of evil-doers and
the reward of good men". Justice was the chief
attribute of the King of heaven, and the earthly
king who represents Him is therefore most truly a
king "when he metes out reward to virtue and
punishment to vice with a just and equal balance".[8]
Princes are "þe mynystris of god to do ry3twisnesse
and bere doun wronges and synne".[9] The secular
political power was ordained by God for the maintenance of justice or righteousness. The king, as
the regent of God's majesty (*vicaris summi regis*),
should do all in his power to imitate the equity of
divine justice in giving like for like - ill for ill,

and well for well. He undertook to do so in his corona-
tion oath, in which he pledged himself to the reward
of the righteous, and the punishment of the evil
(*vindictam malefactorum*).[10] When he so ruled, he ruled
indeed 'like God', creating a likeness on earth of the
divine *imperium* and the exact equity on which it was
founded. The basis of both the *ius divinum* and the *ius
regale* was the just payment of all works, good or ill, so
that all deeds found the return due them in equity:

> Most sacred vertue she (ie Justice) of all the rest,
> Resembling God in his imperiall might;
> Whose soveraine powre is herein most exprest,
> That both to good and bad he dealeth right,
> And all his workes with Iustice hath bedight.
> That powre he also doth to Princes lend,
> And makes them like himselfe in glorious sight,
> To sit in his own seate, his cause to end,
> And rule his people right, as he doth recommend.[11]

This notion of justice as due and exact repayment
was of central importance in the Middle Ages. It
influenced not only their theological, political and
social, but also their economic thinking. Medieval
economic theory was based on the concept of 'the just
price'. All goods and services had an exactly ascertain-
able value for which they could properly be exchanged.
A livelihood from labour or trade was morally blame-
less so long as it observed the principles of "mesurable hire", and remained "a permutacion apertly, a
penyworth for another" (III.256-8). To take more or
less was to create inequilibrium in the scales of justice. It is according to this principle that Conscience
distinguishes between a livelihood honestly earned,
in which repayment is strictly "mesurable" with the
goods or services rendered, and the immoral receipt
of "mede mesureless" (III.246). A just life in socio-
economic terms observes the principle of 'the just
price'. It was this principle that made usury a
capital offence throughout the Middle Ages: the interest
on the loan had no counterbalance, and was therefore
unjust, an offence against the measure and equilibrium
of justice.[12]

And as the *maintenance* of justice by the kings of
earth and heaven consisted in giving to the good what
they had owing to them, and to the bad what they had coming
to them, so the *observance* of justice consisted also in
giving to all their due. That virtue which we today call
honesty or integrity was known in medieval Latin as
iustitia, and in the vernacular as "rightwisnes", "(good)
faith" or "truth".[13] It consisted precisely in giving

3

to all their due, doing by them what one owed (*debet*)
it to them to do. The notion of 'debt' was fundamental to the medieval definition of *iustitia* or
'truth'. And here again one can see the influence of
the paramount importance of equilibrium in the scales
of justice: a just or true man was one who balanced
his books, left no payments outstanding. Cicero had
defined the *iustus* as one who apportions to each man
his own; and Ambrose had repeated his *dictum*, describing justice as giving to each his due. And this -
reddere debitum unicuique - became the standard and universally accepted definition, repeated by Aquinas and
other prominent theologians.[14] The jurist Fortescue
repeats it as *Iustitia unicuique tribuit quod suum est.*[15]
It was a truism, and could be repeated as such by,
for instance, Robert of Basevorn, in his *Forma
Praedicandi* - where the just man who renders to each
his due, pays his debts to God, to his neighbour, and
to himself, is offered as an example of a common
theme susceptible of division and amplification according to the 'art of preaching' the treatise aims to
expound.[16] How central to the concept of justice
were the notions of 'debt' and 'owing' can be seen
from the occurrence of the words in, for instance,
John of Salisbury's account of the Emperor Trajan and
the widow, the classic *exemplum* of zeal for justice; to
Trajan's promise that, should he not return from his
expedition, his successor will right her wrongs, the
widow replies: "It is thou who *owest* this thing ... it
is fraud for one not to render that which he *owes* ...
thy *debt* will not be discharged by the justice which
another does; well for thy successor if he discharge his own *debts*!"[17]

One's 'duty' lies in payment of one's 'debts',
literal and moral, to others. The Latin *debet* means
both 'owes' and 'ought', which are etymologically
related words. The connection between them was more
apparent in Middle than in Modern English, since the
two words had not then yet separated into two distinct
forms with two different meanings. They were more
interchangeable, as can be seen from the definition
of justice given in the *Lay Folks' Catechism* -

> That is to yheld to al men that we augh tham,
> For to do til ilk man that us augh to do

> (418-9)

- or by Hilton ("to ȝelden to ilk a þinge þat it
owiþ to have", where "owiþ" means both 'is owing'
and 'ought').[18]

Perhaps the clearest idea of what this virtue

involved is to be found in the exposition of it given by Aquinas in his *Summa Theologica*. It is "an abiding will to give every man his due"; he is defrauded of that due if he is assaulted, robbed, cuckolded, or slandered - for what is due him must also be considered with respect to persons, things, or dignities related to him. There are negative and positive aspects to justice: it forbids any injury which may rob a man of his due, and demands payment of the respect and consideration due him as a fellow human-being. Under justice fall restitution, religion, devotions, prayer, divine worship, sacrifice, offerings, performance of vows and oaths, natural affection, obedience, gratitude, vengeance, truthfulness, friendliness or affability, liberality, and equity. Offences against it include respecting of persons, homicide, mutilation, theft, contumely, detraction, mischief-making, cursing, fraudulent dealing in buying and selling, usury, idolatry, superstition, sacrilege, perjury, simony, ingratitude, lying, hypocrisy, boasting, flattery, quarrelsomeness, covetousness. As will be apparent, 'due' is interpreted as applying to God as well as man, and devotion and religion are therefore 'due' from one; and the word is interpreted in a moral as well as a legal and financial sense, and filial piety, gratitude, truthfulness, liberality, and affability are all 'due' in justice. The behaviour described would probably be referred to today as consideration, respect, integrity; the Middle Ages regarded it as paying one's debts to God, one's parents, and one's fellow-men, giving them what was 'owed' them, and so justice. All the above virtues relate to justice, because, Aquinus explains, they prevent inequilibrium in human affairs. Justice ensures that others 'weigh equally' with oneself, and that in all respects there is rendered them their due "according to equality".[19] It included even almsgiving, which we might well view as going beyond what strict justice requires, and so a function of generosity. But in the medieval view God had ordained an overall equilibrium between the totality of means available for sustaining life and the totality of human needs. The rich were merely trustees of wealth, charged with the duty of distributing it equitably according to needs. To give to others from one's own superfluity was not, therefore, to go beyond justice, but to perform it - it was a debt owed in justice to others who had needs still unsatisfied; the principle is alluded to in Lear's admonition to "pomp" to "shake the superflux to (the poor), And show the heavens more just" (*King Lear*, III.iv.35-6). Acquisition or retention beyond one's own needs was a kind of robbery, unjustly depriving others of what was due theirs.[20]

There was, of course, Biblical authority for the profound moral significance that thus became attached to the concept of debt-paying. "The wicked borroweth, and payeth not again" (Psalms 37:21), and, of course, *Redde quod debes* ('Pay what thou owest', Mt:18:28). Langland makes of the latter a crucial text, and it is one that encapsulates the essence of justice as the Middle Ages understood it.[21] As quoted in the poem, it refers in context primarily to restitution of what has been wrongfully acquired from others and is thus 'owed' them. But the debt-paying definition of justice underlies nearly all Langland's social and moral thinking, as has been observed.[22] His insistence that deeds should meet with their due rewards and punishments, both earthly and divine, that wrong must be punished (Passus IV), that the labourer is worthy of his hire (*"Dignus est operarius* his hire to have", II.123), on earth and in heaven, that one must reap as one sows, in socio-economic (Passus VI) and in moral terms, his pre-occupation with the social injustice and inequity created by the rich not giving to the poor, his use of need as a proper 'measure' of consumption (I.13-39; XX.3ff), his objection to beggars who do not pay their way socially but "borwen everemo": all these are concerns arising from a deep commitment to the medieval conception of justice as founded on equilibium and balance - on strict retributive equity, on exact 'measure' of give to take, needs to consumption, effort to reward, and on payment of debts.

In fact, the whole subject of debt came to be fraught with a moral significance difficult to recapture. To be literally in debt was to be in a state to which there clung a peculiar degree of infamy. It signalled one had failed in the most obvious way to balance one's moral accounts: God's justice would not tolerate this, and somewhere somehow the score would be evened at one's expense. It is with anxious insistence that poor Hoccleve, for instance, whose salary was in more or less permanent arrears, brings his debts to the attention of his paymasters: "Thy dettes paie lest that thou be shent", he reminds himself, knowing that he must "heere or elles where Rekne of my dettes and of hem answere". Payment of debts was so universally acknowledged to be a prime moral imperative that the notion could be used semi-seriously, with a casual-

ness that indicates confidence the irony will not
be missed. Hoccleve can elsewhere comment of the
rather grim vengeance taken on a prostitute by a
young man she had tricked that, after all, he was
her "dettour" with regard to deceit, and must
therefore "qwyte" (repay) her.[23] Comic caricatures
of the willful wife play sarcastically on the
principle; their insubordination to their husbands,
giving as good as they get in blows and insults,
is an ironic payment of debts. "I shal not in thi
det Flyt of this flett", remarks Noah's wife before
returning the blow he had delivered her; and the
Wife of Bath can reflect with sardonic satisfaction
that she never failed to answer her husbands back:
"I ne owe hem nat a word that it nys quit".[24] And
the old definition of justice as that which pays its
debts still retains enough force even today to make
us aware of the moral significance of the declaration, "I believe in paying my debts"; and to make
even those not otherwise markedly scrupulous
peculiarly anxious and prompt to reimburse friends
for sums, however trivial, expended on their behalf,
as if not to do so would cast a particular moral
stigma on their character generally. In developing
the notion of debt, Langland is thus tapping something very basic in the human sense of fairness.
     To die in debt, in particular, was viewed as a most
grave misfortune or dereliction, presumably because
it appeared to be the literal equivalent of that
spiritual death in debt that consisted of going to
meet one's Maker with all one's sins yet on one's
head, *ie* unatoned. Consider the following passage
from *Henry V*:

> *Williams*: But if the cause be not good, the king
> himself hath a heavy reckoning to make; when all
> those legs and arms and heads, chopped off in a
> battle, shall join together at the latter day, and
> cry all, 'We died at such a place'; some swearing,
> some crying for a surgeon, some upon their wives
> left poor behind, some upon the debts they owe, some
> upon their children rawly left. I am afeard there
> are few die well that die in a battle.

(IV.i.141ff)

One would not today, I think, regard the fact that
one left behind one at death debts yet unpaid a
misfortune quite on a par with the others here
listed. But the speaker plainly does: the soul and

the good name is mutilated by it as efficaciously as the body by swords. The dying took especial care to balance their accounts, morally and literally. They took their last opportunity to pay their debts. Again, the notion was common enough to allow of ironic allusion. "Though I right now sholde make my testament", the Wife of Bath says, she leaves no scores unsettled with her husbands. Skelton in his "flyting" with Garnesche, promises his opponent, "I will nat dy in thy det".[25] But it is Shakespeare who, in *Richard III* (a play full of references to 'tooth for tooth' justice), puts into the mouth of the embittered Margaret the grimmest and pithiest of ironies on this matter; of the death of Edward IV, she comments (IV.iv. 21) that he "pays a dying debt" (meaning that, by the very fact of dying, he pays the debt for the death of her own son Edward).

All sorts of obligations were characterized in terms of debts. There was the sexual "dette of matrimony", or the 'King's debts', the fines, taxes, and "dutes" owed to the Crown.[26] Sin and crime, wrongdoing in secular and theological contexts, were both conceived of as 'debts' owed. The miscreant had borrowed from justice, and was in debt to it to the tune of whatever penalty it took to 'pay for ' the offence. In criminal contexts, the phrase 'paying one's debt to society' is still sometimes heard of the penal system. The same applied to sinners. God had His law, and a penalty was owed for breach of it if the scales of justice were to be restored to equilibrium: whenever we sin, "we renne into dette of peyne".[27] The confessional was essentially the machinery established by the Church for the satisfaction of God's justice. The "dette of synne"[28] was assessed in it, and the penances requisite as payment imposed by the confessor. It was not just a question of, *"Mea culpa*, I'm sorry, and won't do it again". One had to pay back - literally in the case of unjust gains, metaphorically or by compensatory self-deprivation in the form of penances in other cases. It was emphasized by even the most humane of theologians that "þe payn dettid for þe syn"[29] must be paid by performance of whatever penance the competent assessor should enjoin. God in his omniscience knew what fairness, *equitatem rei*, demanded, and any short-fall in repayment would be made up in Purgatory. The confessor, therefore, bore a heavy responsibility: he must know how to *equilibrare penam culpe* (weigh the penalty against the offence) as precisely as possible and must be very expert in the niceties of penitential law.[30]

The supreme day of justice, Judgment Day, was

likewise thought of as a great and final settlement
of accounts, a universal debt-paying. All would then
be required to 'render accounts' of the way they had
spent their money and their lives.[31] Those in debt to
justice would be forced to pay the penalty they owed.
God, for His part, would also pay His debts. Those
who had done good deeds on earth for His sake without
reward had remuneration 'owing' them. Hence Langland
can stress the risk run by those who are rewarded
(financially or otherwise) for their virtues on earth:
such will have no reward in heaven strictly 'due'
them. So those who are rewarded by public admiration
for alms-giving have "(their) hire here and (their)
heven als"; and priests who take monetary reward
"Taken hire mede here as Mathew us techeth: *Amen, amen,
receperunt mercedem suam*" (III.72,253-4). The same idea of
the reward of heaven being payment of a debt, and as
such only strictly 'owing' to such as have expended
what has as yet received no return payment, is found
in the *Ancrene Wisse*, with regard to charity and its remuneration in heaven. If, when asked by God why you
loved such-and-such persons, you reply, "Sire, ha
luveden me", He will simply reply, "þu ȝulde þet tu
ahtest. Her nabbe ich þe nawt muches to ȝelden". If,
on the other hand,"Ȝef þu maht ondswerien, Alle wa ha
duden me, ne na luve ne ahte ich ham, ah, sire, ich
luvede ham for þi luve; þet luve he ah þe, for hit
wes iȝeven him & he hit wule þe ȝelden".[32]
    Related to the importance attached to the notion
of debt at this period is the high occurrence of the
words "hire" and "quyte" in Middle English. Both the
words and the concepts are frequently employed, literally and figuratively. To "quyte" meant 'to requite
or repay in exact mesure so as to be even (or 'quits')
with'. At its most literal, it referred to the moral
right to re-imbursement for cost or labour expended,
a right deeply felt and insisted on by all. Thus
Margery Kemp can talk of 'acquitting the costs' and
'rewarding the labour' of a man who agreed to act as
her guide and protector on one of her many journeys[33]
This, after all, was the most basic way in which one
observed justice, paid to others what was 'due' them
in consideration of cost or labour expended. God was
that perfect justice that "qwyteth every dede"; and
the Virgin Mary promises, for instance, a monk, with
respect to his devotional labour in prayer, "for thy
travaille Shalt thow be qwyt".[34] Again, the word
could be ironically applied, and as often refers to
vengeance as to reward.[35] And the principle it enshrined was so commonly accepted that it could, in
Chaucer's hands, form the basis of rather complex

comic manipulation. The Miller offers his outrage-
ously bawdy fabliau as a tale that will 'quite' the
Knight's grandly dignified chivalric epic (*CT*.I.3127);
whether he is really making a drunken effort to
'match' it, or with mischevous malice to 'pay him
back' for it, is left humorously ambiguous.

That labour or "travaille", in particular, had
a moral claim to 'quittance' was a cardinal point of
justice. This was the wage or 'hire' that was owing
to the expenditure of work. Here, the 'debt' ethic
received reinforcement from an emphasis natural in
feudal society. To achieve the loyalty and support
of his 'meyny', a lord or master needed to be known
as a prompt paymaster. If, like Sloth in Passus V
(427-9), he was dilatory or dishonourable in this
respect, he would find it hard to attract servants.
One's lot could be materially affected by one's master's
readiness or otherwise to pay the debt of wage's owing
his servants.[36] Obviously, therefore, the principle
of the fairness of due 'hire' was one much stressed.
Once more, ironic or metaphorical uses of the notion
indicate the general acceptance of the basic principle
a writer could rely and play on for comic or wry
effect. Troilus can taunt the 'servants' of Love by
pointing to how bad a paymaster is the lord in whose
service they so labour; they see a most inequitable
return for all the 'travail' expended in his livery:

> "Youre hire is quyt, ayeyn, ye God woot how!
> Nought wel for wel, but scorn for good servyse".

(*T&C*,I.334-5)

Friar Daw gives a grim assurance to Jack Upland of
due 'guerdon' (excommunication) for his 'labour'.[37] And
Hoccleve, in a feudal image, declares that his intem-
perate habits have led him into the "servage" of Sickness, "Habundantly that paieth me my wage" (*La Male
Regle*, 116-9) - an irony heightened by the fact that this
was probably the only one of Hoccleve's masters of
whom this could be said. And the glozing Friar of
Chaucer's *Summoner's Tale* can cite in his fluent casuistry
the well-known Biblical authority (Luke 10:7) for the
principle that "the werkman worthy is his hyre" (*CT*.
III.1973). The text itself became proverbial (as
Robinson's note to the line indicates).

And as work earned 'hire' from a just lord, so
did works earn the hire of heaven from the supremely
just Lord: He will "quiten our servise".[38] From this
feudal analogy emerge two interconnected principles
very relevant to *Piers Plowman*: that it is *works* that

must earn that hire - *Do*-wel - principles must be put
into practice; and that it is inconceivable that a
just lord should refuse the debt of hire to good works
done. "*Dignus est operarius* his hire to have", Theology affirms (II.123). This applies in the temporal
world - as is demonstrated in Passus VI, where labour,
and labour alone (intellectual, devotional, or manual)
is affirmed to be deserving of hire - and in the
eternal, where the works of the loyal servant of Truth
will never go unpaid, for such a man serves with Piers

> 'the presteste paiere that povere man knoweth;
> He withhalt noon hewe his hire that he ne hath it at
> even'.   (V.551-2)

In the course of the following chapters on the
Visio, I hope to demonstrate that for Langland such
equities were of the essence of what he calls 'Truth'
(one important meaning of which word was 'justice'[39]),
and therefore also of true Christianity - for God is
Truth, and is first introduced into the poem under
that name. To establish the primacy of this concept
in *Piers Plowman*, I wish to begin, however, at the end,
by considering the conclusion of the poem.
    The final catastrophe, precipitated as it is by
the confessional malpractice of the friars, has
seemed to many readers to result from an evil
disappointingly particular and local, and therefore
to lack the universality of significance one
expects at the climax of a poem of such moral
intensity and scope.[40] The friars were, certainly,
the occasion of much popular complaint and satire
in Langland's day, no doubt much of it justifiable,
but for a poem which has survived the devil and
Antichrist to founder on them seems to reduce its
stature somewhat, to bring it down to the level of
the popular prejudice of the day. It is my belief,
however, that Langland does not overstate the
matter in representing the threat they constitute
to the whole nature of Christianity as he sees it
to be so profound as to cause the poem to break off
in near despair. And by explaining what I take to
be the nature of that threat, I hope to emphasize
the importance in the poem as a whole of the
principle whose violation by them proves to be so
decisive an obstacle to the further progress of a
work that had apparently engaged its author's
energies for upward of twenty-five years.[41]

In the final Passus of his long poem, Langland comes to focus on the struggles of the conscience of the Christian Church to preserve itself intact, to preserve its integrity (or *Unite*[42]), amid the manifold and insidious pressures of this world, against all that is anti-Christ. Towards the end of the Passus, the allegory records the entry of the friars into the church, and when they start to commute penances to money payments within its walls, Conscience resolves to quit it. And the poem closes as Christian Conscience and Christian Church thus part company.

The implications of such a conclusion, in both senses of the word, are profoundly serious. The Church has, apparently, granted official 'admission' to practices so essentially contrary to Christian principle that it and Christian conscience can no longer give each other mutual support, without danger of compromise to the latter, which can now look only to the elusive figures of Piers and Grace (whose geographical location is not known). The close of *Piers Plowman* in fact implies considerable pessimism as to the possibility of Christianity ever becoming, or remaining, an institutional reality, since a Christian church in which Christian conscience is not present truly *nomen habet sine re* (Prol.142) - 'has the name without the substance'. And it may be that the particular events as Langland's imagination has here recorded them adumbrate a more universal truth: the Church will always betray the absolute rigour of true Christianity (a demanding faith, as Langland saw it, "costing not less than everything"[43]) to the softer option represented by the friars. The friars have long since discontinued the practices Langland found so obnoxious, but were he alive today it is unlikely that he would regard the present state of the Church as a happy disproof of the sell-out on Christian justice his allegory accuses it of. It is a church from which all mention of penance (earthly punishment) has virtually disappeared, and which positively deprecates any allusion to Hell, Purgatory, or the wrath or justice of God (divine punishment).

These are concepts crucial to Langland's understanding of Christianity. His God is an exacting God because for him, as or Milton, God can be nothing if not the embodiment of that justice which is "The chief seed that Piers sew" (XIX.409), and which is the informing principle of man's instinctive sense of right and wrong: "Not just, not God",[44] and therefore an exacting God, in a very specific sense -

in the exaction, that is, of the due penalties for
wrong doing , which must be paid on earth (in the
form of penance) or in the afterlife (in Hell or
Purgatory). Otherwise there would be only unfair-
ness and promiscuity in the distribution of His
rewards, and nothing to substantiate the trust that
He "rewardeth ryht as men deserveth". Heaven is not
for free, and sins are not automatically forgiven
on request.

So when Langland's allegory comes to record in
Passus XIX the power the Church has by divine grant
from Christ, the power to administer His mercy, he
is careful to define the exact extent of this power.
The Church's authority in the dispensation of
Christ's mercy was theoretically founded in 'the
power of the keys' granted by Christ to St. Peter,
regarded as the founder and first head and eternal
representative of the Church : the power of opening
and closing the gates of heaven, with which he was
believed to have been invested when Christ spoke to
him those famous words in St. Matthew 16:19 : "And
I will give unto thee the keys of the kingdom of
heaven: and whatsoever thou shalt bind on earth
shall be bound in heaven: and whatsoever thou
shalt loose on earth shall be loosed in heaven".
This power was commonly interpreted to refer to the
power of the Popes, the successors of St. Peter as
heads of the Christian Church, (normally) resident
at St. Peter's in Rome, to remit or impose excommunication; and, in a more general way, to the power
of all the servants of St. Peter, all the clergy, to
grant or withhold absolution at confession.[45] It is
this power, the power to dispense the mercy He had
made available to mankind , that Christ gives after
His resurrection at XIX.183ff. to Piers, who, at
this stage of the poem, represents primarily St.
Peter, but also, in this connection, all those who
partook of St. Peter's privilege, every minor
member of St. Peter's Church, every "Sire Piers of
Pridie" (V.313). It is the power to pardon
("myghte men to assoille of alle manere synnes",
XIX.186), to absolve from sin, to realize in his
official function the historical significance of
Christ Himself, to release from the 'debt' of sin.
However, the metaphorical definition of sin as a
debt, common in medieval theology (the Vulgate
version of the Lord's Prayer, for instance, has
debita where the Authorized Version reads "trespasses"), is one that Langland took extremely seriously.
Debts signify payments due, and the Church's dispensation of the forgiveness of Christ is to be

extended only to those who have fulfilled the injunction Langland represents as attached to Piers's pardon as a condition of its efficacy: *redde quod debes* (Mt.18:28): 'Pay what thow owest':

> 'To hym, myghte men to assoille of alle manere synnes,
> In covenaunt that thei come and kneweliche to paye
> To Piers pardon the Plowman - *Redde quod debes*.
>   'Thus hath Piers power, be his pardon paied,
> To bynde and unbynde bothe here and ellis,
> And assoille men of alle synnes save of dette one'.

(XIX.186-91)

The financial logic implicit in the 'debt' analogy is further developed when the ministers of the Church, here represented by Piers, are likened to: procurators (originally, officers who attended to the interests of the Roman imperial treasury, collecting taxes, etc; the word was applied in the Middle Ages to the agents of churches, religious houses, or secular households or estates); registrars (recorders, including those who kept treasury records); and reeves (who were responsible for the manorial accounts).[46] So, in granting absolution only after assigning such penances as they think needful for atonement, the clergy are to be seen as God's official 'receivers', duly registering by absolution the discharge of their debts by sinners:

> 'For I make Piers the Plowman my procuratour and my
>   reve,
> And regestrer to receyve *redde quod debes*'.

(260-1)

The point is emphasized when Conscience, inviting his Christian labourers to partake of Easter communion (commonly regarded as symbolizing the feast of heaven to which the just will be called when released from the Lent of their lives on earth[47]) specifically delimits those eligible to accept the invitation to such as have 'paid for' their sins in some way, to those who have cleared their debts and "ypaied to Piers pardon the Plowman, *redde quod debes*" (392-3).

In one sense, the sort of 'pardon' Christ made available to mankind, and which it is the business of His church to administer, amounts as Langland describes it to something of a profound paradox. To pardon, or forgive, only such debts as have been paid could be regarded as a contradiction in terms;

14

and XIX.191 might be paraphrased, "and absolve men
of all sins save of the debt sin represents, which
must be paid". But Langland's emphasis is theo-
logically neither inexplicable nor unorthodox.
Christ's own 'atonement' did not issue credit
guarantees for all the future sins of mankind. It
merely paid off that part of the collective debt of
humanity (the death it owed as the penalty of the
Fall) which they could never hope to pay off themselves. He did not so much redeem men, as make it
possible for them to redeem themselves, by cancell-
ing the unredeemable deficit with which all men had
before His time begun life. Similarly with the
power of His Church to pardon and absolve sinners
in His name, through the sacrament of shrift. Such
considerations would make it not entirely illogical
to speak of a 'pardon' given only to such as have
atoned for actual sins committed. But on a deeper
level, the paradox is a resolution of the conflict
of justice and mercy with which Langland has
struggled throughout the poem - and it thus comple-
ments the reconciliation of the four daughters of
God in Passus XVIII. Langland's strong and urgent
conviction that God can be nothing if not equitable
and just, his revulsion at the whole concept of
getting 'pardoned' into heaven, and at that of
unearned reward (or "mede"), needed somehow to
accommodate the central Christian tenets that man
gained heaven through the merciful forgiveness of
Christ, and gained it not by merit, for he could
never earn it, but by supervenient grace, as "mede"
("That oon (mede) God of his grace graunteth",
III.232). The pardon with the imperative condition
'pay your debts' is Langland's imaginative resolution of justice and mercy: Christ and His Church
are thus seen to grant not so much forgiveness of
debts one incurs in life as the opportunity to pay
them. The perfect equity of heaven can admit only
those who have balanced their accounts.

The debt of sin was atoned or paid for,
according to medieval theory, by restitution (the
return of wrongfully appropriated money or goods) or
penance (the undergoing of due punishment for transgressions). This constituted 'satisfaction'. And
it is, of course, precisely because it represents a
violation of this all-important principle of equity,
redde quod debes, that the perversion of the
sacrament of shrift by the friars is seen by Langland at the end of his poem to constitute so profound
a corruption of the whole principle of Christian
justice as to divorce Church and Conscience. By

15

commuting penalties to money payments, by making
absolution conditional, not on restitution or
penance, but on "pryve paiement" (365) in the form
of donations to their orders , the friars paradoxically prevent true payment of the debt of sin. By
paying in money, the penitents are not paying the
penitential penalty at all, but rather buying themselves off it - or they think they are. For the
real perniciousness of such practices rests in the
fact that they lull the Christian community into a
false spiritual security, allowing them to appease
their consciences by assuming that God's justice
can be bribed, that Christianity is less demanding
than it really is, that heaven does not have to be
earned, nor debts paid.

The laxness the community themselves demanded
(nobody wants salvation actually to cost them anything) the friars provide, but their softer option
is a delusive one. They are playing *Duessa* to
Unite's *Una*: preaching and practising a false
Christianity - one which pretends that the sacred
principle of equity can be disregarded; they have
become indeed the false prophets associated in
Revelation with the predicted reign of Antichrist
with which Langland explicitly identifies them
elsewhere (XIX. 222).[48]

A most expressive verb is used to describe the
effects of the measures the friars take to heal the
penitents sick with sin:

> 'He lith adreynt', seide Pees, 'and so do manye
>   othere;
> The frere with his phisyk this folk hath *enchaunted*,
> And plastred hem so esily that hii drede no synne!'

> (XX.378-8o)

Besides its primary sense of 'bewitch, put under a
spell', the verb "enchaunt" had also acquired in
Middle English an extended, idiomatic sense of to
'beguile' by misrepresentations calculated to
undermine resistance to their own falsehood by
being of a kind the hearer will find attractive and
want to believe. One may compare the later similar
use of 'bewitched' ("Heavens grant that Warwick's
words bewitch him not!" *3 Henry VI*, III.iii.112).
Criseyde, for instance, is confident that she can
"so enchaunten" her father with her "sawes", by
appealing to his greed, that he will consent to
her return to Troy (*T&C* IV.1395).Langland himself
uses the word "enchaunted" wnen Mede is talked into

marriage with False by the broker, Favel (C. II.43).
"Escanto" similarly occurs in Juan Ruiz of bawds who
persuade young women into illicit liaisons (sts.709,
916). Hoccleve (*La Male Regle*, 225-272) applies the
term "enchauntours" to flatterers by whom "the peple
is misgyed and led, And with plesance so fostred and
fed" that they fall into a "deedly sleep", as did
Ulysses's crew at the song of the Sirens: a particularly interesting parallel with Langland's
reference here to the soporific state induced by the
glozing friars. His allegory enacts the metaphor
from withcraft underlying the idiomatic usage of the
word: the patients are so 'charmed' by the pain-
killing course of treatment prescribed that they
have sunk into a state of slothful delusion, their
senses soothed to the insensibility that the allegory represents as a sleep induced by a spell or charm -
with perhaps the added implication that the medicine
used is itself a charm.

For belief in the power of charms to cure
illness was still prevalent in Langland's day. In
Passus XVII, the Ten Commandments (summarized as
Christ Himself had summarized them in Matthew 22:
37-40) carried by Hope are described as a 'charm'
against the sickness of sin, which has saved many
thousands (19-22). However, there is evidence from
Passus XIII that Langland regarded literal application to magic and sorcery in time of sickness as
idle and irreligious superstition. Haukyn confesses
that he has been wont when ill to

> 'despise
> Lechecraft of Oure Lord and leve on a wicche,
> And seye that no clerc ne kan - ne Christ, as I leve -
> To the Soutere of Southwerk, or of Shordych Dame Emme,
> And seye that God ne Goddes word gaf me nevere boote,
> But thorugh a charme hadde I chaunce and my chief
>   heele'.

(336-41)

The suggestion of the use of magic by the friars,
then, casts further serious doubt on the nature of
the 'cure' they offer. It is a delusive cure, and
an irreligious substitute for the true medicine
("Lechecraft of Oure Lord") Christianity prescribes.
Indeed , in a manner typical of Langland's frequent
movements from literal to figurative, the allegory
here has been anticipated by a passage earlier in
Passus XX on bodily sickness and charlatan physicians.
Conscience's greatest allies in his struggle against

Life, with its instinctive bias towards ease and so towards Antichrist, are sickness, age, and death. Where persuasion fails, these act as forceful reminders of mortality, weakening by their own rough logic excessive attachment to this world and urging preparation for the next. Life turns in alarm to the venal physicians who are the secular counterparts of the friars to whom the sick with sin later turn, and like them he pays out money only for false security, for "thei gyven hym ageyn a glazene howve" (172). They enable Life to forget that he will die; and the falseness of the confidence reposed in them is plainly revealed when, a few lines later, one of their own number himself drops dead from palsy. Life's hope of a salve against age and death (173-4), his silly trust in physical immortality, is as delusive as that in the spiritual salvation or immortality the spiritually sick believe themselves to have secured when they submit to the cures of the flattering friar. The absolution they receive is a "glazene howve", a sham, a flattering delusion. When Langland calls the friars 'flatterers', he is referring not only to the unctuous hypocrisy of their address, but also to the 'flattering' hopes they inspire in the hearts of their hearers: that is, hopes that correspond more to desire than to rational probability. The verb 'flatter' is related etymologically to 'flatten', and originally meant to smooth, or stroke soothingly. It thus applies to the soothing medicine the friars apply to the wounds of the sick, as contrasted with the rougher plasters of the parish priest (who would have enjoined restitution and penance as conditions of absolution), and to the soothing confidence the penitents are lured into:[49] the confidence that their sickness has been attended to (whereas they are all in fact sinking into an ever-deepening coma), and that heaven can really be attained on these easy terms - at no cost.

For the friar-enchanters transform and denature Christianity, and, like the conjuror of *The Franklin's Tale*, deceive the mind with appearance without substance. Atonement in their hands is no atonement at all, but their victims are oblivious to this, sunk in a pleasing torpor, insensible to shame or desire to amend, not realizing that the painless Christianity the friars are hawking is a sham, *nomen sine re*, and that the penitential payment they believe themselves to be making for their sins is merely formal, and retains none of the essence of true penance:

> ... Contricion hadde clene foryeten to crye and to
> wepe,
> And wake for his wikked werkes as he was wont to
> doone.
> For confort of his confessour contricion he lafte,
> That is the soverayneste salve for alleskynnes
> synnes.

> (370-3)

The picture Langland here paints of a church in
which name and form are void of essential principle
is an alarming and sinister one. Again the prophetic tag of the "goliardeis", *nomen sine re*,
proves applicable. The "goliardeis" had himself
applied it to a king who did not uphold and enforce
the law:

> 'Dum "rex" a "regere" dicatur nomen habere,
> *Nomen habet sine re nisi studet iura tenere'.*

> (Prol.142-3)

A ruler who does not execute the rules of his land
betrays and perverts the office from which his title
derives. The church, too, instituted to rule and
govern the Christian community, has betrayed that
essential rule of justice and equity that demands
men pay their debts to their God and to their
neighbours. In such a situation, the Christian has
only his own conscience, his own God-given sense of
what is just, of the difference between right and
wrong, to guide him; for that conscience can no
longer look to the Church for support and guidance.
When the very institution nominally and formally
dedicated to the upholding of the principles by
which he seeks to live has in fact abandoned them,
it becomes worse than useless. The Christian is at
least on his guard against someone or something
called Antichrist. But name and form have become
treacherous in the church, an insidious temptation
to laxness without the need to acknowledge it to
oneself, to go through the motions of such things
as 'contrition' and 'penance' without the reality
of atonement, of paying one's debts.[50]
     The situation at the end of the poem thus
fulfills the menacing prophecy of Pride, the fore-
runner of Antichrist, at XIX.346ff. He predicts
that guile and deceit will ultimately be his most
powerful weapons, that the very sacrament that
enshrines the sacred principle of equity contained

in the injunction *redde quod debes*, the sacrament of penance, will become for Conscience an untrustworthy test of observance of that principle:

> 'Confession and Contricion, and youre carte the Bileeve
> Shul be coloured so queyntely and covered under our sophistrie,
> That Conscience shal noght knowe by Contricion
> Ne by Confession who is Cristene or hethene.'

His boastful threat is validated at the end of the poem, and it could be argued that the subsequent history of the Christian Church has validated Langland's general point - since all moral rigour has given way to a soft sell softer even than that practised by the friars, who at least imposed monetary penalties for the wrong-doing confessed to them.

Langland's own urgent sense of equity made the whole doctrine of sin and its atonement one of central importance to him. It was, for him, simply unthinkable that a just God could countenance the non-punishment of transgression, and he habitually speaks of sin in legal and financial terms (law and commerce being the spheres in which principles of equity are most strongly operative - everyone agrees that penalties must be imposed on those who break the law, and that those to whom money is owing are entitled to receive it). Sin for Langland is a law broken, and no king or judge with any integrity can suffer the laws of the land to be flouted with impunity; it is a debt incurred, an amount due to rectify a financial imbalance, or inequity. Earlier in Passus XX, Langland had used the following simile to define exactly what it is to confess to friars, who relax the rule *redde quod debes*, and give absolution for money, instead of making it conditional on restitution and penance. It is a complex image, in which legal and financial criteria are intricately interinvolved:

> ... ac shame maketh hen wende
> And fleen to the freres - as fals folk to Westmynstre,
> That borweth, and bereth it thider, and thanne biddeth frendes
> Yerne of foryifnesse or lenger yeres leve.
> Ac while he is in Westmynstre he wol be bifore
> And maken hym murie with oother menne goodes.
> And so it fareth with muche folk that to freres

```
        shryveth;
   As sisours and executours - thei shul yyve the freres
   A parcel to preye for hem, and purchace hem murthe
   With the remenaunt that othere renkes biswonke,
   And suffre the dede in dette to the day of doome.
```

                    (284-94)

To paraphrase:- People prefer to be confessed by
the friars (because they commute penances to monetary donations to charitable institutions - their
own friary, of course, being the one specified).
Such penitents are in fact in the position of which
Shakespeare's Claudius perceived the inherent
falseness, attempting to "be pardoned and retain
th'offence" (*Hamlet*, III.iii.56).   But in
applying to friars instead of to their parish
priests, they do as those who have broken the law
do in going to the courts ("as fals folk to Westmynstre" - Westminster was the seat of the principal
law-courts), only to bribe the judges and advocates
to connive at their crime.   Within the legal simile,
there is embedded a financial one.   The applicants
to "Westminster" (the sinners who apply to spiritual judges, the clergy, for verdict and sentence on
their conduct) have borrowed money ("That borweth")
- that is, they are debtors (representing the debts
of sin - the *debita* of the Lord's Prayer - which
had by church law to be regularly heard by a
competent confessor).   But at confession, the
spiritual Westminster, they do not undergo the
penalty equity would impose: they do not pay their
debts there, but merely apply for cancellation or
postponement of them ("foryifnesse or lenger yeres
leve"), and then proceed to 'make merry' with the
money that is not theirs;   that is, those who
prefer the friars as confessors use the sacrament
not to pay their debts of sin, to make atonement
by restitution and penance, but to evade them,
'making merry' with the proceeds of their sinful or
criminal practices, buying off their consciences by
the monetary donations for which the friars gave
absolution.   The peace of mind is bought not by
payment of the debt, but by evasion of it.   The
word "foryifnesse" at 287 is one of the many in
Langland that serve to fuse vehicle and tenor,[51]
allegory and message, re-inforcing the applicability of image to concept by focusing on both
through the lens of a single word.   Within the
image, or vehicle, of 'debt', it carries a quasi-
technical sense of financial remission: the

debtors are seeking to have their debts cancelled.[52]
But in the context of the tenor, the word applies
also to the 'forgiveness' or absolution penitents
seek at shrift - and particularly that sought from
friar-confessors, which is rather a release or
'forgiveness' of the debt of sin, than true absolution through atonement. Towards the end of the
passage, Langland slightly alters the precise terms
of the financial image. In order to emphasize the
leading notion of a debt left unlawfully and
irreligiously unpaid, the debtors are transformed
from persons who have borrowed but are neglecting
to repay to the executors of wills, who have appropriated the proceeds of estates to themselves
instead of applying them to the purposes enjoined
by the testator. The laws of probate would appear
to have been in a deplorable state in the Middle
Ages, since the rascality of embezzling executors is
a complaint frequently to be met with in the literature of the period. It appears that funds particularly liable to misappropriation were those the
deceased had assigned for the saying of masses for
his soul, or for the other religious purposes
favoured by medieval testators in their last
desperate attempts to settle their spiritual accounts
before going to the divine audit. Men were warned
that measures to build up credit in heaven left so
late were unlikely to be efficacious, if only
because the moneys so assigned would probably find
their way into the pockets of the executors.[53]
Executors were also supposed by law to pay from the
proceeds of the estate any debts the deceased had
left behind him[54] - a duty which has evidently been
neglected here. These men are instead converting to
their own uses the money earned by "other renkes"
and due to "oother menne", and so allowing the soul
of the deceased to remain in Purgatory until his
debt of sin (which would include any literal debts
left unsettled at his death) has been paid off
there; he can stay there till Doomsday for all they
care. This development in the financial analogy
(emphasizing monetary debts as part of the debt of
unatoned sin the dead will pay off in Purgatory)
again has the effect of re-inforcing the link
between tenor and vehicle, between sinners who shirk
atonement and those who do not pay their debts. The
legal element, the idea of buying off the law, is
sustained by the mention of "sisours" - jurors,
presumably here corrupt ones, who had accepted
bribes;[55] while the allusion to the "day of doome"
acts as a reminder that there is an ultimate court

of justice which is unbribable, and which will
enforce the payment of all outstanding debts.

The legal and financial imagery of this passage
is merely the culmination and confirmation of a view
of sin that Langland has been urging throughout the
poem: a view informed by a rigorously precise
sense of equity. I entend to trace the development
of the analogy in detail in the following chapters ;
so it will be sufficient to mention here just a few
illustrations of the preceding history of these modes
of definition. The question of sin and its atonement
is first raised in Passus V, and repayment of the
spiritual debt it represents (*satisfactio, restitutio*) is insisted on by Repentance, the confessor,
who uses the image most markedly at 270-1 and 294-6;
while the important verb *reddere* is introduced in
the speech of Robert the Robber (462-71) which
closes the confession scene - an oblique allusion to
the text *redde quod debes* that is to become the all-
important condition of pardon in Passus XIX, the
principle to be violated by the friars in the
passage quoted above, and in the closing scenes of
the poem.

The most specific analogy with legal procedure
occurs in a speech by the Good Samaritan, this
instance of its occurrence being also perhaps the
most revealing, since one would expect the character
(the embodiment of "charite", after all) to stress
the mercy and forgiveness, rather than the legal
strictness, of the ways of God. He does not,
however. And when the dreamer so to speak pins him
to the wall, and asks him if, in fact, there is
then no hope for a sinner truly repentant but
having neither time nor means for atonement, the
Samaritan is downright evasive. And he points, as if
the analogy were conclusive, to the difficulty such
a problem would prose in a court of law. However
repentant a proven criminal may be, however sorry
the judge may feel for him, he cannot pardon him
without sanctioning insult to the law and betraying
the sacred principle of "equite" that it is the
essence of his function to uphold: the judge cannot
be satisfied until the wrong has been satisfied, by
restitution or by punishment, until "eyther have
equite, as holy writ telleth: *Numquam dimittitur
peccatum, etc*" (XVII.307).[56]

The interconnections between the *Visio* and the
end of the poem are important to an understanding of
both, and of the poem as a whole. For in the return
to the world of the *Visio* which the final *Do-Best*

section of the poem (Passus XIX-XX) partially represents, the friars are the counterparts of the venal
lawyers of the *Visio*. In the latter, the prime
antagonist of Holy Church had been identified as
Mede, and it was Mede's role in the perversion of
the law that Langland had come to focus on in particular, in Passus IV, which provides the climax of
his treatment of this character. It is her
influence in this sphere that Langland identifies
as the most pernicious of the many obstructions she
throws in the way of social integrity and justice.
"'Mede overmaistreth Lawe and muche truthe letteth'"
(IV. 176), declares the King: for where she is,
the law is for sale and can be flouted with
impunity by Wrong, who here attempts to bribe and
buy his way out of the due legal penalties for his
crimes - a state of affairs against which Reason
and Conscience protest. And along with false
beggars, it is venal lawyers who are most string-
ently excluded from the scope of the pardon
expounded in Passus VII:

> Men of lawe leest pardon hadde that pleteden for
> mede.
>   (39)

When the principles established in the *Visio*
are reapplied on a spiritual plane in *Do-Best*, the
same central evil is identified. Though Mede is
not present as a character, she is as an influence
- on the friars, who are selling God's law in a
manner as destructive of the spiritual commonwealth
as the sale of the law of the land was to the
social. The sinners are buying themselves off the
penalties for breaches of God's law as Wrong had
attempted to buy off the King's law in Passus IV.
The friars, like venal judges, are prepared to
relax it for money, for a "pryvee paiement" (XX.
365). As Mede and her entourage had made their
way to "Westmynstre" (II.135,156,161), in an
attempt to get the law to connive at venality ("to
loken if the lawe wolde Juggen (Mede and False)
joyntly in joie for evere", II.156-7), so the
sinners of *Do-Best* turn, "as fals folk to Westmynstre", to courts of confession where they can
rely on being able to buy verdicts of acquittal -
that is, to the saleable absolutions granted by
the friars.
That Langland saw venal confessors and venal
lawyers as strictly comparable is also suggested
by the similarity of the remedy he suggests for the

evil each represents. Oddly enough, it is the same
respect for law, justice, equity, divine and human,
which fills him with such rage against those who
debase and pervert either, that also enables him to
rise above that anger. Friars and lawyers have
that same inalienable right to the necessities of
life as all men have from birth (the very first, in
every sense 'primary', principle laid down by Holy
Church, I. 17-26). If one cannot come by these
necessities by fair means, then one is entitled to
use foul - a point categorically laid down by Nede,
elaborating (at XX. 6-39) on the teaching of Holy
Church in yet another instance of the development of
a point first raised in the *Visio*: food, drink,
and clothing, the means to sustain life, are the
right of every living creature, for God has
created these things "in commune" (I. 20), to meet
the needs of the life He also gave. If you cannot
acquire them honestly, by begging, borrowing, or
earning, then you must steal them. To do so is no
sin, for need can never fall into debt (XX. 10).
It is its own guarantor, or (a legal term) "maynpernour" (" 'Nede anoon righte nymeth hym under
maynprise' ", 17). Langland is here stating a law
(one aspect of the "lawe of kynde", 18) that he
recognizes to be more basic, and an equity more
fundamental, than all others. St. Thomas Aquinas,
discussing the same problem, explains that God, in
his wise purveyance, has ensured that there should
always be an overall balance between life and the
resources available to sustain it. Elaborate
systems have evolved to facilitate fair and orderly
distribution, but if these break down in some way
then one is only restoring an equity ordained by
God, correcting an inequity, in taking what one
needs[57] - "Nede ne hath no lawe, ne nevere shal
falle in dette" - for the balance between basic
needs and what is required to meet them is an
equity that requires to be observed before all
others. Where need dictates what and how much is
taken, this equity can never be breached, for the
act is then sanctioned by the cardinal virtue of
temperance (the virtue that shuns excess or
deficiency, that regulates precise degree). Temperance alone of the cardinal virtues is incapable of
offending against equity (23-33), because it cannot
by definition by guilty of inequilibrium, of
disproportion, of lack of "mesure" (26).
    The passage is an important one, for it enables
Langland to see that, in one way, the lawyers and
friars are only doing what his own need has

counselled and justified to him. Their actions are
partially excused by their needs. Having no assured
source of income, thet get it from the sale of the
laws entrusted to their administration. With a
profound justice, Langland therefore blames ultimately the system, and states that the means of
distribution should be adjusted so that such men
should not be tempted by need to such evil practice.
On the "men of lawe that pleteden for mede" almost
his last word is that,

> Princes and prelates sholde paie for hire travaille:
> *A regibus et principibus erit merces eorum.*

> (VII.43-43*a*)

There would be no lawyers if no livelihood was to be
got from lawyering. And since a system whereby
remuneration is recovered in the form of "yiftes"
(40) and "mede" from the clients themselves clearly
operates to the prejudice of "the innocent and nedy"
(47), Langland makes a peculiarly far-sighted
suggestion. For he seems to be urging here either
some kind of 'nationalization' of advocacy, whereby
barristers are retained on a regular basis to give
their services to all alike by those whose responsibility it is to ensure access to disinterested justice
in the realm (*ie* its governors, secular and ecclesiastical); or some system analogous to 'legal aid',
whereby advocacy is subsidized by the authorities
for the "innocent and nedy".[58] Need amongst legal
officials was, in fact, recognized as a prime factor
contributing to miscarriage of justice. John of
Salisbury had urged that the prince should "from the
public store supply (his) officials with a suffic-
iency for their needs", and others had stressed that
judges, in particular, must have an assured income
sufficient to present their being easily tempted to
sell the law to the rich.[59] Langland is extending
the principle to advocates: let them, like
judges, be paid from the public purse for their
travail, instead of having to seek their due
hire for it from the rich at the expense of the
poor.
    He counsels similar measures for similar reasons
in the case of the friars, with regard to whom his
final word, which has appeared unexpectedly generous
to some critics, is closely comparable: Conscience's
closing prayer notices them by a request, not that
they should all be sunk to the lowesth depths of Hell
forthwith, but "that freres hadde a fyndyng, that *for*

nede flateren" (384 - my italics).[60] Again,
Langland is advocating that regular provision be
made for persons at present driven to sell the law
with whose (properly) impartial execution they are
entrusted.

The parallel between the *Visio* and *Do-Best* is
of particular significance. It is most noticeable
in the recurrence of the agricultural concerns of
Passus VI - since in Passus XIX Christians are again
discovered working the land under the guidance of
Piers that it may bear food to nourish and sustain
the community. In the former case, of course, the
activity is literally exemplary, representative of
the virtues of honest and productive labour;
whereas in the latter, it is a spiritual allegory.
But it would, I think, be a mistake to suggest that
Langland has in some way moved beyond, transcended
the concerns of the *Visio*. What he is doing is
re-applying in an extended sense the principles he
had intellectually struggled through to in that first
section of the poem.

Langland's is essentially an exploratory and
investigative poem, and it follows the sound and
time-honoured heuristic principle of moving from the
known to the unknown. In order to discover how he
may save his soul and gain eternal life in the next
world, his dreamer is first made to understand what
is right and desirable in this world : that a king
should enforce the laws of his land, that criminals
like Wrong should be punished and not allowed to
buy themselves off, that men should earn their
livelihood by their labour, and not expect it
gratis. Langland then proceeds by analogy to apply
his findings to the laws of heaven, the law of God,
and the earning of eternal life ("For the invisible
things of him ... are clearly seen, being understood by the things that are made", Rom.I:20).

In particular what the *Visio* establishes is
that our own natural 'reason' teaches us that
equity is the prime social good: that men should
get their just deserts, that there should be no
disproportion between desert and reward or punishment. It is the dictum of Reason (and it is quoted
as such) that *nullum bonum* be *irremuneratum* and
nullum malum be *impunitum* (IV.143-4). We should
perhaps remind ourselves that Reason for the Middle
Ages was much more of a moral virtue than it is
today: it was the faculty that discerned what was
right (one may compare the French *avoir raison* =
to be right), the intellectual power of distinquish-
ing right from wrong. In the Middle Ages, in fact,

'right' and 'reason' were terms intimately inter-
related. One may note, for instance, the relationship assumed between *recte* (rightly) and *ratio*
(reason) in the following *dictum* of St. Augustine:
"For everything that is done, if it be not *rightly*
done, is a sin, nor can that be anyhow *rightly* done
which proceeds not from right *reason*".[61] And in
the vernacular too, 'reason' and 'right' each
connoted the other, as can be seen from such
phrases as "resoun of ryʒt þat con not rave"
(*Pearl*, 665). Aquinas defined reason as the faculty
by which we "act according to virtue and avoid sin"
(*ST* II-II.cl.2). Reason was, therefore, conceived
of as "the mother of all laws", which ultimately
derived from this innate awareness of what is and
what is not according to justice.[62] In fact,
'reason' came to denote the basic principles of
justice,[63] and should perhaps be translated
'justice' in Langland. Chief Justice Coke, for
instance, declared a statute void because it ran
counter to "common right or reason".[64] And in many
of the recorded occurrences of the word in Middle
English, it is clear that what is being appealed to
is 'right' or 'justice'.[65]
    Reason was, then, the morally discriminating,
judging power of the mind, and it is precisely as a
judge that Reason is introduced by Langland into
his poem. He is sent for to decide the debate
between Mede and Conscience, and when he arrives
he is further required to pronounce upon a case
currently being heard in the law-court between
Peace and Wrong. His entry signals the emergence
of an emphatic confidence in the absolute inviolability of the law of equity quoted above, a
principle affirmed in three successive Passūs - in
the different contexts of crime, sin, and the
earning of a livelihood.
    In Passus IV, Reason's verdict is unequivocal
and categoric. Though Wrong offers monetary
compensation to Peace, Reason is adamant that he
must suffer the legal penalty due to his crime. In
Passus V, the same principle is affirmed in relation
to sin, the violation of God's law, by Repentance,
the spiritual judge or confessor, who must grant or
deny pardon to the sins confessed him; like Reason
(whose presence at the beginning of the Passus,
preaching to the people, provides the only link
between the *dramatis personae* of this Passus and
those of the last), he insists that the debt
incurred by sin be repaid, and he has his own Latin

aphorism to match that produced by Reason: *Numque
dimittitur peccatum donec restituatur ablatum*
(272a).[66]   In Passus VI, again, this same principle
of equity is applied in the social sphere: livelihood must be earned, worked for.   In all three
cases, one must reap what one has sowed.

If reason recognizes this rule as of the
essence of a just state on earth, then no less can
be true of the kingdom of heaven, ruled over by a
God who is justice (or Truth) itself.   There, too,
then, breaches of the law must be paid for, and
eternal life must be worked for: anything else
would be inequitable, and unthinkable of Truth.
The preoccupation in the *Visio* with the King and his
administration of justice and law is paralleled by
the opening of *Do-Best*, in the lengthy exposition
of Christ as a King, laying down laws for the
governance and guidance of his subjects (XIX.26-
139).   As Wrong attempts to buy his way out of the
due legal penalties for his crime, so do the
sinners of Passus XX, when they seek to buy their
absolution from the friars;   in both cases, the
law is wrongly relaxed, through the corrupting
influence of Mede, the desire for which leads law-
courts and friars to give invalid 'pardons'
to wrongdoers.

Similarly, when Piers attempts to establish a
social equity based on an equivalence between
labour and livelihood (only those who have in some
way contributed to the labour of the cultivation of
the land are to share in the harvest), he encounters the problem posed by the determined waster, the
man who simply refuses to work, and demands his
keep free.   Conscience, too, the counterpart of
Piers as 'overseer' of the agricultural community
in that passage of Passus XIX which is the parallel
of Passus VI in the *Visio*, encounters his spiritual
Waster - in the person of Brewer, the man who will
not work for his eternal livelihood, will not pay
the price, *reddere quod debet*.   On discovering
that he must give up the profitable petty frauds,
the injustices, of his trade, and so cultivate
'justice', in order to earn his spiritual 'bread'
(here symbolized by the Eucharist to which
Conscience invites such Christians who have
"laboured lelly" and 'paid their debts', XIX.386-
93), he energetically refuses to undertake that
spiritual labour.   He, like Waster, wants his
living free, and wishes to reap salvation without
cultivating the seeds of the cardinal virtues, as
Conscience is quick to remind him is impossible:

neither he nor anyone else can reap what they have
not sown, and if people will not cultivate these
seeds of virtue, they will spiritually starve:

> 'But thow lyve by loore of *Spiritus Iusticie*,
> The chief seed that Piers sew, ysaved worstow
>   nevere.
> But Conscience be the commune fode, and Cardinale
>   Vertues,
> Leve it wel, thei ben lost, bothe lif and soul.'

> (408-11)

The secular concerns of the *Visio*, then, its
concern with justice and law and social equity,
should not be read simply as implying the initial
limitations of vision in the dreamer, whose mind at
first is preoccupied with the things of this world -
with secular justice, law-courts, and labour for
one's daily bread. In one sense, Langland never
progresses beyond the principles he establishes in
the *Visio*. Given that Christ is a King, and the
Christian community His spiritual commonwealth, it
is first necessary to establish what Reason tells us
should happen in an ideally just state on earth.
The findings are then applied to the Christian
society and the laws that govern it in *Do-Best*.

It is noticeable, however, that in the translation something of optimism is lost. In the *Visio*,
real persons in combination with abstract virtues or
forces, had been able to counter the threats to
equity: the King had been able to give effective
force to the verdict of Reason, and between them
they had been capable of foiling the attempt of
Wrong to bribe his way out of the law; Piers had
been able to summon Hunger to his aid, and this had
forced Waster to at least temporary observance of
the law of natural justice that every man should
work for his living. However, the counterparts of
these undesirables in *Do-Best* are less easily to
be dealt with. Conscience is powerless to resist,
can only protest at, the slothful obstinacy of his
Waster, and of the sinners (the corporate spiritual
Wrong) that seek to buy remission from penalties
from the friars. For conscience, except in a
psychological sense, has no authority. The authorities of this kingdom (Christ, its King, and His
"procuratour" Piers) are not physically sensible
presences, and their representative in the soul of
each man, Conscience, cannot enforce on others the
values he holds by. He can only watch in despair as

they are eroded in the community around him.

Christianity, then, is ultimately unenforcible, except by one's own conscience on oneself. For a post-Romantic readership, this conclusion may not seem so very depressing. The Romantic movement brought with it a new stress on the primacy of the individual heart, and we are used to thinking of religion as something essentially personal and interior. Langland, too, knew that Christianity must derive its vitality and urgency for each believer from an inner conviction (a "kynde know-ynge"). But in the Middle Ages values were more communal and external, and for Langland (for whom, in particular, Christianity derived its reality from its power to shape and regulate external actions and conduct), it is certain that the discovery that his own 'conscience' could do nothing to make Christianity a social and institutional reality in the nominally Christian society he lived in was a grim one.

II: *Law, Obedience, and Authority*

In his insistence on an analogy between Christianity and the law, Langland is giving an emphasis to, pursuing the logic of, a conceptual correlation already existing in the language, organization, and theory of the Christian faith of his day. The expression "Goddis law" was a common one, and it was used to refer to the totality of Christian directives on matters of faith, conscience, and conduct. Langland himself refers to the Christian *law* on a number of occasions in the course of his poem, and examples from elsewhere could be multiplied.[67] The Bible itself provided ample authority for such a conception of Christian faith and morality; the legal phraseology of , for instance, the following is typical of many verses in both the Old and the New Testament: "If his child-ren forsake my *law*, and walk not in my *judgments*, if they break my *statutes*, and keep not my command-ments , then I will visit their transgression with a rod" (Ps.89:30-32).

And for the fourteenth-century Christian, much would have concurred to encourage him to think of his faith in this way. The Church had its own elaborate system of ecclesiastical courts and court-officials, as anyone acquainted with Chaucer's Summoner is aware (a Summoner was the official

responsible for executing summonses to the Church
courts). The Canon Law it administered through them
was a complex, codified, elaborately glossed *corpus*,
and was as enforcible and as authoritative as the law
of the land administered through the secular courts:
a state of affairs totally without parallel in
twentieth-century English society, where we are
conscious of an important division between the laws
of the state, to which obedience is compulsory, and
the laws of the Church, which we regard as unenforcible against us except by our own consciences.
     There was, then, much to give substance to the
common conception of the Christian faith as a 'law'
to which the citizens of God were subject. Priests
were the judges and lawyers of God's law; and,
again, there was much superficial resemblance
between the two professions to encourage such a
view.   Both were learned and literate,   both were
called "clerkes" (in contradistinction to the common
mass of 'lay' folk, both had specialist competence
in their respective laws, and in the Latin language
which in both cases enshrined them). Lawyers were,
in fact, originally members of the clergy, and still
wore the tonsure.[68] Conversely, priests, especially
archdeacons and bishops, were often called upon to
exercise a judicial function in the Canon Law courts.
     The notion of Christianity itself as a body of
dogma and directives designed to regulate and guide
mankind, and so the moral and spiritual counterpart
of the secular law, is especially evident in the
words and images used to describe the phases of
Christian history as the Bible presented it. Here,
the concept of successive 'laws' was one universally
employed. The history of the salvation of mankind
fell naturally into two parts: there was the 'Old
Law' of the Old Testament (when salvation was to be
gained primarily through faith and observance of the
Ten Commandments - at least, provisional salvation,
confirmed at the death of Christ and the Harrowing
of Hell, when the Old Testament faithful were
released from Limbo by the Redeemer, and led into
heaven) ; and the 'New Law' of the New Testament,
when the Old Law was supplemented by the command of
charity laid down by Christ, and under which mercy
and pardon for offenders through His grace was made
possible. Almost as common as this bipartite division, however, was a tripartite one, in which Old
Testament history was in turn seen as falling into
two distinct phases, so that the scheme of salvation
was conceived of as comprising three successive
stages, in conformity with the Trinitarian principle

at the centre of the Christian faith. First came
the *Tempus Naturae*, in which men had only the "law
of nature" (the "lawe of kynde") to guide them:
their own instinctive, God-given sense of natural
justice, of what was right and what was wrong,
'natural' or 'unnatural'; then came the *Tempus
Legis*, when the "lawe of kynde" was supplemented by
the written Law of the Ten Commandments, providing
more precise and elaborate guidance for the citizens
of God; this Law was consummated and completed by
Christ, who inaugurated the final phase in the
history of salvation which was referred to as the
Tempus Gratiae, in which men were ruled by the new
Law of Grace, which both gave and demanded something
more - charity and forgiveness. The representative
figureheads of the three legal eras were Abraham,
Moses (who brought the tablets of the law down from
Mount Sinai), and Christ respectively.[69]
     God's scheme of salvation was thus conceived of
as having manifested itself in the provision of ever
more refined systems of law for His subjects, to
save them from offending against the divine order
and harmony of His state, and from the consequent
punishment all societies reserve for the undesirable forces of *mis*rule that threaten to undermine
their peace. This prominence given to the notion of
law in medieval metaphysics underlines the change in
sensibility that has since taken place.   Their
concept of the relation of the individual to eternal,
essential truths was one with which post-Romantic
notions of self-fulfilment have little to do. Less
importance was attached to individuality, and more
to "auctoritee". The self was a narrow prison of
anarchic "Will" which required the rule of laws
beford it could play any significant part in the
divine order. When they spoke of self-knowledge,
what they meant was the knowledge of the place of
the self in a larger scheme. Abelard's *Scito
Te Ipsum* ('Know Thyself') was, in fact, a treatise
on confession;[70] to know yourself was first and
foremost to know and deplore your lack of conformity
with the moral order; the righteous "find out
themselves" in order that they may "bring themselves
to a better state by weeping and self-chastising".[71]
So the aim of self-knowledge was to identify not the
self, but what in the self prevented its identification with a divine universal order. True self-
knowledge consisted not in finding, but in losing
one's identity, feeling oneself nothing before a
power greater than oneself. He cannot truly "felyn
of hymself so þfastly as he is" who cannot "felen

himself no3t as he is"; it is the proud and self-
involved who "wil not know hemself trewly", because
they know not their own sinfulness nor "how no3t
þei are in here owne kynde anentes God" (*Scale of
Perfection* II (chs.xx,xxvi, pp.67,97). Knowing
oneself came of knowledge and acknowledgement of
God , and so the subordination of one's own identity
to His; it was that wisdom that "Maketh his God
and eek hymself to knowe" (*CT*.III.1202). So it is
that the would-be contemplative, Margery Kempe, can
pray to God, "Make my wil þi wyl & þi wil my wil
þat I may no wil han but þi wil only" (pp.249-50):
for she aimed, in her tragi-comic way, at the
spiritual 'perfection' of the mystic, and this was
achieved "when we put His will before our own so as
to follow His rather than our own" (Abelard's
Ethics, p.13).

According to Anselm, in fact, man's 'free' will
consisted in "the power of not acting contrary to
the will of God":[72] that is, in renouncing its own
freedom and autonomy. In Langland , the will that
recognizes no master but itself is twice shown
(once in a minor, once in a major way) to lead only
to frustration and futility. The folk in the field,
eager to seek truth, are helpless without a guide,
for "while thei wentę here owen wille thei wente
alle amys" (A.VI.5).[73] And the protagonist, Will,
represents himself as having abandoned the search
for truth for many years of his life, in order to
follow his own will, "for wil to have his likyng"
(XI.45). The self-reliant will can, then , in
Langland's world, make no progress in moral understanding. In fact, part of the purpose of submitting to the penances imposed by one's confessor at
shrift was that penitents, "having used their
judgments proudly in contempt of God", might be
"corrected by obedient submission to another
power".[74]

Obedience, "buxomnes", was for related reasons
a virtue much more highly regarded than it is today.
The verb "conform" was used with a positive force
totally absent from the pejorative connotations (of
unimaginative and unintelligent conservatism)
carried by "conformity" today. Paradise, churchmen
never tired of pointing out, had been lost by disobedience to the first and only law imposed on Adam
and Eve, and was to be regained by obedience to
God's commandments.[75] The fruits of disobedience
were chaos and disorder, morally and socially.
Langland's stress on the need for laymen to live "in
lawe", and for religious to obey their 'rule' (eg.

V.45,VII.62,IX.200,XII.34-6), shows that he
shared to a marked degree this identification of
rectitude with regularity, the observance of *regula*
(one may note, in this connection, the word-play at
the end of Part VII of the *Ancrene Wisse*, where
"I will praise thee in uprightness (*directione*) of
heart" (Ps.119:7) is glossed, *id est, in regulatione
cordis*). *Obedite dominis vestris*, the Bible
commanded (Col.3:22) - and very properly, too, it
was felt, for here piety combined with entrenched
interests in the feudal and hierarchical structures
of Church and state to subdue possibly dangerous
self-assertion. Obedience of child to father, wife
to husband, servant to his secular and spiritual
lords, of subjects to the king and his laws,
religious to their superiors: such subservience was
a type and an extension of the need for obedience to
the Lord of heaven and His laws. "Superiors are
intermediaries between God and their subjects",
regents of the authority of God and the laws -
natural, written, and divine - by which He instructs
mankind. "My spyrit schal restyn vpon a meke man,
a contryte man, and dredyng my wordys", God had said;
and the virtues by which beatitude was earned consequently "consist in the good of obedience";
obedience and humility constituted the path to
"complete subjection to God and love", and so to
perfection.[76]

The importance attached to humility is reflected
in the elaborate analysis the subject attracted to
itself. It was conceived of as having twelve
degrees or subdivisions, and these were often
rehearsed. Obedience was, of course, an especially
important element in monastic rules, and monastic
culture had been highly influential in the earlier
stages of the dissemination of Christian values and
concepts. The whole respect for 'authority', and
the notion that salvation was impossible outside
the church, and was to be gained only through the
sacraments and teaching it provided, should really
be seen in the context of this general cultural
emphasis. Such attitudes are attributable not just
to narrow-minded authoritarianism (though doubtless
that played its part in hardening them), but also
to the different sensibility and value-system of the
age. Awe and reverence were concepts more resonant
then than now. Ours is a markedly aweless age. It
is almost impossible to recapture the thrill of
dread originally conveyed by the phrase *Godes egesa*
('the aweful power of God') in, for instance, the
Anglo-Saxon *Seafarer*. The positive value of fear of

God's justice and His power, the "delectability"
even that the Middle Ages discerned in such sensa-
tions of dread and awe, are notions foreign to us.[77]
We revere very little, and institutions not at all.
But in habits of mind that condemned 'individualism'
- intellectual, moral, or social - as presumptuous,
reverence and obedience to authority were held proofs
of a virtuously selfless meekness. The beginning of
virtue was meek deference, intellectually and
morally, to "þe faith and ... þe lawes of Holy
Kirke" *(Scale of Perfection* II.ch.xxi, p.72). Margery
Kempe, anxious to demonstrate the 'perfection' of
her way of life as a result of her mystical exper-
iences, particularly stresses her obedience. "I am
wel plesyd wyth þe, doutyr", she hears God say, "for
þou stondist vndyr obedyens of Holy Cherch and þat
þou wylt obey þi confessour and folwyn hys counsel"
(p.72).   At one point, she and a White Friar who
had come to like and revere her are ordered - she
by her confessor, he by his provincial - to have no
more to do with one another; and thus "be vertu of
obediens" (p.168; cf.p.162),   each humbly consents
to the cessation of an entirely innocent and pious
friendship. Margery frequently refers to how she
"obeyd hir to hir confessowr", and does not think
it unreasonable that he should be angry when she
goes on a long journey without consulting him, for
"sche was hys obedience" (p.247).   Moral leave
from the penitential master was as important as
formal leave from a secular lord. To 'obey' was to
'bow' before the due authority of each.   Such
deference was a small token that one was not
"obstynat ageyns þe lawes of God" (p.38) generally.
Virtue was often seen as internalized obedience:
the obedience of the will to wit, the rule of
reason over the passions. This emphasis on obedience explains and coincides with the reverence
accorded the concept of 'law' at this time. "Under
obedience to be and buxum to þe lawe"[78] was a
desideratum the logic of which Langland's poem
thinks very thoroughly through.
      So when Francis Quarles, the seventeenth
century metaphysical poet, wrote, "I wish a greater
knowledge than t'attain / The knowledge of myself"
(Christ and Ourselves), the words express much of
the essence of the religious instinct of earlier
centuries. The word of God was 'law'; that is, it
was authoritative in every sense of the word,
compelling intellectual and behavioural conformity
to itself. The earlier notion of the *summum bonum*
was one which had a more collective, inclusive

emphasis, based on a concept of a universal order, which required suppression of the self, the conforming of its unruly passions to the rules of a law greater than those of the individual Will. The highest possible phase of spiritual development occurred when the Will found itself in instinctive harmony with the higher purpose it had sought to conform itself to, and lost all its own identity in a total merger of its own motions with those of the divine First Mover, and thus found itself synchronized with the motion of the whole universe. This is the experience that Dante claims in his *Divina Commedia* to have been the culmination of his vision of the Trinity in the *Paradiso*, and his poem closes as he describes it, for no higher can be sought:

> ma già volgeva il mio disio e il velle,
> sì come rota ch'igualmente è mossa,
> l'amor che move il sole e l'altre stelle.

> ("... but now my desire and will, like a wheel that spins with even motion, were revolved by the Love that moves the sun and the other stars").[79]

The modern rather derogatory connotations of the term 'legalistic' have, therefore, to be totally disregarded in assessing the significance of the word 'law' for the medieval mind. Human law itself, the law of nations and states, which is for us the primary sense of the word, was for the fourteenth century only one aspect of a much larger order by which God governed and regulated the universe. To be more precise, it was the middle member of a hierarchical triad of laws, closely similar to that discerned in the three phases of Biblical history described above, designed to ensure order amongst the lowest and most primitive forms of life to the highest. First came the law of nature, the "lawe of kynde", to which all life was subject : even animals and plants obeyed this law, when they did what was 'natural' to their different species; and man obeyed it when he did was was 'natural' to him as a being endowed with a rational and moral soul. Then came 'positive law', the laws human societies devised for their own better governance, codifying, formalizing, and refining the "lawe of kynde"; above that, there was 'divine law', God's law, mediated to man through the Holy Scriptures and the Holy Church. Man's law, 'positive law', was based on natural justice and the law of "kynde", and guided by and obedient to the revealed dictates of divine

law.[80]   Spenser alludes to these three levels of law
in his Legend of Justice, when he condemns those

> Whom neither dread of God, that devils bindes,
> Nor lawes of men, that common weales containe,
> Nor bands of nature, that wilde beastes restraine,
> Can keep from outrage, and from doing wrong.

(FQ V.xii.1)

The officials of the church and the officials of
the law, therefore, were essentially administrators
of different departments or aspects of one larger
law. And the comparability between them, as parallel
mediators of 'law', the divinely ordained instrument
for the government and regulation of mankind, was
frequently noted. Throughout the *Policraticus*, John
of Salisbury conceives and speaks of the secular and
ecclesiastical powers, *imperium* and *sacerdotium*, as comparable agencies of law and government. They form
"the double power", "the one ministering in things
divine, the other presiding over and displaying its
diligence in human affairs"; both are alike ordained
by God, to "improve the life of man" by providing due
regulation and guidance for his social and spiritual
effort. The officials of state and church both minister to God and His justice, mediating to mankind
"the law, both divine and human". Governance and
regulation are the greatest gift of God to the human
race, and so there is "nothing better or more useful
than a prince, whether ecclesiastical or temporal".
It is the function of both and of the officials under
them to prevent subversion of the justice of God, by
promulgating and enforcing His laws in their respective domains, secular and spiritual.[81] Law and
order being sacred to God, the secular authorities
in whom it is vested in its social dimension really
perform a religious function: the prince is "a
minister of the priestly power", and every office
derived from him concerned with "the execution of
the sacred laws" is "really a religious office".
Conversely, priests are properly legal and judicial
officials, for they "administer the divine laws" of
God - "The lips of the priest keep knowledge, and
from his mouth they seek the law" (Mal.2:7); they
are "the fathers of the Church who judge the
world".[82]   Venality in clerics is therefore seen
as a heightened form of the sale of justice. If
it is wrong for judges and legal officials to be
motivated by desire for gain, how much more heinous
is it for "the fathers of the Church, the judges of
the earth" to "delight in gifts" and "run after

fines and forfeitures". It is because the "love of gifts" is incompatible with justice that mercenary preoccupations in the Pope and his servants are as dangerous as in the legal profession. And John sees the venality of sheriffs, etc, and that discernible in "the ecclesiastical judges" as the twin most crucial threats to the moral law and order of the society of his day.[83]

Priests and judicial officials were, therefore, conceived of as comparable mediators of the law. The parallel between the two professions is put to creatively imaginative use by the author of the fourteenth-century alliterative poem, *St. Erkenwald*. This is a poem about the significance of the transition from paganism to Christianity. The theme is announced in the prologue, which recounts a series of such transitions by narrating the story of the original conversion of the ancient British, their subsequent relapse into heathenism, their re-conversion by St. Augustine, and the re-dedication of their pagan temples to Christian saints. At this early stage of the poem, however, the difference appears to be a largely nominal one: the same churches and 'idols' continue, with only their denominations changed. For the really fundamental difference effected by the transition (the difference between spiritual life and death) is not one that is sensibly apparent; but it is to be dramatically revealed in the subsequent course of the poem - in the transition from hell to heaven of the soul of the virtuous pagan judge, whose uncorrupted body had been found in the precincts of St. Paul's: this occurs the moment he is baptized, that is, formally received into the Christian Church. Without Christianity, man, however virtuous, is debarred from entry into eternal life, which he cannot gain by his own unaided efforts: that is the real inner significance of the transitions related in the prologue.

At the heart of the poem is a scene that focuses in one dramatic cameo the entire nature of the contrast the work as a whole is concerned with: the confrontation between a bishop (St. Erkenwald) and a judge, the official embodiments of God's law and man's law respectively. The equivalence between the two in everything but Christianity is emphasized. Each is dressed in the full regalia appropriate to officials in whom the majesty of two different laws is 'vested': Erkenwald is dressed in full pontificals (130),[84] - that is, mitre, crozier, and episcopal robes; these

accoutrements finding their counterpart in the
crown, sceptre, and mantle of the judge, whose
insignia of office combine the two roles most
identified with the law - those of judge, and king
(who was regarded as the head of law, and whose
prime duty it was to uphold justice and law in his
domains). For, as a mark of respect for the
integrity with which he had administered the law,
the judge's body had been buried with the insignia
of judicial and monarchical office: over his coif
(the badge of the legal profession),85 which he
still wears (83), had been placed a crown, and in
his hand a sceptre. Both men are specifically
associated with the administration of different
levels of the 'law', with their see/seat at London:
Erkenwald is bishop "At love London toun, and the
laghe teches" ("laghe" here meaning 'the faith',
the Christian 'rule' of life), and "Syttes semely in
þe segge of Saynt Paule mynster" (34-5). The law he
administers is that of the king of heaven, "þe
Prince þat Paradis weldes" (161), whose servant he
is. The judge too describes himself as a "lede of
the laghe", though this law was "þe laghe þat þen
þis londe usit" (200), where the meaning is both
the pre-Christian *faith* (as in 34)86 that then
prevailed in England, and the highest kind of law -
man's law, positive law - then (before Christ)
available to mankind, in contradistinction to
divine law. He, like Erkenwald, had his seat in
London, which was under his jurisdiction, as it
was under Erkenwald's ("To sytte upon sayd causes,
þis cite I ȝemyd", 202). He, too, in his administration of the law, was the servant of a king,
though that king was "a prince of parage of
paynymes laghe" (203: "laghe" carrying the same
significant double meaning of 'faith' and 'legal
system' as in 200). The judge discharged his
duties with an integrity and conscientiousness
(229-56)87 comparable with that shown by Erkenwald
in his episcopal office. They are both zealous
guardians of their respective laws. It was the
judge's task to bring an unruly people newly
emerged from war (214-5) to a higher degree of
order by imposing the rule of man's law, positive
law, upon them (231-2). It is Erkenwald's to
enlighten his only recently converted flock as to
the nature of the divine "laghe", and this he
effectively does in the course of the poem, illum-
inating them by his preaching (159-76), and by the
revealing miracle he procures for them through his
prayer (122-7). The implication obviously is that

Erkenwald is looking at a mirror·image of himself as
he would have been had he not been a Christian (and
similar honours were certainly bestowed on his body),
and that the lawyer is the secular counterpart of the
priest. Both are instrumental in the guidance and governance
of mankind, leading them through the successive
degrees of the ladder of law (natural, positive,
divine) to the ultimate perfect order of heaven.
This poem uses the parallel to point to the salvation available through the law of Christ and the
final age of grace, unobtainable through observance,
however strict, of the laws of Abraham and Moses,
natural or positive law.

The two laws are frequently brought together in
Dante. Dante, of course, as is well known, held
extremely specific views on the question of the
relation of Church to state; he was an early
preacher of Montesquieu's doctrine of the separation
of powers, and was adamant that neither should
encroach on the other's jurisdiction.[88] But he saw
them as ordained for comparable functions, the one
to govern and guide man to his perfection as a
social being, the other to perform a similar role
with regard to the fulfilment of his spiritual
potential. But the justice by which kings and
emperors ruled their states on earth was divinely
inspired, and earthly justice was a propaedeutic
for the understanding of the perfect justice by
which God governs. In the *Purgatorio*, for instance,
it is from the idyllic beauty of the Valley of the
Princes that Dante is conveyed to the gates of
Purgatory proper, which he enters through the three
steps of contrition, thenceforward to proceed
through the seven terraces designed for the penitential correction of each of the seven deadly sins.
He is carried from valley to gates in a visionary
dream - by an eagle, the emblem of the Roman empire,
and for Dante symbol of the ideal justice and
order in government toward which secular states
aspired.[89] Through the apprehension of the meaning
of rule, governance, and justice on earth, that is,
Dante is spiritually prepared to enter the realm of
God's justice, the penal correction of sin in this
life, through the sacraments of confession and
penance, and in the next, through the purgatorial
penitentiary. The transition and the mode of
conveyance are significant: it is the common
principle of justice that links God's law and man's,
and makes the latter ' a degree to' the perfect
equity that reigns in heaven.

And, in fact, the parallel between the secular

and sacred law, and therefore the comparability of
lawyer and priest, came especially to the forefront
of the medieval mind where the administration of
the sacrament of shrift was concerned : the
correction of wrong-doing. This, of course, is
especially pertinent to Langland, and in particular
to matters already discussed : the bearing Passus
IV (the court-room scene of the *Visio*) has on the
end of the poem, which concerns shrift; and the
juxtaposition of Passus IV with Passus V, which are
concerned with legal penalties and the atonement
required in shrift respectively. The long simile
in which sinners applying to confessors are compared
to "fals folk" applying to Westminster may also be
recalled here. For it was as a confessor that the
role of the priest as a judge administering the
laws of the heavenly kingdom was most apparent.
The sacrament of shrift required him to hear and
pronounce upon cases of conscience; to conduct an
investigative trial, by close questioning of the
penitent, into the exact nature and extent of the
latter's transgressions; and finally to pronounce
verdict and sentence - in the form of an injunction
to restitution, and/or the imposition of penances.
For punishment, the payment of debts, is essential
to the equity of justice, the informing principle
of the divine law, and of all lesser laws which
derive from it. Sin is an evil, but punishment is
in itself a good, not an evil, since it is an
aspect of justice, and, in the words of St. Thomas
Aquinas, "by punishment, the equilibrium of justice
is restored".90

    To relax penalties and punishments, especially
those due to sin, was therefore a betrayal of
justice, and Langland was by no means the first to
object to the practice on those grounds. Even
before the existence of the friars, such relaxation
was loudly denounced, especially where it was
granted in consideration of 'charitable' donations
to the church. This was to sell justice; to allow
absolution to be purchased by 'alms' rather than by
penance was a sin committed "in fraud of the
justice of God". These are the words of the
twelfth-century John of Salisbury. That the abuse,
and concern about it, predated the friars is also
testified to by Abelard, who severely censures
those clerics who unlawfully remit penalties, and
so *iniuste* pervert the supreme justice of God,
summam Dei iusticiam.91 Nor did the friars, when
they did appear, acquire a monopoly over the
practice of giving absolution in exchange for

donations to the house or order of the confessor, on the grounds that "unto a povre ordre for to yive Is signe that a man is wel yshryve" (*CT*. I. 225-6). The fourteenth-century Spaniard Juan Ruiz castig- ates monks who absolve penitents from penance in exchange for cash donations (st.503ff).After the creation of the first orders of friars, however, in the early thirteenth century, such confessional malpractice became especially associated with them. Accusations about their "sellynge of shrift", their relaxation of penances and restitution in return for donations, were frequently re-iterated;[92] and Langland's complaint that penitents were abandoning their parish priests in favour of the easier absolutions obtainable from them findsechoes from elsewhere - from, for instance, Bishop Brinton, a prelate of some standing in his day.[93]

The analogy between the confessional and the court-room that led to the outcry against such practices as a 'sale of justice' was basic to the function of shrift as the Middle Ages conceived of it. The New Testament itself, in I John 3:4, provided a definition of sin (ἡ ἁμαρτία ἐστὶν ἡ ἀνομία) where "its essence is conceived of as the deviation from the law of God or the transgression of such law".[94] The terms 'trespass' and 'trans- gression' themselves were used to refer both to offences against secular law and to sin. To sin was to pursue or to refuse that which justice forbids should be done or left undone.[95] And a large part of penitential theory and practice in fact originally derived from the law-courts. It was based on the concept of an offence against the law, and the consequent need to satisfy justice by paying the penalty equity demanded.

Abelard, in his *Ethics*, for instance, a work much concerned with shrift, the theory and proper practice of it, makes considerable use of the terminology of and analogy with the law. Many key words and concepts were common to both juristic and penitential theory: in particular, the notion that the offender owed a *penae debitum* (a debt of penalty or punishment) due to the justice (*debitum iusticiae*) he had robbed.[96] *Restitutio, satis- factio debita, emendae* are all essentially concepts derived from the principle of equity, and were used in a legal as well as a penitential context, as were the terms *absolutio, reddicio* and *reddere*.[97] The confessor was conceived of as the competent spiritual 'judge' of his parish, and the term *iudex* is frequently applied to him in penitential literature.

He holds the *locum iudicis*; it is his function to
'moderate' (a legal term) or administer the penalties prescribed by law (*statuendae satisfactiones*)
in the particular case before him. His office is
that of a magistrate (*magisterium legis*), and he
delivers judgment (*arbitrium*) on the penitent.
Again, he is the *spiritualis iudex*, the penitential
judge of his parish; such priests should be
iuriperti, expert in penitential law, not, like
unskilled 'advocates', applying one rule to all
cases.[98] *Iuriperti*, 'skilled in the law', applied
literally to responsible confessors: for there was
a large body of ecclesiastical law relating to
penances, and they would need to be familiar with
such penitential canons (*instituta canonum*) in
deciding and assigning the satisfaction proper in
particular cases.[99] Those from whom this judge was
competent to hear confessions constituted his
jurisdiction (*jurisdictio*)[100]; their confessions
were cases (*causae*) brought before him for decision
as to the type and magnitude of guilt and the
penalty due it;[101] they themselves were his
subjecti, subjects to his penitential authority;
the penance he assigned was the sentence (*sententia*)
pronounced on them.[102] The confessional itself was
referred to as the 'court', or *forum* in Latin (whence
the modern word 'forensic'); the *forum penitentiale*
was conceived of as one of the two courts before
which the sinner was brought by the church: the
confessional being the private analogy of the open
ecclesiastical court (the *ius fori* and the *ius poli*
thus constituting the double church court before
which the Christian was answerable for offences
against the laws of God of which it was the guardian).
The all-important doctrine of restitution (the
obligation to restore whatever money or goods had
been wrongfully acquired) had itself been developed
from Roman Law principles; the concepts of 'mortal
sin' and 'restitution' were, in fact, "the theological equivalents to the Roman Law remedies of
voiding the contract and seeking full redress in
law".[103]
    The equity essential to justice was the chief
criterion by which the spiritual judge was to
determine satisfaction. He represented divine
judgment, *divinum iudicium*, and behind him stood
God, *iudex iustus*, and the *horrendum Dei iudicium*
which could never ultimately be evaded (*Ethics*,
pp.118,80,84).   In ensuring, therefore, that
equity was satisfied by atonement and restitution,
the priest bore a particularly grave responsibility,

for any disproportion between offence and penalty or penance would be made good on the sinner by God, who would sentence him to pay off the balance of punishment due in Purgatory or Hell (*Ethics*, p.109). For God's justice was not to be baulked, and there awaited in the future the great Day of Judgment itself, when justice would be universally, openly, and exactly dealt to all, the supreme court of the universe, capable of reversing the erroneous decisions of lower courts, and from whose own sentences there could be no appeal.

Doomsday: the Middle Ages were more conscious of the etymology of that word than we are today - "Domes dæg", the Day of Judgment. On that day, God as King of the universe would preside in person over the court "þer alle oure causeȝ schal be tryed" (*Pearl*, 702), to pronounce the sentence of His own law on all His subjects. The vividness with which the medieval mind apprehended the analogy with the courts of their own day may be illustrated from a fifteenth-century poem by Friar Herebert, in which, with metaphysical wit, he attempts to bribe the judge, by pointing out that, "Seththe he my robe toke ... He is to me ibounde". Judges, like all feed servants in the Middle Ages, of whatever rank, received robes from their paymaster (whose livery they thus wore) as part of their wages. In the case of judges, the paymaster was of course the King, and they were forbidden, for obvious reasons, to accept robes or fees from anyone else.[104] Herebert is suggesting that, since Christ accepted the garb of human flesh from mankind, the court at Doomsday will be as it were in our pocket, for the judge will have accepted robes from us. It is a witty way of dealing with the significance of the redemption by pursuing the legal analogy indicated in the term "Domesday".[105]

It was perhaps the very concept of Doomsday (which prospect dominated the metaphysical outlook as the great representation of it over the west door did the churches) which most sharpened the awareness of a 'law' of God. Certainly, the abstract notion of the law was vested with a sacred solemnity far exceeding the respect in which it is still generally held today. One current definition of it ran: "Law is a sacred sanction commanding what is honest and forbidding the contrary" (*Lex est sanccio sancta iubens honesta et prohibiens contraria*); and if priests were not infrequently regarded as sacred judges, the officials of the law could, conversely,

be termed *sacerdotes* (priests). For they administered what was sacred. The fifteenth-century
judge and legal theoretician, Sir John Fortescue,
explains the application of the term to the members
of his profession thus: "*Sacerdos enim quasi sacra
dans vel sacra docens, per ethimologiam dicitur,
quia ut dicunt iura leges sacre sunt, quo eas
ministrantes et docentes sacerdotes appellantur*"
("For a priest is by etymology said to be one who
gives or teaches holy things, and, because human
laws are said to be sacred, hence the ministers and
teachers of the law are called priests").[106] It
ought, perhaps, to be remembered that in the Old
Testament, to which Fortescue, like his predec-
essors in the field of juristic theory, turned in
true medieval manner for his Biblical "auctoritee"
(particularly, of course, to the Books of Judges
and Kings), lawyers and priests were in very fact
identical.[107] The state religion and the state law
were one and the same thing, and the Levites were
therefore the official authorities in both fields.
And in medieval Christendom, the Bible was conceived
of as the supreme exemplar for the legislation of
individual states: King Alfred in fact prefaced
his laws with models of Biblical legislation.[108]
Indeed, the separation of the two functions of
church and law belongs to a fairly late stage of
civilization, and is a relatively modern phenomenon.
The example of Iran at this very day may serve to
remind us that the older norm has not faded entirely
from the memory or practice of all the states of
the modern world.

   This particular dissociation of sensibility had
certainly not taken place in Langland's mind, and
the constructive and imaginative use to which he put
the analogy between human and divine law, how he
develops it, will be the subject of the following
chapters. The peculiar Langlandian rigour and
integrity that conveys itself even through the most
confused, diffuse, and bad-tempered parts of his
uneven, but uniquely absorbing, poem is, I believe,
partly the result of his refusal ever to lose sight
of the principles of justice and equity in his
investigations into matters secular and sacred, his
uncompromising faith in the absoluteness of Law.

NOTES

1. See, for instance, R. Kirk, 'References to the Law in
   Piers Plowman', *PMLA* lxviii (1933), 322-7; G. Mathew,
   'Justice and Charity in *The Vision of Piers Plowman*',
   Dominican Studies i (1948), 360-6; P.M. Kean, 'Love, Law
   and *Lewte* in *Piers Plowman*', *RES* n.s.xv (1964), 241-61;
   M.W. Bloomfield, *Piers Plowman as a Fourteenth-Century
   Apocalypse* (New Brunswick, New Jersey, 1961). As M.E.
   Goldsmith points out in *The Figure of Piers Plowman*
   (Cambridge, 1981), it is Bloomfield who has "most plainly
   stated that justice is Langland's theme" (p.115); she
   herself refers to "the teaching about justice and mercy
   which pervades *Piers Plowman*" (p.76), and has many
   pertinent observations to make on the subject. The most
   recent major contribution to the critical literature on
   this aspect of the poem is A. Baldwin, *The Theme of
   Government in Piers Plowman* (Cambridge 1981), to which
   the reader is referred for a fuller bibliography of
   relevant studies (p.92, n.5).
2. See *Policraticus* IV.vii (translation from J. Dickinson,
   The Statesman's Book of John of Salisbury (New York,
   1927), p.33); W.F. Bolton, *Alcuin and Beowulf* (London,
   1979), pp.146-7, 162; *Fortescue on The Governance of
   England*, ed. C. Plummer (Oxford, 1885), pp.206-7; J.W.
   Baldwin, *Masters, Princes, and Merchants: The Social
   Views of Peter the Chanter and his Circle*, 2 vols
   (Princeton, New Jersey, 1970), vol.ii, p.171.
3. Prol.136. All references to the poem are from *The Vision
   of Piers Plowman: A Complete Edition of the B-text*, ed.
   A.V.C. Schmidt (London, 1978), unless otherwise stated.
4. *Libro de Buen Amor*, ed. with facing translation by R.S.
   Willis (Princeton, New Jersey, 1972), st.933.
5. *Policraticus* IV.ii (p.6).
6. *An Edition from the Manuscripts of Book II of Walter
   Hilton's Scale of Perfection*, ed. S.S. Hussey (Ph.D.
   thesis, University of London, 1962), ch.xliii, p.213;
   Pearl, ed. E.V. Gordon (Oxford, 1953), 1.595; *Piers
   Plowman by William Langland: An Edition of the C-text*,
   ed. D. Pearsall (London, 1978),V.32 (all references to
   the C-text are from this edition).
7. See (Dante's?) letter to Can Grande della Scala (*Latin
   Works of Dante Alighieri Translated into English*, tr.
   P.H. Wicksteed (Temple Classics, London, 1904), p.348.
8. *Policraticus* IV.i,VI.xxvi (pp.4,5,266).
9. *The Lay Folks' Catechism*, ed. T.F. Simmons and H.E.
   Nolloth, E.E.T.S. o.s. 118 (1901), 11.587-8 (Wycliffite
   version).
10. See T.P. Dunning, *Piers Plowman: An Interpretation of
    the A-Text* (Dublin, 1937), p.46; J.W. Baldwin, ii.157,
    i.307.

11. *The Faerie Queene*, V (The Legend of Artegall or of Justice) Prol.10. All references to Spenser are from *Spenser: Poetical Works*, ed. J.C. Smith and E.de Selincourt (Oxford, 1912).

12. See G. O'Brien, *Medieval Economic Teaching* (London, 1920), pp.102ff, 133, 177.

13. *cf.* "The iustest man alive, and truest did appeare" (*Faerie Queene*, V.vii.2).

14. On this definition of justice, see also Goldsmith, p.30; Bloomfield, pp.104, 131.

15. *Sir John Fortescue: De Laudibus Legum Anglie*, ed. and tr. S.B. Chrimes (Cambridge, 1942), p.52.

16. *Three Medieval Rhetorical Arts*, ed. J.J. Murphy (Berkeley, Los Angeles, 1971), p.180.

17. *Policraticus* V.viii (p.106).

18. *Scale of Perfection* II xxx (p.124).

19. *Summa Theologica* II-II.lviii-cxx; translations from J. Rickaby, *Aquinas Ethicus: A Translation of the Principal Portions of the Second Part of the Summa Theologica*, 2 vols (London, 1896).

20. See, for instance, the quotations from Jerome and Albertus Magnus cited by Dunning (pp.56, 75) and O'Brien (pp.80ff).

21. For further discussion of this text, and its relation to justice, see Bloomfield, pp.104, 131; and R.W. Frank, *Piers Plowman and the Scheme of Salvation* (New Haven, Connecticut, 1957), pp.106ff.

22. By G. Mathew, *art.cit.*, 363.

23. *La Male Regle*, 1.375; *Balade to My Maister Carpenter*, ll.11-12; *Jonathas and Fellicula*, ll.600-1. All references to Hoccleve are from *Hoccleve's Works: The Minor Poems*, ed. F.J. Furnivall and I. Golancz, E.E.T.S. E.S. 61, 73 (1892, 1897).

24. *The Wakefield Pageants in the Towneley Cycle*, ed. A.C. Cawley (Manchester, 1958), *Processus Noe*, ll.222-23; *Canterbury Tales* III. 425. All references to Chaucer are from *The Works of Geoffrey Chaucer*, ed. F.N. Robinson (2nd ed., London, 1957).

25. *CT* III. 424-5; *John Skelton: The Complete English Poems*, ed. J. Scattergood (Harmondsworth, 1983), *Agenst Garnesche* (iii), 1.173.

26. For examples of these expressions, see *CT* III.130; *The Book of Margery Kempe*, ed. S. Brown Meech and H.E. Allen, E.E.T.S. O.S.212 (1939), p.11; Skelton's *Upon the Dethe ... of the Erle of Northumberlande*, 1.66.

27. *Lay Folks' Catechism*, ll.125-6 (Wycliffite version).

28. *Ibid.*

29. *Scale of Perfection* II.vii (p.18).

30. See *Peter Abelard's Ethics*, ed. with facing translation D.E. Luscombe (Oxford, 1971), pp.89, 113; J.W. Baldwin, ii.97.

31. *Cf.*, for instance, *Libro de Buen Amor* (st 1653): "Quando a Dios *dierdes cuenta* / de los algos e la renta (When you render account to God of your wealth and your income) ..."

32. *Ancrene Wisse, Parts Six and Seven*, ed. G. Shepherd (Manchester, 1972), p.28.

33. *The Book of Margery Kempe*, pp.239, 243.

34. Hoccleve, *The Story of the Monk who Clad the Virgin*, ll.75-6, 102.

35. Of rebels executed in 1415 a contemporary verse comments, "here travell was quyte ful well" (quoted by V.J. Scattergood, *Politics and Poetry in the Fifteenth Century* (London, 1971), p.129); The Wife of Bath uses the word to signify 'getting her own back': "I quitte hem word for word"; "But he was quit, by God and by Seint Joce! I made hym of the same wode a croce" (*CT* III.422, 483-4).

36. As the case of poor Hoccleve demonstrates; and *cf Libro de Buen Amor* (st.1366): "quien a mal omne sirve siempre sera mendigo (he who serves a bad master will always be a beggar)".

37. See *Jack Upland, Friar Daw's Reply and Upland's Rejoinder*, ed. P.L. Heyworth (Oxford, 1968), *Friar Daw's Reply*, l.905.

38. *Medieval English Lyrics*, ed. R.T. Davies (London, 1963), no.65, l.16.

39. This is perhaps most clearly evident in the use of the words 'true' and 'truth' to characterize Trajan and his exemplary zeal for justice in Passus XI (141,151,157-8, 163); *cf*.n.13 *supra*.

40. *Cf*. Bloomfield: "... the introduction of the friars may seem anticlimactic ..." (p.148).

41. On the dating of the A, B and C versions of the poem, see Schmidt, p.xvi.

42. The term *Unite* in the final passūs should be interpreted as referring not only to 'brotherly love and harmony', but also to the *simplicity* or singularity of the truth on which the church is founded, as opposed to the *duplicity* by which the friars falsify that truth. Compare the truth represented by Spenser's *Una*, and falsely simulated by *Duessa*, in Book I of *The Faerie Queene* (and *cf* "truth is one", and right is ever one", *FQ* V.ii.48). It was, in fact, a commonplace of medieval exegesis that "the singular number is always taken *in bono*, the dual *in malo*" (Bolton, p.72); *cf*. Dante in the *De Monarchia* (I.xv.12-15): "... 'being one' is seen to be the root of 'being good' and 'being many' the root of 'being bad' ".

43. The phrase is T.S. Eliot's (*Four Quartets*).

44. *Paradise Lost*, IX.701.

45. See, for instance, *Abelard's Ethics*, pp.111-125 ("... so that the loosing of sins is the equivalent of their forgiveness and their binding the same as their being retained or imposed", p.125).
46. See *OED*, *sv* Procurator, Registrer; and *Langland: Piers Plowman: The Prologue and Passus I-VII*, ed. J.A.W. Bennett (Oxford, 1972), n to II.110.
47. See, for instance, the sermon for Easter Day in *Mirk's Festial*, ed. T. Erbe, E.E.T.S. E.S. 96 (1905), p.131.
48. He was not the only one to do so. The identification became, of course, especially popular in Wycliffite polemic; see, for instance, *Jack Upland*, p.54; *Upland's Rejoinder* (11.329, 373) also associates them with the "false brothers" and those "*qui penetrant domos*" of 2 Cor.II:26 and 2 Tim.3:6, as does Langland (XIII.69a; XX.341).
49. *OED sv* Flatter $v^1(7)$ is relevant here: "To encourage or cheer ... with hopeful or pleasing representations; to inspire with hope, usually on insufficient grounds" (the word is used in this sense at XX.110).
50. That hypocrisy would be the chief threat faced by the church in its last age was a common idea, and one to which Langland's poem gives particularity - though he was not alone in associating the friars with the hypocrisy that would characterize the reign of Antichrist (see D.W. Robertson, *Chaucer's London* (New York, 1968), p.194, for other examples). On the related theory that the church would in the course of its history be threatened by (successively) persecution, heresy, and hypocrisy, see J.A. Burrow, 'Words, Works and Will: Theme and Structure in *Piers Plowman*', in *Piers Plowman: Critical Approaches*, ed. S.S. Hussey (London, 1969), pp.111-124 (pp.113-4).
51. The terms are those used by I.A. Richards to analyze metaphor (*The Philosophy of Rhetoric* (London 1936), Lectures V and VI, *passim*): the 'vehicle' is the image, the 'tenor' the matter figuratively 'conveyed' by it.
52. "Foryifnesse or lenger yeres leve" here may be compared with Hoccleve's request to his debtors for "respyte to sum lenger day" (*Balade to my Maister Carpenter*, 1.18).
53. For these and other charges levelled against executors in contemporary literature, see *Winner and Waster*, ed. I Gollancz (Oxford, 1921; re-issued Cambridge, 1974), 11.441-4; *Libro de Buen Amor*, sts 1538-41; Scattergood, *Politics*, pp. 32, 324.
54. See E. Jenks, *A Short History of English Law* (5th ed, London, 1938), pp. 65, 131.
55. On the corruption prevalent in the jury system (packed juries, bribed juries, perjured juries), see *De Laudibus*, pp.173-4.
56. "This sin is not forgiven until what has been taken is restored". Repentance had also quoted this *dictum* of

St. Augustine (V.272*a*).

57. *ST* I-II.xcvi.6; II-II.lxvi.7: Aquinas taught that
private property was ordained by Providence for the more
efficient satisfaction of needs; any superfluity
remaining after the needs of oneself and one's dependents had been met was therefore due to the poor, to
relieve their needs, was in fact their 'debt'; it was
lawful, therefore, for anyone in real need to relieve
his distress from the property of another, since the
necessities of life were his due. Need thus provided a
dispensation from all breaches of law committed under its
instigation. This became the orthodox position on the
question, and the same principles were often repeated
(see O'Brien, pp.68-9, 86). This consensus as to the
absolute claims of need is discussed by Dunning, p.33;
Bloomfield, p.136; and A. Baldwin, p.9; see also J.W.
Baldwin,i.125. *Necessitas non habet legem* ("Nede ne
hath no lawe") was in fact a principle of Canon Law,
well-known enough to be quoted outside theological or
juristic *compendia*, in semi-serious or ironic contexts:
Juan Ruiz cites it ("coita non ha ley", st 928) in
relation to an amorous predicament, and it appears as
"nede has na peer" in *The Reeve's Tale* (*CT* I.4026).

58. In what appears to be the earliest version of the poem,
Langland says, "Of prynces ant prelatus youre pencyoun
schal aryse", repeating an earlier point he had made
about physicians and their pay - "Of princes ant prelatus
here pencyoun shal aryse" (*Piers Plowman: The Z Version*,
ed. A.G. Rigg and C. Brewer (Toronto, 1983), VII.270-3,
VIII.47-9. The reference to 'princes' and 'pension' in
both cases suggests that he does have in mind a regular
income from the state authorities, rather than that he is
merely advocating that both professions should charge the
rich enough to enable them to give their services free
to the poor (a possible alternative interpretation).

59. *Policraticus* V.x (pp.112-3); J.W. Baldwin, i.191.

60. *Cf.* X.320-1 (and the parallel lines at C.V.173-4): in a
reformed church, friars will not be excluded, but will
have a due share in its patrimony, and so find "bred
withouten beggynge to lyve by".

61. *De Utilitate Credendi*, cap.xii (quoted Dunning, p.37).

62. See A. Baldwin, p.10; 'reason' was, therefore, conceived
of as the basis of 'natural' (unwritten) law (*ibid.*
pp.21-2).

63. *Ibid*, p.42.

64. A.K.R. Kiralfy, *Potter's Outlines of English Legal
History* (5th ed, London, 1958), p.24.

65. In Dunbar's *Ane Drem*, for instance, (*The Poems of William
Dunbar*, ed. J. Kinsley (Oxford, 1979), no.51), Reason
objects to the inequitable distribution of rewards at
court, claiming that "The ballance gois unevin" (ll.61-70,

96-100).

66. See n.56 *supra*.
67. The common expression *lex divina* is used, for instance, by Fortescue (*De Legibus*, p.100), and Abelard (*Ethics*, p.74). The phrase was equally common in the vernacular, and can be instanced from such widely differing contexts as Hoccleve's *Invocacio ad Patrem* ("sende us grace Thy lawes keepe",l.60); *The Book of Margery Kempe* ("obstynat ageyns þe lawes of God", p.38); the orthodox *Lay Folks' Catechism* ("the lawe and þe lare þat langes till halikirke", l.29); the Wycliffite *Jack Upland* ("Cristis lawe",pp.56, 59, 65).
68. See D. Brewer, *Chaucer in his Time* (London, 1963), p.133; *Potter's Outlines*, p.269; and Skeat's note to Prol.210 in the separate edition of the *Visio: The Vision of William Concerning Piers the Plowman*, ed. W.W. Skeat (Oxford, 1869).
69. *Cf. Policraticus* VIII.xviii (p.350): "For the earliest fathers and patriarchs followed nature, the best guide of life. They were succeeded by leaders, beginning with Moyses, who followed the law, and judges who ruled the people by the authority of the law; and we read that the latter were priests". Abelard's *Dialogue Between a Philosopher, a Jew and a Christian* (PL 178. 1652A-1658A) is a philosophical enquiry into the relationship and distinction between the three laws. Langland himself refers to these three eras / laws in Will's encounter with (successively) Abraham, Moses, and the Samaritan/ Christ(XVI-XVII).
70. This was the co-title of his *Ethics* (*ibid*, p.xxx).
71. The words are St. Gregory's (quoted by Dunning, p.149).
72. Quoted by Luscombe, *Ethics*, p.xvi.
73. All quotations from the A-text are from *The Vision of William Concerning Piers the Plowman*, ed. W.W. Skeat, 2 vols (Oxford, 1886).
74. Abelard, *Ethics*, p.99.
75. For examples, see Bolton, p.78; and Robertson, p.67.
76. Aquinas, *ST* II-II.civ.5; Margery Kempe, p.41; Abelard, *Ethics*, p.129; Bloomfield (quoting Gregory), p.60.
77. On humility, the authority of the church and the 'fear of God', see in particular, J. Leclercq, *The Love of Learning and the Desire for God*, tr. C. Misrahi (New York, 1961), pp.201, 206, 246, 216.
78. C-text, IX.220.
79. All references to *La Divina Commedia* are from *Dante: The Divine Comedy* (Italian text with facing translation), tr. J.D. Sinclair (Oxford, 1971).
80. 'Natural' law governed both man's animal and his rational nature: thus sex and love of offspring, for instance, on the one hand, and love of one's neighbour and innate knowledge of right and wrong, on the other, were both the

result of its operation (see Aquinas, *ST* I-II.xciv.2; also P. Dronke's essay "Arbor Caritatis" in *Medieval Studies for J.A.W. Bennett*, ed. P.L. Heyworth (Oxford, 1981), pp.207-43, p.233, n.51). In its latter manifestation, it was held to denote those principles of justice which it seemed connatural to man to recognize, obtaining in societies of differing political and theological persuasions: *ius naturale est quod apud omnes homines eandem habet potestatem* (Fortescue, quoting Aristotle, *De Laudibus*, p.39). See also Fortescue's *De Natura Legis Nature* in *The Works of Sir John Fortescue* collected and arranged Thomas (Fortescue) Lord Clermont, 2 vols (London, 1869). For an analysis of all three laws and their relationship, see Aquinas *ST* I-II.XC-C; Fortescue, *De Laudibus* and *Governance*, *passim*. Human or 'positive' law should never be "ayenst the lawe of God, or ayenst þe lawe off nature" (*Governance*, p.117).

81. VII.xxi, xx; V.iv.v; VIII, xxiii; VII.xix (pp.315, 302, 79, 81, 399, 299).

82. IV.iii; V.v,xvi (pp.9, 80, 154).

83. VIII.xvii, xxiii; V.xvi (pp.346, 408, 151). Further evidence of the equivalence perceived between the ecclesiastical and the secular hierarchy comes in the pairing of ranks often encountered in the literature of the time: thus a duke and an archbishop, an earl and a bishop, etc. were regarded as of equal status (see *De Laudibus*, p.123; *Governance*, p.239).

84. All quotations are from *St. Erkenwald*, ed. H.L. Savage (New Haven, Connecticut, 1926).

85. *Cf Winner and Waster*, ll.149-52. The coif was strictly the peculiar badge of the sergeants-at-law (*De Laudibus*, p.125), from whose ranks judges were appointed. Judges continued to wear the coif; they also wore robes of minever, as does the judge in this poem (l.81).

86. For 'law' in this sense, *cf The Squire's Tale*: "As of the secte of which that he was born He kepte his lay, to which that he was sworn" (*CT*. V.17-18).

87. These lines seem intended to recall the oath sworn by justices when they took up office (for which see *De Laudibus*, p. 204).

88. For Dante's views, see his *De Monarchia*, and *La Divina Commedia*, *passim*. Montesquieu (*L'Esprit des Lois*) was, of course, referring to the separation of the judicial, legislative, and executive functions of government, not like Dante, to the separation of ecclesiastical and secular power.

89. *Purgatorio*, VII-IX; *cf Paradiso*, XVIII-XX.

90. *ST* II-II.cviii.4; punishments, being medicines for the prevention of sin, "have the quality of justice in so far as they are checks upon sin" (II-II.xliii.7); failure "to punish according to the judgment of reason" was a sin

(II-II.clviii.8). Again, Abelard refers to those who feel more repugnance at penance than at their sins as offending against "the just judgment of God which they fear in the form of punishment, hating equity rather than iniquity" (*Ethics*, p.79).

91. *Policraticus* VII.xxi (pp.316, 320); Abelard's *Ethics*, pp.109-11, 118; the latter similarly censures leniency extended to the dying (in consideration of bequests to the church) where restitution should be insisted on (p.84).

92. See, eg, *Upland's Rejoinder*, 1.144; for further examples, see Frank, pp.106-7(n); Bloomfield, p.131.

93. See Robertson, p.191.

94. A. Keiser, *The Influence of Christianity on Old English Poetry* (University of Illinois Studies in Language and Literature, v, 1919), p.98.

95. St. Augustine, *De Duabus Animis*, xi.15 (PL 42.105).

96. Abelard, *Ethics*, p.90; and, in a legal context, *Governance*, p.202; *De Laudibus*, p.64.

97. For examples, see Bennett, note to IV.86; *De Laudibus*, pp.86, 112, 134, 163.

98. Abelard, *Ethics*, pp.118, 104, 106; J.W. Baldwin, ii.42, 97; i.301; ii.76, 43.

99. J.W. Baldwin, i.54; *Ethics*, p.108.

100. J.W. Baldwin, ii.97; *Lay Folks' Catechism*, 1.1166 (Wycliffite Version), p.96 (Latin version); *Libro de Buen Amor*, sts 1146, 1154.

101. Abelard's *Ethics*, p.121; J.W. Baldwin, ii.42, 43.

102. Abelard's *Ethics*, p.106; J.W. Baldwin, ii.97; *Libro de Buen Amor*, st 1155.

103. J.W. Baldwin, i.242; ii.131; i.51-2, 135, 265.

104. Davies, *Lyrics*, no.28, 11.19-21. On judges' robes, see *Governance*, pp.223, 310; *De Laudibus*, p.126. Judges did not, however, always observe this article of their oath (see Scattergood, *Politics*, p.365).

105. Elsewhere one finds Mary or Christ being appealed to as 'advocates' to plead the sinner's cause there (*Libro de Buen Amor*, sts 1641, 1717).

106. *De Laudibus*, pp.6-8; see also Chrimes's note on the definition of law and the etymology of *sacerdos* here repeated by Fortescue (*ibid*, p.147).

107. Cf n69 *supra*.

108. F.M. Stenton, *Anglo-Saxon England* (Oxford, 1943), pp.272-3.

CHAPTER II

REGNUM, *SACERDOTIUM*, JUSTICE, AND MERCY

I: *The Prologue*

If the B and C versions of *Piers Plowman* do represent subsequent revisions of the A text by the poet himself, as is generally agreed, and as seems most likely, then the additions made in the course of those revisions must be of particular interest to the critic. For Langland's style suggests trial and error, and the A text may well have been written to no preconceived plan at all; it breaks off abruptly and inconclusively at the end of Passus XI,[1] as if its author had found that his experimental steps (or *passūs*) had after all only led him down a no-through-road. But the B revision must have been undertaken with some knowledge of the future course of the argument, at least as far as the point it had reached on the first attempt at pursuing it, which includes the whole of the *Visio*. Where, therefore, the poet, in retracing his steps (for they are retraced, and not substantially altered), pauses to emphasize or elaborate a point, one is entitled to assume that one's attention is not being trifled with: that the point is importantly relevant to the overall significance of the work.

The first substantial piece of additional material occurs in the Prologue itself; and since the introductory passages of any work must always play an especially significant role in identifying the nature of the questions to which it will address itself, the matter Langland saw fit to insert here ought to prove particularly pertinent. And the extra lines are in fact precisely calculated to foreground the whole question of governance and the rule of law, and to suggest that Church and State have analogous responsibilities to the respective laws they administer. Before proceeding to examine the passage in detail, however, and its relation to the context into which it is introduced, it will be as well to give some account of that context.

The Prologue as it stood in the A version, then (that is, excluding from consideration the lines added at the time of the B version), proceeded roughly as follows:- The poet falls asleep, and sees in dream the various grades of human society going about their daily business ("Werchynge and wandrynge as the world asketh", 19), that business being allegorically represented as a 'field' of activity poised between the moral poles of good and evil, signified by a "tour on a toft" and a "deep dale" (14-15). In the remainder of the Prologue, various pursuits are selected for moral comment, that is, analyzed from the perspective suggested by the "tour" and the "dale". Ploughmen are commended for their honest labour, and so are recluses who have devoted their lives to prayer and contemplation (20-30). Thereafter, however, the moral emphasis is negative, and the remainder of the groups dealt with are selected that their vices may be condemned rather than their virtues applauded. These are:- minstrels, not the "giltlees" type, but the tellers of bawdy jokes ("japeres and jangeleres, Judas children") - the Benny Hills rather than the Arnaut Daniels of the minstrel world (33-9); beggars who feign disabilities to impose on the charity of others, and whose lives are spent in drunken belligerence and laziness (40-5); pilgrims and palmers who gad off to shrines abroad, and fabricate stories about their adventures there ever afterwards (46-52); hermits who, though dressed as hermits, do not in fact live as recluses, but roam about the country with no fixed employment (53-7); friars (58-67) - the two most frequent charges levelled against this unpopular brotherhood concerned their abuses in preaching and in the confessional, and both are mentioned here: that they twisted Holy Writ to suit their own purposes by 'glozing' it ("Glosed the gospel as hem good liked"), and that they gave absolutions for money, and therefore favoured and were favoured by the rich ("chief to shryve lordes");[2] pardoners who con the commons into buying the papal 'indulgences' which purported to remit the temporal penalties due to sin (68-82); parish priests who, when their parishes are impoverished, repair to London to seek more profitable employment as chantry priests (83-6). The material added at the time of the B revision was inserted at this point, the list originally continuing with:- lawyers, wearing the distinctive badge of the order of sergeants-at-law, the coif, against whom the allegation is that they are more interested in money than in justice (211-6); and ending (the scene having apparently shifted as and when the parish-priests did to London, where, in

the courts of Westminster, sergeants of law were
most commonly to be seen) with the itemization of
various types of city crafts and trades, with the
echo of whose songs and street cries the Prologue
closes.

The criterion through which this piece of
social 'complaint' is focused is clearly occupational. The dreamer is concerned with ways of
earning a living, with men "werchynge and wandrynge
as the world asketh". Against the yardstick
provided by the honest labour of the ploughman are
measured two types of inequity in the obtaining of
a livelihood. For the miscreants subsequently
listed clearly fall into two categories: the shiftless (those who do nothing at all to earn their
"lyflod"), and the venal (those who come by it by
selling what should not be for sale - that is,
spiritual and moral truth, religion and justice).
For the antithesis between the ploughmen (who
"swonken ful harde", 21) and the groups mentioned in
33-57 is plainly one based on the popular 'winner-
waster' polarity alluded to in the assertion that
the ploughman "wonnen that thise wastours with
glotonye destruyeth" (22). The winner-waster
opposition has here been adapted to allude to a
second contrast, that between hard 'swinking' and
greedy 'eating', a vernacular version of an
antithesis found elsewhere in the literature of
occupational morality ("*Quid ergo dicemus de illis
qui in nullo laborant, tamen omnia devorant?*" asks
Robert of Courson[3]): the antithesis between gain
proportionate to and therefore justified by labour,
and disproportionate consumption. The first set
of antitypes to the ploughmen are, then, the social
parasites, and Langland's principal objection is in
each case that they do nothing to earn their
"lyflod", are too idle to do an honest day's work.
The minstrels, the purveyors of vacuus popular
entertainment (and many modern fathers feel the same
about today's pop-singers), simply never do any
real work, and should do, for they "han wit at wille
to werken if they wolde" (37). The beggars
"Faiteden for hire foode" (42) - scrounged it by
feigning disability or distress, when the real
motive for their begging was "sory sleuthe" (45);
they may perhaps be said to represent the
fourteenth-century equivalent of the Social
Security scroungers of our own day. The objection
to those types of pilgrims and palmers that are
next described is obviously that these ostensibly
pious journeys are made simply for the sake of

having a holiday, a jolly get-together and a good gossip (they "plighten hem togidere" and "Wenten forth in hire wey with many wise tales", 46-8) - and dining out for ever after on the tall travellers' tales they bring back with them (49-52). The hermits nominally dedicated to the life of a recluse, but in fact roaming the countryside, are simply "Grete lobies and longe that lothe were to swynke" (55), donning the hermit's garb simply to give some colour to their vagrant existence: they have "shopen hem heremytes hire ese to have" (57). The peripatetic life-style of most of the groups mentioned reflects their lack of 'fixed' employment, and makes them stand, not only against the ploughmen, as wasters to winners, but also against the genuine recluses, devoted to a life of prayer, who "Coveiten noght in contree to cairen aboute" (29).

Langland then, however, characteristically proceeds to complicate the moral diagram he has been drawing. For the vicious clerics and lawyers he goes on to scrutinize do not stand against the ploughmen quite as wasters against winners. These men are certainly active enough in the pursuit of gainful employment, and would in fact have been recognized as 'winners' (friars and lawyers are grouped under Winner's banner in *Winner and Waster*).[4] So perhaps getting something for nothing may not be the only cause of occupational inequity; there is also getting it for the wrong things, and the kind of inequilibrium here consists in false rather than inadequate measure; this offence to commutative justice[5] lies in the exchange for money of activities which should never be measurable in money or goods, and Langland's alliterative emphases incisively point to the incongruity between them:

(Friars)	Prechynge the peple for profit of the wombe ...
	For coveitise of copes construwed it as thei wolde. (59,61)
(Priests)	And syngen ther for symonie, for silver is swete. (86)
(Lawyers)	Pleteden for penyes and poundes the lawe. (213)

"Charite hath ben chapman" (64) is perhaps the most telling alliterative conjunction of all, since it points to the radical incompatibility between the whole nature of the clerical vocation ("charite", essentially something given freely), and what may be exchangeable for money and thus the object of "chapmanhede" (of which Langland does not disapprove in itself: it is "a permutacion apertly - a penyworth for another" (III.258), and thus perfectly equitable). It is with the pardoner, however, that Langland's imagination (nearly always best stimulated by anger) most vividly succeeds in betraying exactly the illegitimate use being made by this sect of all their vaunted paraphernalia: it is being used to "blere the eyen" (the idiom was the medieval equivalent of our modern 'pull the wool across the eyes'[6]) of the people, to deceive and to disguise beneath an officiously imposing display what is in fact a money-making enterprise. These abstract notions Langland's allegory translates into crudely physical gestures, as the pardoner is pictured literally dimming the sight with his "brevet", by boxing his hearers about the head with it, and literally using his "rageman" to rake in the profits:

> He bonched hem with his brevet and blered hire eighen,
> And raughte with his rageman rynges and broches.

> (74-5)

The Prologue closes by transposing into rowdy music the two vices of idleness and venality with which it has dealt. We hear the songs in which shiftless labourers idle away the day:

> As dykeres and delveres that doon hire dedes ille
> And dryveth forth the longe day with *'Dieu save
> Dame Emme!'*

> (224-5)

- lines which find a parallel in Passus VI, where Langland again associates shirking with idle popular songs, the vacuous activity used by wastrels as a substitute for real labour:

> Thanne seten somme and songen atte nale,
> And holpen ere this half acre with 'How trolly lolly!'

> (115-6)

In the Prologue, the song of the loafing labourers
is succeded by the raucous antiphon of inn-keepers
and caterers, lustily uttering their wares in the
hopes of attracting custom:

> Cokes and hire knaves cryden, 'Hote pies, hote!
> Goode gees and grys! Go we dyne, go we!'
> Taverners until hem tolden the same:
> 'Whit wyn of Oseye and wyn of Gascoigne,
> Of the Ryn and of the Rochel, the roost to defie!'

The sloth and greed the dreamer has seen in the
world could hardly be more tellingly expressed.[7]
     Already, then, we see Langland's concern with
inequity, imbalance between input and output,
between what is given and what is taken, particularly as this concerns "labour" and "lyflod", an
issue to be more thoroughly explored in Passus VI,
but which is also to act as a touchstone for more
metaphysical investigations into what input
justifies what out-take. The dreamer is primarily
aware here that people do not "geten gold ...
giltlees" (34); they get it unfairly, and it is
thus distributed inequitably, going to the lazy and
greedy ("ye gyven youre gold glotons to helpe"),
and not as a true counterbalance for honest work
or real need, the vicious sharing the silver that
"the povere peple of the parissche sholde have if
they ne were" (82). That the dreamer's first
question to Holy Church in the following Passus
should be "... the moneie of this molde that men
so faste holdeth - Telleth me to whom that tresour
appendeth" is, therefore, not surprising. How is a
livelihood properly come by? What kind and what
degree of "labour" constitutes the 'just price'
of it, what is the proper measure for "mesurable
hire?"

     Furthermore, within the moral *schema* of the
Prologue as described above, there is some evidence
of an attempt to correlate secular and spiritual,
active and contemplative. This is especially
relevant to the passage added in the B revision, and
to what I see as an essential principle of Langland's
procedure as a whole: his application to spiritual
matters of the rules he derives from his pre-
occupation with law and justice in the secular
world. He trusts his sense of justice and equity,
and does not seek to transcend the kind of
observance of it he realizes to be essential in a
well-governed and equitable state on earth. At the

beginning of the Prologue, two types of legitimate "labour" are offered as positives against which to judge the illegitimate activities that follow. First come the types of honest secular labour in the active life, the ploughmen:

> Somme putten hem to the plough, pleiden ful selde,
> In settynge and sowynge swonken ful harde.

(20-1)

These are paralleled, in alliteration and idiom, two lines later by their counterparts in the contemplative sphere, whose spiritual labour is prayer:

> In preieres and penaunce putten hem manye,
> Al for the love of Oure Lord lyveden ful streyte.

(25-6)

The devotion to the obligations of the employment the two groups have respectively committed themselves to is mirrored in the voluntary restrictions they impose on themselves in time and place: they do not leave their 'posts', or take time off for tea-breaks or holidays. The ploughman stays at the plough, allows himself little leisure ("pleiden ful selde"), the recluses stay in their cells - the phrase "ful streyte" fuses the moral and physical strictness, straitness, of their lives. By contrast, the various categories of shirkers whose itemization follows lead a vagrant life of perpetual holiday, of unfixed employment, as already noted. Again, there is an analogy suggested between secular and spiritual 'wastrels'. The minstrels and beggars who do no real 'active' work, but merely roam the countryside, are juxtaposed with the vagrants of the spiritual world, the sham pilgrims and hermits, who do no real devotional labour, and for whom shrines and the garb of a recluse are merely an excuse for leading a vagabond and shiftless existence.

Most importantly, however, when Langland turns to the venal, the clerics who turn religion to their own profit, and are thus guilty of "symonie" (the friars, pardoners, and parish priests), are juxtaposed with lawyers who hold justice and law up for sale. The implications of the juxtaposition would not have been lost on a medieval audience, as I trust the preceding chapter will have demonstrated: the clergy are selling God's law, as the "clerkis of mannes law" are selling that of the human King. When justice itself is for sale, divine and secular, what hope of a just society, spiritually or politically? And it is between these two types of "clerkes" that the extra material added in the B revision occurs. It is quoted in full below, the well-known fable of the rats and mice alone being omitted, save for its concluding lines:

> Bisshopes and bachelers, bothe maistres and doctours –
> That han cure under Crist, and crownynge in tokene
> And signe that thei sholden shryven hire parisshens,
> Prechen and praye for hem, and the povere fede –
> Liggen at Londoun in Lenten and ellis.
> Somme serven the King and his silver telle,
> In Cheker and in Chauncelrie chalangen his dettes
> Of wardes and of wardemotes, weyves and streyves.
> And somme serven as servaunts lordes and ladies,
> And in stede of stywardes sitten and demen.
> Hire messe and hire matyns and many of hire houres
> Arn doone undevoutliche; drede is at the laste
> Lest Crist in Consistorie acorse ful manye!
> I parceyved of the power that Peter hadde to kepe –
> To bynden and unbynden, as the Book telleth –
> How he it lefte with love as Oure Lord highte
> Amonges foure vertues, most vertuous of alle vertues,
> That cardinals ben called and closynge yates
> There Crist is in kyngdom, to close and to shette,
> And to opene it to hem and hevene blisse shewe.
> Ac of the Cardinals at court that kaughte of that
>   name
> And power presumed in hem a Pope to make
> To han the power that Peter hadde, impugnen I nelle –
> For in love and in lettrure the eleccion bilongeth;
> Forthi I kan and kan naught of court speke moore.
> Thanne kam ther a Kyng: Knyghthod hym ladde;
> Might of the communes made hym to regne.
> And thanne cam Kynde Wit and clerkes he made,
> For to counseillen the Kyng and the Commune save.
> The Kyng and Knyghthod and Clergie bothe
> Casten that the Commune sholde hem communes fynde.
> The Commune contreved of Kynde Wit craftes,
> And for profit of al the peple plowmen ordeyned
> To tilie and to traveille as trewe lif asketh.
> The Kyng and the Commune and Kynde Wit the thridde
> Shopen lawe and leaute – ech lif to knowe his owene.
> Thanne loked up a lunatik, a leene thyng withalle,
> And knelynge to the Kyng clergially he seide,

'Crist kepe thee, sire Kyng, and thi kyngryche,
And lene thee lede thi lond so leaute thee lovye,
And for thi rightful rulyng be rewarded in hevene!'
    And sithen in the eyr on heigh an aungel of hevene
Lowed to speke in Latyn - for lewed men ne koude
Jangle ne jugge that justifie hem sholde,
But suffren and serven - forthi seide the aungel:
" 'Sum Rex, sum Princeps"; *neutrum fortasse deinceps!*
O qui iura regis Christi specialia regis,
Hoc quod agas melius - iustus es, esto pius!
Nudum ius a te vestiri vult pietate.
Qualia vis metere, talia grana sere:
Si ius nudatur, nudo de iure metatur;
Si seritur pietas, de pietate metas'.
    Thanne greved hym a goliardeis, a gloton of wordes,
And to the aungel an heigh answerde after:
'Dum "rex" a "regere" dicatur nomen habere,
Nomen habet sine re nisi studet iura tenere'.
    Thanne can al the commune crye in vers of Latyn
To the Kynges counseil - construe whoso wolde -
'Precepta Regis sunt nobis vincula legis!'
    With that ran ther a route of ratons at ones ...
'For may no renk ther reste have for ratons by nyghte.
For many mennes malt we mees wolde destruye,
And also ye route of ratons rende mennes clothes,
Nere the cat of the court that kan you overlepe;
For hadde ye rattes youre raik ye kouthe noght rule
    yowselve.
    'I seye for me', quod the mous, 'I se so muchel
    after,
Shal nevere the cat ne the kiton by my counseil be
    greved,
Ne carpynge of this coler that costed me nevere.
And though it costned me catel, biknowen it I nolde,
But suffren as hymself wolde so doon as hym liketh -
Coupled and uncoupled to cacche what thei mowe.
Forthi ech a wis wight I warne - wite wel his owene!'
    (What this metels bymeneth, ye men that ben murye,
Devyne ye - for I ne dar, by deere God in hevene)!
    Yet hoved ther an hundred in howves of selk,   etc.

                                        (87-211)

Though such a lenghthy insertion may theoretically
appear to mask the significance of the original
juxtaposition of clerics and lawyers, it in effect
emphasizes that significance, by providing an
examination of the origins, the *raison d'être*, the
authority and nature of the two laws they respectively represent. A larger and more intellectualized
justaposition (between allegorical accounts of the

foundation and nature of Church and State authority)
replaces the former one, and imposes on the latter
sections of the Prologue as a whole an elaborate
chiasmic structure - whereby the investigations
into the origins and power of Church and State are
flanked by examples of the actual contemporary
corruption among the lower officials responsible
for administering the laws of each: venal clerics
(58-99);   St. Peter's Church and its power (100-111);
the King and his responsibility to law and justice
(112-210);   venal lawyers (211-216).   The juxtaposed accounts of church and state within the added
lines serve to focus the attention squarely on the
subject of authority.   This was a matter on which
the classic position had been formulated by Pope
Gelasius I at the end of the fifth century,
according to whom all authority was "divided into
two spheres, the *sacerdotium* (spiritual) and the
regnum (temporal)".   This notion clearly underlies
Langland's lines, and in treating *sacerdotium* and
regnum together he is following earlier ethical
theologians who had likewise found that "since
princes and prelates were those assuming the
responsibilities of government, they performed many
functions in common and could be treated together".[8]
      In this addition, then, Langland proceeds to
the top of each of the institutions concerned, and
goes back in time to examine in that figurehead
the whole nature of the authority vested in him
(and so in his servants), and how it ought to be
exercised.   As far as the Church is concerned,
he links his enquiry to the foregoing matter by
first continuing his illustration of the mercenary
orientation of the contemporary clergy (already
exemplified in the practices of friars, pardoners,
and parish priests) by turning his attention to
the same vice as manifested by the episcopacy - the
bishops.   This is, in one sense, already to go to
the top of the ecclesiastical hierarchy, for in
every diocese the bishop was the supreme authority,
the ecclesiastical 'king',[9] and the rank of bishop
is used elsewhere in the poem to symbolize that of
the highest authority: in one of the many
definitions of Do-Wel, Do-Bet, and Do-Best, the
responsibility for enforcement of rule undertaken
by Do-Best is expressed in the fact that he "bereth
a bisshopes croce" (VIII.96);   and in Passus XV (39-
42), the authority the rank connoted is revealed in
the dreamer's rehearsal to Anima of the many grand-
sounding titles by which it was variously referred
to - Bishop, Presul, Pontifex, Metropolitanus,

Pastor, as well as Episcopus (the etymological sense
of which is 'overseer'). The bishops here, like the
Church officials referred to before them, are
represented as neglecting their proper duties, to
pursue lucrative secular employment in the service
of the crown or of other nobles of the land, the
particular examples given being the frequency with
which they are found presiding over the royal or
manorial courts. The breach of trust thus committed
with respect to their true offices is made clear
from 88-91, in the first of three instances in this
added passage where Langland defines the real
nature of authority from the logic implied by the
title and symbols of the office in question (*cf*.
the attention to Peter's keys, and to the word
'cardinal' at 100-7; and to the word *Rex* at 141).
Here, he pauses to emphasize what the "crownynge"
(tonsure) and "cure" (cure of souls, pastoral
responsibility) possessed by bishops really
betokens or signifies ("in tokene And signe"), what
they really 'mean'. They epitomize the comple-
mentary aspects of any office that involves government: the care that belongs to responsibility, and
the crown of authority. The duties that properly
belong to such spiritual authority are then listed,
the conduct of the sacrament of shrift being the
first mentioned. For bishops hold office "under
Crist"; they are the servants of the King of
Heaven, and it is their prime duty to administer
His justice in the court of confession, hearing
cases, and dispensing sentence and pardon, in the
form of penance and absolution. This they were
especially obliged to do in Lent;[10] when, as at
other times, the bishops are, however, to be found
in London, corruptly serving the interests of a
King other than the one whose robes they wear. It
is specifically financial and legal offices held
under the Crown that Langland mentions:

> Somme serven the King and his silver tellen,
> In Cheker and in Chauncelrie chalangen his dettes.

There is probably some secondary emphasis on the
word "his" in each of these lines. It is the
payments due to the King of Heaven through the
debts of sin that, as "registrer(s) to receyve
redde quod debes", they should be collecting,
judging cases of conscience in the confessional,
not Crown cases in the Courts of Exchequer and
Chancery, or other matters in the manorial courts,
where they "in stede of stywardes sitten and demen".

They are not stewards, they are bishops, and are
usurping secular judicial functions to the detriment of their true offices as spiritual judges in
spiritual courts.   On these false justices who
have neglected His law Christ himself will pronounce
sentence on the Day of Judgment, His court on that
day being appropriately referred to as "consistorie",
the diocesan court over which the bishops should be
presiding;   and His sentence as a 'curse', the
formal term for the interdictions pronounced in the
Church courts.[11]   Christ, the supreme Bishop and
Judge, will condemn them with a justice both
poetic and exact: from the "*consistorium palatii
summi regis in quo leges et iura discernet*".[12]
Behind and beyond the courts over which the bishops
actually preside lie the neglected Church courts
and courts of confessional, and the Court of God
at the Day of Judgment.

From the office of Bishop, Langland moves to
that of the bishops' Bishop, the Bishop of Rome,
the Pope, to examine the whole nature and origin
of clerical authority.   He goes right back to
first principles, directing his attention to the
very first Pope, St. Peter, and to the text that
provided the basis of his authority, and that of
his successors in the See of Rome: the words that
gave the power to bind and to unbind, to open and
close the gates of heaven, ever afterwards
betokened by the keys that were St. Peter's symbol,
and that of those who succeeded him as heads of
the Church, the Popes.   It was on this text that
the clerical power of excommunication rested: the
power to debar sinners from the sacrament, to close
the gates of the Church upon them, in symbolic
expression of the closure of the gates of heaven
also.   The gates were opened, loosened, by
absolution, in the with-holding or granting of
which at shrift even the lesser clergy exercised
the power of the keys.[13]   In accord with what
principle ought these penalties and pardons of the
divine law to be administered by its officials?
Langland's answer to this question comes in his
account of how he conceives Peter to have 'left'
his power.   In justice and in equity, the gates of
heaven must be opened to those who obey the prime
tenet of the New Law (Charity, or Love), and
exercise the four cardinal virtues (Justice,
Temperance, Fortitude, Prudence) on which the
Natural and Old Law depend.

John of Salisbury compares the cardinal
virtues to the four rivers of Paradise, because

they "flow like primary rivulets from the original
source of honour and right living ... and beget
from themselves the streams of all other good
things". Derived from Aristotle, they belonged to
the 'natural' law; that is, knowledge of them was
innate, did not depend on the Christian revelation.
In this, they contrasted with the theological
virtues (faith, hope, and charity), which did not
derive from natural justice, and could be possessed
only by Christians ("a solis fidelibus possidentur"),
and were "a product of God's grace, rather than
man's good intentions". The cardinal virtues, on
the other hand, were the product of "reason" and
"nature", and were normally regarded as part of
the pre-Christian, natural law;[14] hence they are
cited, for instance, by the pagan in Abelard's
*Dialogue Between a Philosopher, a Jew, and a
Christian*, the three *personae* of which represent
the Natural, Old, and New Laws respectively.[15] The
theological virtues were, therefore, normally
regarded as superior, and Langland does progress
to these (XVI-XVII), but only to return to and
re-emphasize the cardinal, the 'political' virtues
"which suit men living in society"[16] (XIX.277ff).
It is rather striking, in fact, that the essential
power of the Church, the agency for the revealed
truth of Christianity, is then and here associated
with them rather than with the theological virtues.
Christianity does not, for Langland, supersede the
Natural Law, but perfects through its new law of
love man's innate and primary perception of truth,
and gives to the virtues he cultivates according
to those natural lights the ability to open for him
the gates of heaven (which they could not do
before Christ and the Church He founded provided
atonement for original sin). Christianity, in
short, gives efficacy to natural social justice.
This fulfilment of the Old and New Laws is also
what true Christians are seen to be cultivating at
the end of the poem, "that love myghte wexe Among
thise foure vertues, and vices destruye"(XIX.312-3).
For this is what must and will open the gates of
heaven to individual mortals. The equity of this
analysis is here in the Prologue re-inforced by the
etymological pun on 'cardinal'. The word derives
from the Latin *cardo*=hinge, and it is on the
exercise of the cardinal virtues, therefore, that
the gates of heaven must truly 'hinge'. The
equilibrium between reward and desert is emphasized
by the pun: the hinges of the gates of heaven are

precisely the 'hinge' or cardinal virtues. That is, they will open to those who deserve it, and not otherwise. By claiming that Peter's power was thus left to every Christian to exercise on his own behalf, Langland is certainly not denying that the Church has any authority to give or with-hold pardon, excommunicate, or absolve. He is merely stating the principle according to which the power of the keys ought to be exercised, and perhaps denying the efficacy of absolutions given or with-held where they do not accord with the character and conduct on which salvation truly 'hinges'. He would not have been the first orthodox Catholic to do so.[17]

In stating the abstract truth of the matter, Langland's allegorical mode in this added passage has naturally shifted towards personification allegory ("he it lefte with love ... Amonges foure vertues"). This makes the contrast between ideal theory and actual practice, between the cardinal virtues and the Cardinals of the Curia that "kaughte of that name", the more marked. The true ruling principle is exercised only by abstractions, the actual rule of the church by those who should embody it (Peter's successor, the Pope, and his Cardinals) is rather different: or so Langland implies by a somewhat heavy dark hint.

The reference to the proper "eleccion" of the Pope, and to his "court" (the Curia), and to the "kyngdom" of Christ, prepares for the transition to the following passage, on the 'election' of a king, and the proper governance of *his* kingdom. Having returned to first principles in the case of the clerks of God's law, by examining the office of the Pope, the head of the Church, and its origins, he now adopts the same procedure with respect to the clerks of man's law. He turns his attention to the King, the "heed of lawe" (XIX.472), whose servants they are, and to the origins and the rationale of kingship.

As he had pointed to the divine authority on which the Church as an instrument of government rested, so his allegory now legitimates the institution of secular rule, regality, in several different ways. As Langland describes it, kingship properly derives not from an arbitrary imposition by one powerful man, but by a natural process and by the common consent of all ranks of society, who create a king for their own better ordering and functioning, as instructed by "Kynde Wit" (natural

reason). A century later, Sir John Fortescue was
to distinguish two types of monarchical rule: the
absolute, and the 'political'. The former orig-
inated in an initial usurpation of power, the latter
by a natural political process, as a result of the
will of the people themselves. Langland's account
here of the true *raison d'être* of kingship
corresponds closely with Fortescue's of the origins
and nature of 'political' monarchy.[18]

It was, in fact, quite common in discussions
of the origin and rationale of kingship to
attribute it to the natural will of the people for
effective government and justice, to see an
implicit social consent to its desirability, and
so to declare that it was, essentially and
originally, 'elective' in nature. It was what
people 'chose' as the best way of ensuring law and
order;[19] that is, common assent to dominion was
assumed. Kingship was, therefore, consonant with
and arose by the operation of the 'natural law'
("*naturaliter tamen et legis naturae institutione
sortitum est*"[20]); it was the 'natural' means of
giving authority to law, order, justice. Hence it
has here the sanction of political "Kynde Wit";
and the prominence given to this abstraction in the
creation of the supreme ruler amounts to an
allegorical emphasis on the proper basis in the
Law of Nature ideally possessed by man's law
(written/positive law). For the laws which the
King here proclaims by deliberate act, or 'shapes',
are framed at the instigation of "Kynde Wit", and
designed to further a natural social desideratum:
that, for the optimum efficiency of the political
whole, every individual's role and duties should
be precisely defined: "ech lif to knowe his
owene". That phrase seems especially applicable
to a state of affairs in which various classes have
been accused of usurping functions that do not
properly belong to them: where a pardoner has
preached "as he a preest were" (68), and bishops
"in stede of stywardes sitten and demen". Such
confusion of roles results in serious moral as
well as political disorder.[21]

Arising, then, from man's natural reason,
and thus from the Law of Nature, positive law,
being an impulse toward order, was further regarded
as divinely inspired, and sanctioned by God. It
is this sanction that the "lunatik" now requests,
calling down God's blessing on the newly founded
king-dom. That the prayer should be put into the
mouth of a lunatic is a prime example of the

peculiar piquancy and density of Langland's allegory. He had the misfortune to be at once a realist and an uncompromising idealist; hence even while he states the ideal truth, part of his mind labels the trust that it can ever be so in fact as foolish, or "lunatik", and belonging to a "clergial" ivory tower. However, the lunatic's prayer appears to be heard, for it is immediately answered by the descent of an angel.

The angel's primary function at this point is to add the third dimension of Law, divine law, to the natural and positive law already represented by Kynde Wit and the King; and to demonstrate that positive law, besides being founded on the *Lex Naturae*, is also the obedient guarduan of divine law. For the justice it is the King's function through his laws to uphold is sacred, and a part of divine law; it is the *iura regis Christi specialia* that he administers. And the two phases of law of which Abraham and Moses were the types are therefore now supplemented with the *Lex Christi*: the law that gave and required mercy. The King must temper justice with the mercy of the New Law, and if he does so he will himself enjoy that mercy. The angel further establishes that, though the king's power may be absolute with respect to the positive law that emanates from him, he is himself subject to the divine law. On the vexed question as to whether the king, as "heed of lawe", was above his own laws, opinions varied; but all agreed that divine law was supreme over positive law. In the *Policraticus*, John of Salisbury had defined the position as follows: the king was not subject to the laws of his own statutes, but he was to the divine law of eternal justice, the rule of which was equity. This the angel affirms: the king must exercise his power with care, for he is himself subject to the *iura regis Christi*, the unalterable equitable principle of which is that one must do as one would be done by. It is thus by an angel that this central axiom of justice (the principle under-lying all three levels of law, obtaining "before the law (*ie*, in the *tempus naturae*), under the law, and still under the new covenant of grace"[22]) is intro-duced into the poem: as a given from above, not itself subject to discussion. Form mirrors content in the measured parallelism of the three successive lines in which the principle is enunc-iated (136-8), and it is a principle that other texts repeated by Langland in the *Visio* will also enshrine: *Eadum mensura qua mensi fueritis*

remecietur vobis; Date, et dabitur vobis; while
Qualia vis metere, talia grana sere is a rule due
to become literalized in Passus VI. It is the rule
of *quid pro quo*, of equilibrium between reward and
desert, and it is to be applied by Langland as a
touchstone to all the questions he raises - crime,
sin, labour, and even, as here, to mercy and
forgiveness: in the sense that these are given
only to those who show them to others, who pay for
them in kind (a point later to be emphasized by
Holy Church and the Good Samaritan).[23] And here
again the natural law is sanctioned and reinforced
by the revealed law of Christ and Christianity: as
St. Peter's keys had proved to be the cardinal
virtues, so the primary principle of all law ('do
as you would be done by'), which formed the basis
of natural law,[24] is given direct restatement by
an angelic expositor of the *iura regis Christi*.

Langland has thus fused in one speech two
apparently contradictory features of the divine
law: the mercy of the *Lex Christi*, as opposed to
the *nudum ius* of the laws of Abraham and Moses;
and the strict equity axiomatic to divine as to
all derivative justice. There is much that is
potentially problematic, however, in Langland's
making the former actually itself operative only
on the latter principle. If the king is to show
mercy in enforcing the law, to forgive its
penalties, in order that he may sow what he hopes
to reap, that will necessarily entail that the
recipients of his mercy shall not have reaped as
they sowed. In observing that rule on his own
behalf, he will be relaxing it on behalf of others;
and if it is sacred, they will then fall into that
one unpardonable sin of debt - a penalty owed, but
not paid. The paradox resultant on applying the
rule of equity to charity is thus that, though it
must always be equitable to give what has not been
earned (thereby to earn similar grace - a word
related to *gratis*, 'free' - for oneself), it must
always be inequitable to receive it. It is
Conscience's famous 'turned page': the text that
reads at the foot of the *recto*, *Honorem adquiret
qui dat munera;* but overleaf on the *verso*, *Animam
autem aufert accepientium* (III.335-353).

The angel appears indifferent to the knotty
problems he has posed for minds merely mortal, but
there is one person present who has the traditional
sauce of the "goliardeis" to point them out. His
objection, marring the confident idealism of the
tone, is with some irritation dismissed by the

narrative voice as a cavil from a too-clever
"goliardeis, a gloton of wordes", which presumably
applies principally to his "clergial" etymological
reasoning. If the angel counsels the king to
relax rules, on the principle that one must reap as
one sows, the "goliardeis", on the same principle,
would prefer to see them enforced. A ruler who does
not keep the rules is scarcely worthy the name, he
reasons: *Dum 'rex' a regere dicatur nomen habere,
Nomen habet sine re nisi studet iura tenere ("non
autem regit qui non corrigit"*, as this popular
medieval tag quoted by him was glossed by
Isidore[25]). He would perhaps prefer that criminals
should reap their lawful deserts on earth, than that
the King should reap his in heaven. And before we
too readily dismiss his interjection as an ungen-
erous quibble against the sublime principle of
mercy, we should perhaps recall the state of the
legal system in the Middle Ages.[26] It was not for
the unhappy, but for the rich and powerful, that
the penalties of the law were most frequently
waived. And by the time we come to Passus IV, we
may be more inclined to admit the merits of
rigorous enforcement of rules as against the
'mercy' requested for Wrong by Mede: Reason at that
point certainly takes the goliardic rather than the
angelic line. However, the goliard's interjection
is at present ignored by narrator and *personae*, and
idealism re-asserts itself as his quibble is
drowned in the spontaneous profession by the
Commons of a loyal obedience so total as almost to
suggest that there will, in any case, be no
criminals to occasion the problem to arise.

What the Commons proclaim is their own version
of a central tenet of the Civil or Roman Law: *quod
principi placuit legis habet vigorem.*[27] The obedience due to the king is absolute, as he is the
embodiment of the law which emanates from him: let
the king study to be just, the Commons not to
quibble or "jangle" but obey.

At this point, it is worth considering why
these three *dicta* on the law are in Latin. The
etymological reasoning of the goliard, of course,
would not work in English, and as a clerk he would
in any case be familiar with Latin. For the angel's
Latin, again, explanations are not lacking: it
provides an appropriate shift to a higher register
for this spokesman of the divine law; and the text
itself gives a further specific reason for the
choice of the learned tongue by this messanger of
God:

>   ... for lewed men ne koude
> Jangle ne jugge that justifie hem sholde,
> But suffren and serven - forthi seide the aungel:

This could mean either or both of two things: (a)
the Commons must not learn to excuse themselves by
arguing the merits of mercy; they should "knowe
(their) owene", and it is not theirs to reason why,
but simply to obey, and the angel's admonishment is
for the king's ears only - if the king is over-harsh,
that is a matter between him and his Maker, and it
is not for his subjects to 'jangle' learned arguments in their own 'justification'; or (b) the
common mass of people upon whom the force of the law
falls are simple, inarticulate people, unable to
afford lawyers or to plead their own causes with
the eloquence that might earn them some mitigation
of sentence - their only advocate, therefore, is the
injunction to mercy laid down by the divine law,
which must act as 'learned' counsel for them.[28]
Either interpretation of the lines would afford a
sufficient reason for the angel to speak in a
language not at the command of the uneducated
laiety. The Commons, however, apparently know
enough Latin to utter their avowal of obedience at
145 in that tongue. Poetic licence may no doubt
properly be invoked to sanction the inconsistency,
but it does suggest that some instinct prompted
Langland to group the three speeches together
through the common denominator of Latin. All three
concern law, justice, equity, the duties of those
who enforce it and of those upon whom it is
imposed. Latin serves not only to make the passages,
to foreground their content, but also to make the
reader pause and ponder. For Latin demands to be
'construed'. When Langland invites us to 'construe'
at 144, he is asking us to do more than simply to
English the texts in question. In fact, this is
the first of three occasions in the *Visio* on which
Latin texts are specifically offered for 'construal';
(*cf.*IV.145,VII.106); and in each case, the text is
one that enshrines a principle of justice or
equity. These evidently need to be parsed for their
significance as well as their grammatical sense.
Here we must construe not only the Latin but also
the problem posed by it of whether and when mercy
may properly be granted, and the implications of the
absolute obedience ideally owed by a people to their
lawgivers.
  One of those implications immediately becomes
apparent in the fable that follows: that maxim

from the Roman Law would require them to "suffren and serven" even where they felt themselves rather persecuted than governed by their overlords. For Langland procedes to subject ideal theory to the test of reality. As he had compared the ideal exercise of the authority of the Church with its reality, by contrasting an idealized past, person-ifications and abstractions with real persons (St. Peter, Love, and cardinal virtues with today's Popes and Cardinals), so he now adopts the same procedure in his analysis of the authority of the state. The transition is the more marked here because of the emphatic downward shift in alleg-orical mode - from generalized representative figures and personifications to animal fable. The fable refers recognizably to the contemporary English scene, not to the remote realms of theory. Gone is the ruler revered by his people, counselled by Kynde Wit and angels, and tempering justice with mercy; authority is now represented as capricious and tyrannical, figured by the pounces of a cat on mice. Gone, too, is the unquestioning obedience of a fervently loyal "commune", to be replaced by cowed and malcontent rats and mice, who are evidently little tempted to say 'Amen' to the 'common' cry of 145.

The fable told here was a popular one, and Bishop Brinton had recently used it with precisely the application to contemporary English politics apparently intended here.[29] But Langland does not give it quite the same emphasis as it usually had. The traditional point of the tale was the ironic one that, when it came to it, the rats and mice were too cowardly to put their ingenious plan into operation. Langland makes this point, but his version does not end there, for he appends to it another moral which supersedes the former, and constitutes the real lesson of the fable in the context in which he has used it. The rats and mice fail - but it is just as well they do, for without authority nature reverts to the anarchy of uncontrolled self-seeking:

> 'For many mennes malt we mees wolde destruye,
> And also ye route of ratons rende mennes clothes,
> Nere the cats of the court that kan you overlepe;
> For hadde ye rattes youre raik ye kouthe noght
> rule yowselve.'

The moral Langland draws, then, is that any law, any authority, however vicious its representatives,

is better than none.   The human will requires
government and rule;   it cannot rule itself, for
self-interest is too strong.   Even where the king
is a "sherewe", that maxim from Roman Law should
still apply;   it is still better to "suffer and
serven", to "knowe" and "wite" one's own as subjects,
than to attempt to evade his laws, for the alternative is "The maze among us alle" (192).   Tyranny
is preferable to anarchy and insubordination:
"Ffor som what of tyranndise may be bettre isuffred,
þan þe harm þat comeþ ʒif men ben vnobedient to þe
prince, and breken his law".30

The additional passage, then, transforms the
Prologue from a descriptive complaint to a thesis,
an essay with a theme and an argument: institutional authority, sacred and secular.   Langland has
examined it as it ideally should be exercised, and
as it actually is, and has drawn a conclusion:
that we need it, however sadly it may have fallen
away from ideal theory, declined from its origins
and *originalia* (first principles).   His Prologue
has now established a point, not just a mood, or a
state of affairs: the necessity for authority and
rules, from however corrupt a source they emanate.
The moral of the fable probably applies as
much to degenerate 'cardinals' as to kings, for by
juxtapositions and parallels Langland has implied a
comparability between his analyses of divine law
(at 100-111) and secular law (112-210), the two
sections being framed by the account of the
ministers of each: the venal clergy of 58-99, and
the venal lawyers of 211-6.   Within each of these
sections his procedure has been the same.   He has
focused upon the office from which all authority
in the respective institutions derives: that of
Pope and King.   He has examined the 'original'
basis of the power of each.   He has found divine
sanction for that power (God knows   men need
government):   St. Peter, the first Pope, received
his authority from Christ Himself;   and the office
of King is in accordance with Kynde Wit (itself a
gift of God) and is conversant with divine truth.
He has employed the logic of etymology to point to
the principles implied in each of the rulerships:
since the gates of heaven hinge on the 'cardinal'
virtues, the church is ruled by cardinals, who
should take more care to live up to the name they
have appropriated;   it is a ruler's job to ensure
that rules   are kept.   The timeless ideal is in
each case contrasted with the contemporary reality:

the cardinal virtues that elect a soul to heaven
find but a sad parody of themselves in the unseemly
schism of 1378, which produced rival popes elected
by opposing factions of the cardinalship; the just
ruler and his obedient commons are very imperfectly
represented in the England of 1377-8 as represented
by the fable of the rats and mice. Each revealing
picture of reality is provided with a coda inviting
the reader to draw his own conclusions, for the
author himself is reluctant to do so:

> Ac of the Cardinals at court that kaughte of that name
> And power presumed in hem a Pope to make
> To han the power that Peter hadde, impugnen I nelle –
> For in love and in lettrure the eleccion bilongeth;
> Forthi I kan and kan naught of court speke moore.
>
> What this metels bymeneth, ye men that ben murye,
> Devyne ye – for I ne dar, by deere God in hevene!

The precise significance of these professions of
prudent reserve is hard to guage. Criticism of this
general kind was common enough, and not likely to
involve any risk to the personal safety of its
authors; and if it were, Langland has already said
quite enough to incur it. So they can scarcely be
genuine. As rhetorical ploys, they are, again,
common enough, but it is not like Langland to be
coy.

It is very possible that he was genuinely
anxious to avoid the sin of 'scandal'. Scandal, in
the medieval signification of the word, is a
fascinating subject, since it referred to behaviour
that would not today be thought of as wrong, and
might even be applauded, and so, as a 'lost sin',
belongs to a totally different ethical climate.
Basically, it was to give occasion of sin to others,
to do or say something that might cause them morally
to 'stumble' (*scandalum* = stumbling block). It was
most frequently applied, however, to words or
behaviour that exposed authority, sacred or secular,
to criticism, revealed faults in ecclesiastical or
temporal governers, and so, by precept or example,
encouraged (sinful) disrespect for or disobedience
to them. "To give publicity to accusation and
censures against the fathers" was to incur "the
curse of Cham, the undutiful son, who did not hide
his father's shame" (Ham revealed to his brothers
the nakedness of the drunken Noah, Gen.9:22).
"Indulgence and reverence" were due to all the
clergy, and to publish real or imagined faults on

their part was to incur the sin of scandal, since it endangered the authority of the church, and the preservation of obedience and reverence to the institution was more important than knowledge of the morality of its member officials. Hence Abelard excuses Peter for not confessing openly his denial of Christ, because "what was being protected was the shame of the church" (which he was to found) "rather than his own". Disobedience to or abuse of secular rulers could also constitute scandal. So, for instance, defiance of the wrongful commands of a lord or a king was only legitimate where it could be done discreetly and *sine scandalo*, that is, without such open defiance as might tempt their subjects to disrespect and insubordination.[31]

So Langland perhaps thought it genuinely dangerous to encourage the damaging criticism by the "commune" of their spiritual and secular overlords his analysis might provoke: the fable, after all, establishes that he thought obedience necessary even where the authority is corrupt - people ought, in their own interests, to "suffren and serven", for they cannot rule themselves. And there is evidence from a subsequent passage in the poem that he was not unconcerned about the sin of scandal: in Passus XI (86-106), he similarly professes to Leaute that he hardly 'dares' publish abroad the vices of the friars he has perceived. A modern reader could be forgiven for experiencing some amazement at these lines; whatever may be Langland's faults, timidity is not one of them, and he himself admits elsewhere to having denied his betters the reverence they were probably accustomed to (XV.5-9). It is evidently the moral rather than the personal risk he alludes to in Passus XI: the danger of committing and fuelling insubordination to the secular and spiritual authorities. The recipient of his doubts on that occasion is probably relevant. Leaute connotes faithful obedience, and it is that which might be compromised. And it is this fear which Leaute's reassurances seem designed to allay: it *is* lawful for "lewed" men to "arate" vice, and, though one should not be the first to publish faults, where they are generally known (and respect has already been sacrificed) there can be no danger in denouncing them. It is precisely on these grounds that John of Salisbury excuses himself from the charge of scandal in denouncing certain clerical vices: "I shall say then that a city çannot be hidden which is set upon a hill, and that it is vain to try to keep from public knowledge things which are

done in the sight of nations".[32] Langland's reservations here, then, seem to have been on the score
of the possibility of incurring himself and provok-
ing others to dis-leaute to authority: *ie*, committing the sin of scandal. And it may be that in the
Prologue, too, this possible result of his comments
is the cause of his professed reluctance to pursue
his implied criticisms of the rulers of church and
state: a probability heightened by the fact that
in the C version the decision not to 'impugn' the
Papal Court is taken "for holicherche sake" (138):
ie, to preserve respect for the authority of the
church.

At any rate, a real or pretended reluctance to
scandalize the authority of the church or the
monarchy, by more explicit emphasis on how the
latter-day representatives of both have betrayed a
trust he has shown to be sacred, forms a common
coda to Langland's account of each.

But the most significant parallel between the
two passages concerns not their epilogue, but their
focus. In each case, the question raised concerns
justice and mercy, and the relationship between
them - when mercy may justly be granted. St.
Peter's keys concern the power of granting or with-
holding absolution: who deserves to have their sins
forgiven them, and the gates of heaven, that supreme
gift of mercy and grace, opened to them? When may
the king grant the mercy divine law enjoins without
prejudice to the rules it is his business as a
ruler to enforce? And, in both cases, there is a
presumption that mercy itself is subject to the
rules of justice and equity: that, though
essentially a free gift of grace, it nevertheless
must be earned, and is given in return for something
that may be put in the scales against it, that may
'match' it, to preserve the rule of *quid pro quo*.
The *cardines* of heaven will respond to the cardinal
virtues; the receipts of mercy will be in proportion to the expenditure of it, according to the
angel; while the goliard is adamant that 'rules'
must never be bent in the interests of it.

Langland, then, revised the poem to bring
questions of law and institutional authority
immediately to the fore, to suggest a correlation
between sacred and secular law, and to establish the
primary importance of 'rule'. The first step to
Do-Wel is for the Will to accept constraints on its
own liberty, to obey laws, God's and man's; which
is why, in the many definitions of the hierarchical
trio of Do-Wel, Do-Bet, and Do-Best, Do-Wel is often

identified with what is law-abiding, obedient,
"lele", accepting of authority.[33] "Let every soul
be subject unto the higher powers, for there is no
power but of God", the Apostle had said (Rōm.13:1),
and "that the Lord commands obedience to duly
constituted authority" was a belief universally
subscribed to:[34] in Langland's words, "holy churche
hoteth alle manere peple Vnder obedience to be and
buxom to þe lawe" (C.IX.219-20). The concern with
"the double power" immediately apparent in the
Prologue as revised is, interestingly enough,
reflected in the reading constituency by which the
poem was early adopted. For it emerges from a
recent investigation into this matter that it was
chiefly those involved in "spiritual and temporal
governance" who read and possessed the poem, and
who evidently found much of interest and relevance
in its exploration of the "historical precedents
and foundations of both temporal and spiritual
imperatives".[35]

II: *Passus I*

Having established in the Prologue the importance of authority and obedience to it, it is to an
institutional figure that Langland first turns in
Passus I - for guidance and instruction in the
rules of the divine law, that he may obey it, and
so save his soul. He turns to her as to an
"auctoritee", and in so doing, he resumes the
subject of the first and higher of the two *regimina*
he had dealt with in the passage added to the
Prologue: the Church, and the divine law it was
instituted to administer. The dreamer's first
specific question arises naturally out of the
various types of unjust gain he has witnessed: what
constitutes a rightful claim to 'money' (44-5)? On
this matter, however, his question elicits no very
clear guiding rule, for he has addressed it to the
wrong law. Holy Church is the guardian of the laws
of the spirit, and her primary concern is with the
dues of God, not the coin of Caesar. And though
she talks constantly of what will save and sustain
life, medicine and money, her interest is in the
salve of salvation, and in the true coin by which
an eternal "lyflod" is earned. And that bodily
and spiritual life are sustained diversely is one
of her first *dicta*:

> 'Al is nought good to the goost that the gut asketh,
> Ne liflode to the likame that leef is to the soule.
>
> (36-7)

The false "phisyk" that proves so fatal to spiritual life at the end of the poem renders Holy Church's references to medicine significant. The first occurs at 35:

> 'Mesure is medicine, though thow muchel yerne'.

She is referring to wrongful over-consumption of the necessities of life. And the word "mesure" is a significant one, since it relates to equity: consumption should be exactly commensurate with needs, otherwise an inequilibrium, an inequity, ensues - and so a sin. This she illustrates by *exemplum* in the story of Lot and his daughters, where excess (in drink) led to deadly sin. This may be more relevant than at first appears to the Prologue, where inequitable types of obtaining a "lyflod" had twice been characterized as "glotonye":

> And wonnen that thise wastours with glotonye
>   destruyeth.
>
> (22)

> Thus ye gyven youre gold glotons to helpe   (76)

"Lyflod" cannot be inequitable where it exactly equals in "mesure" what is needed to 'lead' the 'life' God gave through the sustenance He also gave (14-26): "And therefore temperance (*ie* "mesure") accepts the necessities of this life, as a rule or measure of the things one uses, so that, to wit, they should be used according as the necessity of this life requires".[36]   To take more is inequitably to encroach on the needs of others.

Holy Church's medicine of "mesure" is, in fact, finely balanced between the literal and metaphorical. In the context of literal over-indulgence in food and drink, it may be compared with the professional advice of that austere "leche" Hunger, who also prescribes moderation as a remedy against gastric ailments (VI.257-74). But the lines that follow (quoted above) suggest Holy Church is thinking of it primarily as something nutritious for the soul, even though it may not be for the body, and therefore a spiritual medicine. It thus provides a pivotal point in her transition from these physical aids for the sustenance of physical life to the sovereign panacea for spiritual health she is to proceed to: the truth whose first principle is that Love is "triacle of hevene" (148) and "leche of lif" (204).

Similarly, that truth is also "tresor the trieste on erthe" (137), a rule that Holy Church repeats refrain-like in response to the dreamer's question about "moneie". Money is needed to purchase life in heaven as well as life on earth (everything in Langland has its price, obeys the rule of *quid pro quo*), and the best coins with which to purchase that "lyflod" are 'true' ones.

The many meanings of that central medieval abstraction "treuthe" are all operative in this first Passus. As it means 'justice', it emphasizes the equity on which the divine law as Holy Church describes it turns, observing always the principle of reciprocity. For the virtue of truth, as it means general integrity or 'good faith', is rewarded with 'true' coin: money that does not betray the trust of the payee, but proves true (authentic) on the assay, when "tried". Feudal truth, in the sense of loyal obedience to the will of one's overlord, is also distinctly present. For the foremost attribute of truth as Holy Church expounds it is that it imposes an obligation of obedience:

> 'The tour upon the toft', quod she, 'Truthe is
>   therinne,
> And wolde that ye wroughte as his word techeth.
> For he is fader of feith and formed yow alle', *etc*.

(12-14)

Truth is not definable without reference to something else, for it is demonstrated when one is true *to* something, and in this case that something is the word of God, His commands, His laws. And it is this feudal-social sense of truth as obedience to the dictates of a lord who has rightful authority over you that provides the main link with the subject-matter of the Prologue. That had established that kings and their laws must be obeyed, that the will must bow to the authority of rule and rules. This obedience to His word, which (like the king's) *is* law, is also the prime requirement of the King of heaven. The true man is thus the 'law-abiding' one (as in the phrase 'a true man or a thief'), the man

obedient to the divine law. Again, however, one
may note the reciprocity, and thus the equity,
implied in the above lines. The Truth in question
is both subject and object of truth, both demands
and gives 'good faith'. The line "For he is fader
of feith and formed yow alle" has a number of
implications. The "fader of feith" is in one
sense, of course, the father, or author, of *the*
(Christian) Faith; but the context operates to
assimilate this doctrinal Faith to the moral virtue
of 'good faith' (for "faith" is one of the synonyms
of truth - compare Troilus's "Where is youre feith
... where is youre trouthe?" *T&C* V.1675-6). God
may demand 'faithful' obedience, *for* He is Himself
a 'faithful' Father, as the ensuing lines demonstrate - He has not gone back on His gift of life,
but has 'faithfully', and "of his curteisie" (20),
provided the means of sustaining it ("*Qui dedit
majora, id est vitam et corpus, dabit et minora, id
est victum et vestes*"37). He has faithfully
provided for His "meynee", and they therefore should
be faithful to Him: "inferiors owe it to their
superiors to provide them with service, just as the
superiors in their turn owe it to their inferiors
to provide them with all things needful for their
protection and succour".38 The "for" also refers to
God's entitlement to the authority of an overlord:
who has a better title to property than He who
fashioned it Himself from His own materials?

The feudal interpretation of truth thus
initially attached to the word recurs later on in
the Passus. Faithful obedience to commands is the
primary point made by Holy Church in her definition
of her own identity, as it had been in her definition of the Truth of which she is the representative
authority:

> 'Hole Chirche I am,' quod she, 'thow oughtest me
>   to knowe.
> I underfeng thee first and the feith taughte.
> Thow broughtest me borwes my biddyng to fulfille,
> And to loven me leely the while thi lif dureth'.

> (75-8)

Again one notices the double meaning of "feith":
when the dreamer was received into the Church at
baptism, he was received into the Christian Faith;
but in instructing him in that Faith, the Church
instructed him also in the 'good faith', the
"leaute", that it demands: for "biddyng to fulfille"

and "leely" again suggest that aspect of truth that denotes loyal 'faithful' obedience to the expressed will of Him one subserves. (The image is feudal: Holy Church is imagining herself as a lord who accepts a young page into his household, an act which imposed a mutual obligation: on the child to serve loyally and obediently, on the lord to provide for, or, in the Middle English idiom, to "fynde" him - as, it was at once established, God does). It is both meanings of "feith" that the dreamer takes up, when, in response, he begs Holy Church to intercede for him,

> 'And also kenne me kyndely on Crist to bileve,
> That I myghte werchen His wille that wroughte me
> to man'.

> (81-2)

He is asking to be instructed in the faith, and also in good faith to its author - in faithful obedience to His will. The lines recapitulate precisely the points made in the opening exposition of Truth. It is the true faith of Christianity, and so must involve true faith to and from its God: obedience to Him who has given you (and, here, also restored you to) life. As so often in Langland, there has been a time-lag between a principle expressed and the "kyndely" understanding of its purport by the dreamer. It is this emphasis on obedience to the expressed will of one's lord that proves the relevance of the material added to the Prologue. Langland had juxtaposed the Church and its authority with the King and his authority; from his investigation of the latter, he had established that the precepts of the overlord are law, and we need law. He is now applying his findings to the King of Heaven and His law. Before one can obey that, however, one needs to ascertain what it is, as the dreamer is attempting to do.

It is also the feudal implications of truth - loyal obedience to one's lord - that provides one of the chief links between truth and love. For the climax of Holy Church's exposition comes when she asserts the essential principle of truth to be love, and the last seventy odd lines of the Passus are given over to a demonstration of the importance of this supreme virtue of the New Law. The link between the two abstractions is worth some attention, as it is not immediately apparent why truth (integrity, good faith) should necessarily imply charity. The first hint of the transition comes at

86: "I do it on *Deus caritas* to deme the sothe".
This precedes by some sixty lines the point at
which the centrality of love to truth is specifically introduced, and seems at first to be a somewhat disconnected anticipation of the later
development of the argument, with little apparent
relevance to the immediate context. Holy Church is
citing the text as support for the proposition
that, "When alle tresors arn tried ... Treuthe is
the beste" (85), and she proceeds to commend truth
in word, work, and will, in the man who is "trewe
of his tonge and telleth noon oother, And dooth
the werkes therwith and wilneth no man ille" (88-9),
and therefore, conforming himself to the nature of
God (Truth), becomes himself "a god" (90). The
text most pertinent to what precedes and what
follows would therefore seem to be *Deus Veritas*, not
Deus Caritas. The applicability of the latter
rests, in fact, on word-play on "dereworthe" and
"deere": truth is "as dereworthe a drury as deere
God hymselven" (87). The economic as well as the
spiritual sense of "deere" needs to be borne in
mind in reading this line, if we are to appreciate
how the text *Deus caritas* establishes truth to be
the greatest of 'treasures'. Holy Church has
established that Truth is the first name of God,
the lord of the "tour"; truth must, therefore, be
a most valuable commodity, since God is also
car-itas, dear-ness. In fact, Holy Church is not
at this point seriously introducing the subject of
love, but only establishing the 'dearness' of the
treasure of truth by a punning reference to *caritas*;
though that pun provides an interesting link
between Langland's social and his spiritual preoccupations - his interest in how money is come by,
and his emphasis on charity as the indispensible
price of heaven.
It is at 142 that Holy Church really gives
her demonstration of the relevance of love to truth.
In answer to the dreamer's request for some means
toward a "kynde knowynge" of this invaluable
commodity, she replies that,

> 'It is a kynde knowynge that kenneth in thyn herte
> For to loven thi Lord levere than thiselve'.

Norman Blake has pointed out that modern ortho-
graphic conventions regarding capitalization are
often prejudicial to the polysemy that may be
inherent in medieval texts,[39] where the lack of
such conventions meant that the distinction between

common and proper nouns, and thus between dis-
cursive and allegorical statement, was far more
fluid and ambiguous. This is a case in point. If
the editorially capitalized 'L' in "Lord" is disregarded, the logical link with what has already
been asserted of truth may become more clear.
Truth is obedience to the word and will of one's
lord (13, 82); what informs it is therefore an
instinctive, "kynde", habit of holding him more dear
than oneself ("If a man love me, he will keep my
words", John 14:23). The removal of the capital
makes the feudal nature of the reasoning more
apparent. And one further link with the feudal
truth that is obedience is provided. The dreamer
must love, for,

> 'Thus witnesseth his word;   worche thow therafter'.

> (147)

The prime requirement of Truth is obedience to His
command (13). The Bible on several occasions
states that all the commandments, "all the law and
all the prophets", are contained in the injunction
to love.[40] If the dreamer therefore wishes to
"work as his word techeth", "werchen His wille that
wroghte me to man", to be true and faithfully
obedient to the divine law, he must observe its
prime clause.

There is one further piece of negative
evidence for the importance to the concept of truth
here of loyal obedience to one's feudal overlord.
As God is identified with Truth, so is Lucifer
with False, the lord of the dungeon in the "deep
dale" - "Fader of falshede - and founded it
hymselve" (64). He had come by that title by his
own voluntary act of disobedience. He had formerly
been chief of the ten orders of angels knighted by
the King of Heaven, and thus sworn to fealty to
Him, "To be buxom at his biddyng" (110). He "fel
fro that felawshipe", however, when he refused any
longer to be a fellow-servant with his fellow
angels, and "brak buxomnesse" (113-4), in a
treacherous rebellion against his liege lord. The
act by which False, the antithesis of Truth,
originally came into being is thus demonstrated to
have been an assertion of will against obedience to
law, which is the "biddyng" of the King, the
precepta regis.

Feudal 'truth' to one's lord and His bidding is, therefore, one meaning of the word operative in this Passus. In a broader sense, the word was often used to refer to that general righteousness and integrity that in Latin went by the term *iustitia*,[41] and in this sense 'truth' was often used as a synonym for 'just', as in the following lines from Spenser:

> The iustest man alive, and truest did appeare.
>
> (*FQ* V.vii.2)

> When Iustice was not for most meed outhyred,
> But simple Truth did rayne, and was of all admyred.
>
> (V.Prol.3)

And the sense 'justness' or 'equity' is also centrally relevant to Langland's use of the term. It is, of course, precisely to demonstrate the equity of the divine law that Langland has chosen to designate God and the Devil by terms (Truth and False) which may also apply to the conduct that determines in which of their respective abodes one will spend eternity. Truth for the true, and False for the false: a judgment that in itself observes true, not false, measure. The exactness of the *quid pro quo* is emphasized by Langland. Those who are true "Mowe be siker" (132) of salvation: they need not fear treachery in God's promise to them. Those who are false justly find that the looked-for gain likewise proves false, betrays the trust placed in it. The devil is in league with the flesh and the world, which like him are 'liars' and "wolde thee bitraye" (39). The prime Biblical examples of false acts (the disobedience of Adam and Eve, the murder of Abel by his brother Cain, the betrayal of Christ by Judas) were all committed at the instigation of a force that proved false to the perpetrators: "Judas he *japed* with Jewen silver ... He is letters of love and *lieth* hem alle" (67-9). The wages of sin, or falseness, are paid in false coin: That trusten on his tresour bitrayed arn sonnest" (70) - a treasure unlike the treasure of truth, which can stand the 'trial', and proves sterling. It is the "Jewen silver" for which Judas betrayed Christ, and which he afterwards found so worthless. The false angels likewise found that they had been lied to:

'For thei leveden upon hym that lyed in this manere:
Ponam pedem in aquilone, et similis ero Altissimo'.

(119-119*a*)

And the gain looked for by Lucifer himself from his
treachery likewise proved deceptive. Trusting by
it to become *similis Altissimo*, he found instead
that he fell at once to the *lowest* depths of Hell
(126). And such similarity with God as he already
possessed as an angel "lovelokest to loke on after
Oure Lord one" (112) he instantly lost, as did
his fellow-conspirators, all at once transformed
into the "lothliche forme" of "fendes liknesse"
(117,121). For he thereby renounced the very
quality of truth whereby man is most assimilated
to God, for he "Who is trewe ... is a god by the
Gospel, agrounde and olofte, And ylik to Oure Lord,
by Seint Lukes wordes" (88-91).
    Such conformity and disconformity to the image
of God is relevant to the rule of like for like
that dominates the Passus, and which represents
one's state in the afterlife simply as a realization of one's moral condition on earth. The
prepositions in the following passage, for instance,
are carefully chosen:

'And alle that werchen with wrong wende thei shulle
After hir deth day and dwelle with that sherewe;
Ac tho that werche wel as Holy Writ telleth,
And enden as I er seide in truthe, that is the beste,
Mowe be siker that hire soules shul wende to hevene,
Ther Treuthe is in Trinitee and troneth hem alle'.

(128-33)

Those who work 'with wrong' will find themselves
just that: with that very "sherewe" who "Wrong is
yhote" (63). While those who 'end in truth' will
likewise do precisely that - end in (the "tour" of)
Truth. The rule applies not only to the true and
the false, but also to the giving and the ungiving,
the charitable and the covetous, in the discussion
of love at the end of the Passus, which is itself
an extension of that on truth. Chastity without
charity "worth cheyned in helle", Holy Church
insists (188,194). But the chains are self-imposed,
for,

> 'Thei ben acombred with coveitise, thei konne noght
>   out crepe,
> So harde hath avarice yhasped hem togidirers'.

(196-7)

The bonds of hell, therefore, merely perpetuate those evident in the life of the covetous, spiritually and literally. Literally, because the above image obviously partly refers to a back weighed, encumbered, by money-bags, and to treasure-chests firmly 'hasped' against giving. They also describe a spiritually hampered and constricted state, for "combered" was a word used also with reference to the weight of sin, as it is a few lines later (203; and *cf*. II.51). The weight of the money accumulated encumbers the soul, and will lead to "combraunce" in Hell - the word was also used of divine punishment, and here refers back to the chains of 188 and 194. Conversely, those who unlock their money-chests to give will simultaneously unlock the chains of Hell and the gates of heaven; unlocking their goods to others they will unlock God's grace to themselves; disburdening themselves of the bags that encumber the covetous they will be themselves disencumbered of sin:

> '*Date, et dabitur vobis* - for I deele yow alle.
> And that is the lok of love that leteth out my
>   grace,
> To conforten the carefulle acombred with synne'.

(201-3)

Strict observance of commutative and distributive justice is thus seen to be of the essence of the operation of the divine law which rests on equity.[42] Justice is that which renders to all what is due them. God practises it - and so must man. For it is significant that Holy Church uses that important word *reddere* (pay, render up) in connection with the coin due to Caesar and God respectively:

> '*Reddite Cesari*, 'quod God, "that Cesari bifalleth,
> *Et que sunt Dei Deo*, or ellis ye don ille'.

(52-3)

Man must pay his spiritual and social debts, give to

his king and his God what is 'due' them - obey their laws, or offend against justice and equity.

Although it is the emphasis on obedience and justice that provides the most important link with the discussion in the Prologue of the King as law-giver and the necessity for rule and obedience, one should notice that there are more specific parallels drawn between the spiritual and the secular body politic. The necessity for outward rules to govern the will is matched by the positing of a type of inner state and an inner economy: even within himself, man should subject his will to the authoritative dictates of his reason and his "kynde wit", for, he himself being as it were a minor, his fortune is properly under the control of the latter as his guardians and trustees:

> 'For rightfully Reson sholde rule yow alle,
> And Kynde Wit be wardeyn youre welthe to kepe,
> And tutour of youre tresor, and take it yow at nede'.
>
> (54-6) [43]

An interestingly specific analogy between God and King as upholders of justice and law, of truth, in their respective realms occurs at 94-110:

> 'Kynges and knyghtes sholde kepen it by reson -
> Riden and rappen doun in reaumes aboute,
> And taken *transgressores* and tyen hem faste
> Til treuthe hadde yetermyned hire trespas to the end.
> For David in hise dayes dubbed knyghtes,
> And dide hem sweren on hir swerd to serven truthe evere.
> And that is the profession apertly that apendeth to knyghtes,
> And naught to fasten o Friday in fyve score wynter,
> But holden with hym and with here that wolden alle truthe,
> And never leve hem for love ne for lacchynge of silver -
> And whoso passeth that point is apostata in the ordre.
> But Crist, kyngene kyng, knyghted ten -
> Cherubyn and Seraphyn, swiche sevene and another,
> And yaf hem myght in his majestee - the murier hem thoughte -

> And over his meene meynee made hem archangeles;
> Taughte hem by the Trinitee treuthe to knowe,
> To be buxom at his biddyng - he bad hem nought ellis'.

Knighthood is here regarded as theoretically
fulfilling the duties of a police force in the
enforcement of law and order: protection of the
innocent, pursuit of the guilty.   The function of
knighthood was, in fact, commonly conceived of as
consisting in the execution of justice and judgment,[44]   and their role is so represented here and
elsewhere in the poem (VI.27-8;   XIX.246-8).   And
the polysemy of the word 'truth' allows Langland to
interpret at 100 the prime chivalric virtue of
truth (good faith)[45] as implying the knight's
responsibility to the upholding of truth as it
denotes justice and law in the lands of the King
they serve.   The *milites* are in this respect the
earthly equivalent of the aristocratic *militia* of
heaven, the angels, the ten orders of whom Langland
represents as ten orders of knighthood created by
the King of kings, and sworn to fealty to Him.
Obedience to their overlord, and observance of his
law, his "biddyng", knights and angels have in
common, and enjoy exalted status over the "meene
meynee" in recognition of the solemnity of their
commitment.   The analogy between the secular and
the sacred is supported by various instances of
word-play.   The *transgressores* pursued by knights
reminds one that there are also transgressions
against God's law.   Those who show undue favour in
the enforcement of law, enforce it unequally, are
"apostata in the ordre", a semi-pun on "ordre",
since the term 'apostate' generally referred to
defectors from religious orders or to heretics
against divine law.   It is here applied to
renegades from the various 'orders' of knighthood,
and that word provides a neat transition to the
discussion of the orders of angels that follows,
introduced by an apt use of the conventional periphrasis for God, 'King of kings'.
   Once the transition from truth to its informing principle, love, has been made, the image of a
heavenly body politic, with its own structure of
agencies for the enforcement of its laws, recurs,
appropriately adapted to the new emphasis, at
159-62:

> 'Forthi is love ledere of the Lordes folke of hevene,
> And a meene, as the mair is, bitwene the kyng and
>   the commune;

> Right so is love a ledere and the lawe shapeth:
> Upon man for his mysdedes the mercyment he taxeth'.

The lines describe the effects on the divine
political system of the New Law of love, established
by Christ (whose birth and passion are recounted at
153-8). The folk of the Lord of Heaven, the
citizens of God, are now governed by His appointed
representative Love, who 'mediates' His law upon
them. Like the mayor who administers the King's
law in earthly cities (a mayor's duties are similarly
referred to at III.76ff), he is thus a medium for
the transmission of law. A law administered by Love
suggests both justice and mercy, and the two are
held in a perfect if fragile equilibrium in the pun
on "mercyment": Love exacts the due fines or
penalties, but does so with mercy - with perhaps a
suggestion that the very penalty imposed by the New
Law is the injunction that the pardoned *transgressores* show similar mercy to others (this is what
Holy Church proceeds to insist on).

The importance of mercy in the scheme of the
divine law as it was modified in its third phase of
Lex Christi returns us to the problem posed in the
Prologue by the oblique altercation between the angel
and the goliard. How does one reconcile the mercy
which is divine with the strict enforcement of
rules, the perfect equity that is also divine? Holy
Church appears, not surprisingly, to side with the
angel on this issue. As the angel had warned the
king to be *pius* as well as (*not* rather than, be it
noted) *iustus* in his power to enforce the law, so
Holy Church warns the "myghty to mote" to show
mercy and "ruthe" in their dealings with the
"povere" (175-6). And she repeats the warning with
the same emphasis on the fact that, the principle of
the divine law being equity, those who wish to
benefit by the New Law of love and mercy must also
observe it,

> 'For the same mesure that ye mete, amys outher ellis,
> Ye shulle ben weyen therwith whan ye wenden hennes:
> *Eadem mensura qua mensi fueritis remecietur vobis*'.

(177-178*a*).

The rule is re-iterated in a context that demonstrates
more fully its logic. It follows on an account of
the incarnation and passion of the founder of the New
Law, who Himself obeyed His own precept, and died

begging mercy for His murderers (169-71). He made
it possible for divine justice or truth to
accommodate mercy. And it is at this point of her
exposition - when she has thus described the transition from the Old to the New Law - that Holy Church
suddenly proclaims 'truth', which has hitherto
figured as the supreme virtue, to be after all not
the most reliable of treasures: without love, in
fact, it will avail one nothing (179-84). The
mercy of the New Dispensation, then, is available
only to those who obey the New Law of love; others,
however "trewe", will be judged by the strict truth,
the *nudum ius*, of the Old. That is perfectly fair:
each man will be judged by whichever law he has
chosen to live by.

The relationship between truth and love in the
passus, then, and Holy Church's shift of emphasis
from the one to the other, is intimately related to
the transition from the Old Law to the New Law her
discourse describes, and thus to the relationship
between justice and mercy on earth and in heaven
(*nudum ius* and *pietas* in the King; God's truth and
His loving mercy). It is therefore worth tracing
the connection between the two virtues as Holy
Church defines them. Love does not at first
appear as a virtue separate from truth that might
supersede it in pre-eminence. Love is the instinct
to love one's lord that results in truth to him
(142-7). Truth is defined by love in answer to the
dreamer's query about its essential nature. Love is
the inner state on which behaviour that is true
depends. But after the account of the incarnation
and passion, the two start disconcertingly to
diverge; and these lines would seem to indicate
that truth can exist separately from love, which it
does not necessarily imply, and to which it is
inferior:

> 'For though ye be trewe of youre tonge and treweliche
>   wynne,
> And as chaste as a child that in chirche wepeth,
> But if ye loven leelly and lene the povere
> Of swich good as God sent, goodliche parteth,
> Ye ne have na moore merite in Masse ne in houres
> Than Malkyn of hire maydenhode, that no man
>   desireth'.

(179-84)

The effect is highly characteristic of Langlandian
allegory, which has a noticeable tendency to pull

the rug from under the reader's feet, denying him
such firm ground as he had believed himself to have
reached. Salvation always depends on a perfection
that is a receding point. So the one certainty of
truth that Holy Church appears to offer similarly
ends in revealing only its own deficiency in
relation to a higher virtue. The passus is
Langland's first illustration that for the Christian
the pursuit of perfection is a ceaseless one.
Everything that seems to promise the journey's end
proves to be only a bend in the road that leads one
off in a new direction, and points to something
beyond itself.

However, before the Passus is complete, Holy
Church has gone some way to re-establishing the
identity between the two virtues she had initially
implied. In the lines quoted above, and more
specifically in the paragraph that follows, Holy
Church seems to be defining the truth/love antithesis
in terms of the familiar chastity/charity one.
Truth is that strict honesty of conduct that 'knows
its own'; it does not take dishonestly, but equally
it does not give of its own. It does not know
generosity, free gift, for that is not a principle
of truth, or of strict justice. Charity is that
which parts with its own. But in the lines
immediately following those quoted above, Holy
Church substitutes a different definition of the
polarity, from which it emerges that truth stands to
love not as chastity to charity, but as faith to
works:

> 'For James the gentile jugged in hise bokes
> That feith withouten feet is feblere than nought,
> And as deed as a dorenail but if the dedes folwe:
> *Fides sine operibus mortua est &c.*'

(185-87a)

This is to state the matter rather differently, and
very much more interestingly. Truth without love
is as faith not realized in action. Love is not
something separate from truth, but truth in act,
truth in deed. The word-play on "feith" and "feet"
makes the point even more incisively: faith,
unless put into action, is not a fact. Again it
appears, then, that truth cannot really exist
without love, if the relationship between them is as
that between "feith" and "feet". Without the love
that gives, it is as faith without works, a theory
without practice, a principle never acted upon, a
potential never realized. If man is to be true to

his God and his neighbour, pay to all their dues,
he must love, and that love must express itself in
the act of giving: "love" and "lene" are very
frequently correlated in Langland, who insists on
the "workes" that make actuality of the "wordes",
and for whom love meant primarily parting with one's
money to the poor and the needy ("Whoso leneth
noght, he loveth nought", XI.179). And, in fact,
in the example she gives of 'chastity without
charity', Holy Church does not conclude that the
conduct of the covetous but 'chaste' chaplain,
locked in his covetousness as his money is in his
chests, illustrates truth without love. "That", she
declares, "is no truthe of the Trinite, but trecherie
of helle, And lernynge to lewed men the latter
for to dele" (198-9). Not to love (or, more
properly, not to "lene", which is the action of love)
is not to be true but to lack charity; it is to be
untrue, to withhold from the poor the debt due them.

And as love itself thus proves ultimately not
to supersede truth, but to be contained within it,
so does mercy once more prove to lie within the
province of justice. It is dispensed on the equitable principle of *quid pro quo*, the good Old Law
principle of "measure for measure"; for Holy Church
emphasizes the angel's warning, *Qualia vis metere,
talia grana sere*, by citing a couple of texts of
similar purport:

> *Eadem mensura qua mensi fueritis remecietur vobis.*
>
> (178*a*)
>
> *Date et dabitur vobis.* (201)

The love and mercy of the New Law, then, do not
represent something higher or other than the truth
and justice of the Old. For Langland, nothing is
superior to truth and justice, and even mercy cannot
violate the equity essential to the divine law.
Love is not above the law; it is truth to the New
and highest law of the Trinity, and mercy the
supreme equilibrium of the scales of justice: *Date
et dabitur vobis*. This, however, still leaves the
problem posed by the goliard in his 'answer' to the
angel unsolved: should miscreants be dealt with in
truth to the law, and rule and rules thus upheld,
or should they be given mercy as one hopes to
receive it? It is not what he hears from Holy
Church that is to settle Langland's mind on this
question, but what he sees and hears of Mede, whose

false provides the negative antithesis of the
positive value of the truth preached by the true
church.

NOTES

1. The equivalent of Passus X in the B text (A.XII is not
   generally thought to be by Langland).
2. See III.53-63 for an example of 'glozing' the sins of the
   rich. For other examples of arguments adduced by venal
   confessors to play down the need for restitution and
   penance (though not with respect to friars), see
   Policraticus, VII.xxi (p.316); for 'glozing the Gospel',
   see Chaucer's *Summoner's Tale*, *CT*,III.1789-96, 1918-26.
   For a summary of the various charges levelled against the
   friars, see Robertson, p.185.
3. J.W. Baldwin, ii.44,134. The concerns of Peter the
   Chanter and his circle have, in fact, much in common with
   those of Langland. They, too, were primarily ethical (as
   opposed to mystical or scholastic) theologians, and so
   shared his social, occupational, and economic preoccupations.
4. *Winner and Waster*, 11.149-87.
5. Justice was either commutative or distributive: commutative justice concerned equality of thing to thing in
   exchanges; distributive justice governed equality of
   thing to person in distributing or apportioning (see
   Aquinas, *ST* II-II.lxi).
6. For examples, see Skeat's note on the line.
7. Langland is not the only writer of his age for whom the
   London market-place, with its rowdy gluttony for food and
   money, seemed to present the very image of unregenerate
   humanity, trapped in a frenzy of venality and sensuality
   ("How bisie they ben aboute the maze", I.6). Henry of
   Lancaster compares his heart to a city market-place in
   which "most men are drunk, and taverns are situated near
   and all around the market, so that men eat and drink so
   much that they can only leave them with great difficulty,
   they are so drunk, and their bellies so full; and the
   cooks and taverners do not stop crying their good food
   and the   good wine ... And those things signify the evil
   acquaintances and the dirty words from which evil deeds
   follow" (*Le Livre de Seyntz Medicines*, quoted by Brewer,
   pp.223-4); and in *Winner and Waster*, the same scene is
   represented as the most appropriate setting for a Waster's
   debauch, a place where the avaricious can tempt the
   prodigal into an orgy of gluttony (11.472-95).
8. J.W. Baldwin, i.161-2.
9. For the conception of a bishop as the ecclesiastical
   counterpart of the prince, *cf* Leclercq, p.163.

10. Lent was the time of penitential purification in prep-
    aration for Easter, and so the busiest time of year
    for confessors; even those who were not otherwise
    regularly confessed took care to be shriven before
    taking the Easter sacrament (*cf* the reference to those
    who delay shrift "Fro Lenten to Lenten" at XX.362).
11. *Cf, CT* I.655,660-1; III.1347,1587.
12. J.W. Baldwin, ii.63.
13. The power of the keys, the binding and loosing power,
    was regularly interpreted in this way, as consisting in
    (1) the imposing or relaxing of sentence of excommunic-
    ation; and (2) the granting or withholding of absolu-
    tion in the confessional ("ut tale sit peccata solui
    quantum ea remitti, et eadem ligari quantum ea retineri
    vel imponi", Abelard, *Ethics*, p.124; *cf* J.W. Baldwin
    i.51). It was in the church's power to administer the
    potential forgiveness granted sinners by its founder,
    Christ, that its essential identifying function rested:
    "where remission of sins is, there the Church is" (St.
    Augustine, *Tractat*.X in I.Joann.V.3, quoted by Dunning,
    p.41).
14. *Policraticus*, IV.xii (p.59); *Lay Folks' Catechism*, p.78;
    Bolton, p.166; Bloomfield, p.134.
15. See n.69 to ch.I *supra*.
16. Abelard, *Ethics*, p.xxii.
17. *Cf* Abelard, *Ethics*, p.119 ff.
18. *Governaunce*, pp.109-118.
19. See J.W. Baldwin ii.111,115; *Policraticus*, V.vi(p.83);
    Governaunce, p.172; D.R. Pichaske and L. Sweetland,
    'Chaucer and the Medieval Monarchy: Harry Bailey in the
    Canterbury Tales', *Chaucer Review* xi (1976-7), 179-200.
20. Fortescue, *De Natura Legis Nature*, I.c.xviii.
21. *Cf Policraticus*, VIII.xvii (p.335), where law is defined
    as providing, amongst other things, "a rule defining
    duties". Containment within appointed bounds was, in
    fact, an important aspect of the balance and equilibrium
    essential to justice, and so forms a recurrent theme in
    Spenser's Legend of Justice: where "heavenly justice" reigns,
    both men and elements "doe know their certaine bound",
    and in the golden age "all men sought their owne, and
    none no more" (*FQ* V.ii.36; Prol.3).
22. *Policraticus* IV.vii (pp.33-4); see p.1 *supra*.
23. I.175-8; XVII.232ff; and *cf Lay Folks' Catechism*: "For
    he shal find merci that mercifull is, And man withouten
    merci of merci sal misse" (ll.378-9).
24. See p.1   *supra*.
25. *Etymologiae* IX.c.3. This was only one of several possible
    senses to be made of the often-repeated commonplace the
    goliard rehearses. Isidore's and other uses of it are
    discussed by Plummer, *Governance*, pp.181-2. Anna Baldwin
    (p.12ff) is of the opinion that the goliard is primarily

asserting the king's obligation to obey the laws himself;
but the implications of "answerde" is surely that the
goliard is saucily 'answering the angel back', and
countering the latter's deprecation of *nudum ius* with
the argument that preserving rules intact (*iura tenere*)
is what 'ruling' is all about.

26. John of Salisbury even went so far as to say that there
was no sin so great that the experience of legal process
could not constitute a penance sufficient for its atonement (V.x,p.119). The prevalent corruption and insuff-
erable delays (*dilaciones ingentes*) formed frequent
matter of complaint (see, eg, *De Laudibus*, pp.131,173-4).

27. This is from the Institutes of Justinian, and it and
medieval attitudes to and interpretations of it are
discussed by Plummer, *Governance*, pp.184-5.

28. I incline rather to the former explanation, since it
accords better with the emphasis on 'knowing one's own',
and with the moral of the fable that is to ensue: that
the governed are better advised to leave the business of
government to their governors, should not take it into
their own hands, but "wite wel (their) owene"; and
since it seems to have been a common assumption that laws
and judgments are not for subjects to question (*cf* J.W.
Baldwin, i.209) - as the subjects themselves here seem
to accept in their declaration of 145.

29. See Schmidt's note to Prol.146, and the notes on the
fable in *Piers the Plowman*, tr.J.F. Goodridge (Harmondsworth, 1966), p.264.

30. Aegidius Romanus, *De Regimine Principum* III.ii.34, in
the Middle English translation (quoted by Plummer,
Governance, p.179).

31. *Policraticus*, IV.iii (p.10), VIII.xvii (p.347); Abelard's
Ethics, p.102; J.W. Baldwin, i.108; ii.148,156,161,
170.

32. *Policraticus*, V.xvi (p.155).

33. IX.200,204; XII.34; XIII.115.

34. J.W. Baldwin, i.167-8.

35. Anne Middleton, 'The Audience and Public of *Piers
Plowman*', in *Middle English Alliterative Poetry and its
Literary Background*, ed. D. Lawton (Cambridge, 1982),
pp.101-23.

36. Aquinas, *ST* II-II cxli.5; *cf* pp. 5-6 *supra*.

37. *Glossa Ordinaria* on Mt.6:25 (*PL* 114.105-6).

38. *Policraticus* VI.xx (p.243).

39. N.F. Blake, *The English Language in Medieval Literature*
(London, 1977), p.75.

40. The most important text on this matter is Mt.22:37-40.

41. For an excellent discussion of the term *iusticia*, see
Goldsmith, pp.5-6.

42. See n.5 *supra*.

43. For *tutor* in the sense of a guardian who has control over his ward's wealth, *cf* Robert of Courson's statement on whether a man is bound to restitution of what he has received to the damage of his ward: "Lex enim dicit quod si quis est tutor pupilli non potest alienare bona pupilli" (J.W. Baldwin, ii.178).

44. To knights it belonged "to letten wrongs and theftes to ben done, and to maintaine Goddis lawe ... to rulen the puple by law and hardiness" (G.R. Owst, *Literature and Pulpit in Medieval England*, (Cambridge, 1933), p.550); to them "the charge of Iustice given was in trust, That they might execute her judgements wise" (*FQ* V.iv.2).

45. *Cf Sir Gawain and the Green Knight*, ed. J.R.R. Tolkien and E.V. Gordon (2nd ed. revised N. Davis, Oxford, 1967), ll.619-69.

CHAPTER III

MEDE AND MERCY

I: *Passus II*

The second passus, like the first, begins by
focusing on a female figure, Langland's procedure
in these initial stages of the poem being a
dialectic one. Mede is dressed in rich scarlet,
where Holy Church had been clothed in linen: an
allusion to the contrast in Revelation between the
whore of Babylon, decked in scarlet and precious
stones, and the bride of the Lamb "arrayed in fine
linen, clean and white" (Rev.17:4,19:8). Where
Holy Church offers the metaphorical treasure of
truth, Mede offers treasure of an only too 'ravish-
ing' (II.17) literalness. The antithesis is
heightened by Holy Church's description of her rival
at the beginning of the passus. From this (20-46)
it emerges that both ladies are on the marriage
market, and are open to offers; both have suitors,
Holy Church a "lemman" called Leautee, Mede an
intended called False, her union with whom is about
to be solemnized; both have dowries settled upon
them - Holy Church's is the mercy of salvation
(God "hath yeven me Mercy to marie with myselve"
(31), she declares); Mede's portion is wealth of a
more tangible kind, but the precise nature of her
dowry is to be the subject of more detailed
analysis later in the passus. The notion of dowry
is an interesting development, providing a new
angle from which to explore the problem of rewards
and penalties, monetary, legal, and spiritual -
"mercy or no mercy" - which preoccupies Langland;
and neatly reflecting his conviction that they
should be in strict accord with the course of life
one 'espouses'.

Most importantly, as Holy Church had been
intimately associated with Truth, so is Mede with
False. And as justice and obedience had proved to
be an important element of the truth Holy Church had
represented, so does the marriage of Mede and False
turn out to be a matter largely of violation and
corruption of law. In fact the antithesis between
the 'truth' of Passus I and the 'meed' of Passus II
proves Langland's concern to be primarily with
justice. For it was to truth as it connoted
impartial integrity in the administration of justice
that meed was traditionally opposed. Lady Munera

(for whose gifts the term 'meed' is used as a synonym[1]) is the first opponent Spenser's Knight of Justice must overcome, and meed is the chief foe of the truth/justice that once prevailed:

> When *Iustice* was not for most *meed* outhyred,
> But simple *Truth* did rayne, and was of al admyred.

(*FQ* V.Prol.3)

The opposition between meed and truth, in fact, nearly always occurs in a legal or judicial context. Of a just suit lost through bribery of the judge by the other side, Margery Kempe comments, "þat is rewth þat mede xuld spede er þan trewth"; and of a complaint he lodged before the ecclesiastical court which the officials were bribed to let drop, Skelton says that "mayden Meed ... made truth to tryp". Truth was a virtue particularly associated with the conduct of the law ("Naght ought a juge ... Othir wey deme þen trouth requireth"; "(corrupt) men of lawe ... lovyn trewþe in non plas"), and its arch-enemy was money: in a corrupt state, "ʒeft is domesman", and good judges are those who "for lukyr trewthe will not despise". The traditional anti-thesis could be wittily adapted by Pope in his reference to 'poetic' justice and the scales "Where, in nice balance, truth with gold she weighs" (*Dunciad* i.53). "Lawe haþe put Meede in gret distresse", runs one (ironic) fifteenth-century verse, again illustrating how the common polariz-ation of meed and truth was understood.[2] Meed and covetousness were always assumed to be the especial enemies of justice, with which they were held to be incompatible.[3]

Langland has broadened the usually specifically judicial application of the 'truth-meed' antithesis to give it a more universal significance. For Holy Church's truth is clearly more than just rigorous integrity on the part of lawyers and judges, and Mede corrupts "alle manere of men, the meene and the riche" (56), not just legal officials. Justice and injustice in their narrower senses do play a central part in the duality between Holy Church's Truth and Mede, but Langland is also in a much larger sense contrasting *iustitia* - good faith and integrity generally - with the greed for gain that forms the chief temptation to break the laws of God and man. He has, furthermore, assimilated into the common judicial opposition, between truth and meed, the influential theological contrast between charity and

cupidity, whereby all virtue was seen as reducible
to rightly directed love, and all sin to perverse
love: "The Law ordains nothing except charity and
prohibits nothing except cupidity".[4] For Mede is
set not only against the 'truth' of Holy Church, but
also, in the "coveitise" associated with her,
against the love or charity the latter declares to
be the informing spirit of truth: Holy Church had
taken those who are "acombred with coveitise" as her
example of 'chastity without charity', and her parting injunction to the dreamer is,"lat no conscience
acombre thee for coveitise of Mede" (II.51). And
the two ladies are represented as alternative
objects of love (II.32,35) and marriage. Langland
has, in short, given a characteristically legal and
judicial definition to the charity-cupidity
antithesis by presenting in terms of truth v. meed.

Mede's essentially illegitimate nature is at
once apparent, for one of the first things we learn
about her is that "she is a bastard" (24).[5]
'Bastard' was a synonym for the Latin term
illegitimatus, and Langland often uses the concepts
of whoredom and bastardy to exemplify the licence,
the lawlessness that characterizes crime and sin:
they are the results of sexual activity outside
lawful wedlock, a lawless state whose 'issue' is
lawless acts, the bringing forth of "barnes ayein
forbode lawes" (III.152).[6]

With the appearance of Mede, the second of the
two legal systems described in the Prologue re-
appears. Passus I had been concerned with the
first: the Church and the law of God. Against that
truth stands Mede, the corruptness of whose
influence is measured by her effects on man's law,
as the King and the laws of the land, the forces of
positive law, now re-enter. With her, too,
Langland starts to investigate the second of the two
vices he had discerned in the Prologue: venality -
especially venality among the "clerkes", spiritual
and secular (the idle are due to be dealt with in
Passus VI). And as it is Mede who is eventually to
lead him to confront the angel-goliard issue more
decisively (in Passus IV), so it is she who
promises to provide the more specific answer to the
question addressed to Holy Church: to whom does
money belong? The scene the dreamer now witnesses
(the attempt to marry Mede to False) suggests that
it is in danger of becoming in fact if not by right
the property of False - *ie*, that it is gained
dishonestly, and crime does pay. People get rich

by falseness to all levels of the law.

Holy Church at once indicates the primary danger of Mede to lie in her corrupting influence on the law:

> 'That is Mede the mayde', quod she, 'hath noyed
> me ful ofte,
> And ylakked my lemman that Leautee is hoten,
> And bilowen hym to lordes that lawes han to kepe.
> In the Popes paleis she is pryvee as myselve'.

> (20-3)

This is the first of many occasions on which Leaute and its cognates (leel, lelly) are associated with "law". The proximity of the word to "lawes" here, and the grammatical co-ordination of the two statements in which they respectively figure, emphasizes the etymology of the word (derived from Latin *legalitas*):[7]   law-ty, law-ness, the quality of being law-abiding. Holy Church's "lemman", then, is one who is faithful, "leel", or true, to her laws (carrying out his baptismal vows to "loven (her) leelly the while (his) lif dureth", I.78). The conjunction with "lemman", of course, also suggests amorous truth or fidelity, so that, "leautee" thus flanked by "lemman" and "lawes", the allegory and its further significance are pointedly brought together. Mede acts against the interests of Leautee: that is, those who are innocent of any breach of the law are misrepresented in the courts by those who have an interest in so doing, and who are motivated by the hope of gain, or who have been bribed, taken "mede", to bear false witness (the suborning of witnesses was a prevalent vice in Langland's day). Mede thus causes justice to miscarry. Her influence in the courts of "lordes" is immediately followed by a reference to her high connections in another court, the Papal Curia: the first of a series of occasions in the Mede sequence in which Langland conjoins corruption of the spiritual and secular authorities, the representatives of law.

Holy Church then proceeds to the subject of the dowries of herself and Mede. Hers is mercy, and is given on the equitable principle of 'measure for measure' which Langland has already established guides God's dispensation of it: it is given to the "merciful" (that is, to those who have showed it), and to those who have observed "leelly" the bidding of Holy Church (32). Equally equitably, this reward will be foregone by those who choose to unite themselves to Mede, rather than to Holy Church:

> 'And what man taketh Mede, myn heed dar I legge
> That he shal lese for hire love a lappe of
>   *Caritatis*'.

(34-5)

The love of material reward expels that higher kind of love which is *caritas*: Mede is taken *super innocentem*,[8] and is therefore taken in violation of charity. Those who receive it will accordingly find that the *caritas* of God, His loving mercy, is closed to them. Mercy is for the mercyfull, and those who have denied charity to others will be denied it themselves.

The lines also suggest another principle from equity that Langland is to make use of his invest- igations into the question of reward and punishment, spiritual and secular. To be rewarded (or to be punished) twice over is not allowed. Mercy (the "mede" of God, as Conscience later explains) and material meed are mutually exclusive. Take the one, and you cannot take the other. You cannot have two wives, or marry one woman and have the dowry of another. You must lie in the bed you make, and must not expect to have your cake and eat it. God will reward only that desert which has as yet gone without meed. This argument is to be developed as the sequence continues.

Also undeveloped at this point is the full relevance of the Psalm Holy Church cites in support of the position just outlined. She now quotes only one line from it: *Domine, quis habitabit in tabernaculo tu* (39)? In context, this is enigmatic, and it is not until later that we are permitted to read on, when Conscience 'turns the page', and the following verses of the psalm declare its relevance to the question of the two kinds of meed. Holy Church seems to wish the dreamer to win through himself to the truths she is adumbrating from what he is now to witness. She not only hangs fire herself, but advises him to do likewise:

> 'Know hem there if thow kanst, and kepe thee from
>   hem alle,
> And lakke hem noght but lat hem worthe, til Leaute
>   be Justice

103

> And have power to punysshe hem – thanne put forth
>   thi reson'.

> (47-9)

The dreamer is to suspend judgment until the real
position at law of Mede and False becomes apparent:
until he sees how true justice would deal with them.
He is then to pronounce his verdict – put forth
his "reson". This is precisely what Langland does:
he puts forth his character Reason to pronounce on
Mede and Wrong only at the end of the Mede sequence,
the intervening space being necessary for gaining
a full knowledge of her nature from her actions and
from the teaching of conscience.

Again one notes in the above lines the
correlation of Leaute with law and justice. The
true judge is one who abides strictly by the law.
The "til" suggests that Leaute is at present
lacking in justice, and this in fact turns out to
be the case. For in what follows it is not actually
the marriage between Mede and False *per se* (the fact
that the rewards of this world go to the false, who
come by them dishonestly) that primarily concerns
Langland. That issue is quickly decided before the
end of the first of the three passūs devoted to Mede.
It is the danger that the influence of her gifts
will persuade the law itself to connive at the
crimes of the false who possess her; that the law
will cease, through her, to punish crime. The
present Passus is concerned largely with the legal
officials and documents that bestow a false colour
of legality on the proceedings; with the projected
journey to Westminster, so that the union may be
officially legitimated by the courts there; and
with the proper routing of False by the law at the
command of him who is 'head of law', the King. The
next concerns the testing of yet more vital centres
of law now exposed to her blandishments: the King
himself, who seems worryingly disposed to be
lenient with her; and that inner law-giver
Conscience, who is invited to accept her to wife.
And in the final passus of the sequence, which
represents a decisive victory over her, the scene
suddenly becomes precisely that of a law-court, in
which the issue raised is specifically whether or
not the law may be relaxed because of her intercession. Then Reason puts forth his reason: it
should not. The three passūs successively declare
the importance of asserting law, true judgment,
against Mede: official, internal, and external

judgment. At the end of Passus II, "constables and sergeaunts" are dispatched to arrest her and her followers; at the end of Passus III, Conscience - *lex intellectus*[9] - denounces her; at the end of Passus IV, Reason, "the mother of all laws", rejects her, an inner power pronouncing judgment in an outer court. It is the supreme importance of the integrity of the law that Langland is asserting. Outer law, outer judgment, is what gives force and efficacy to those inner judgments and discriminations between right and wrong made by conscience and reason. Law and judgment preserve the reality of the distinction between right and wrong, between truth and false, and are thus indispensible in the guidance and governance of the community. They must remain absolute.

Reason and Conscience, the inner faculties that provided an instinctive or "kynde" norm of morality, were thought of as the basis of the natural law of "kynde", on which positive law was based.[10] The Court of Chancery was, in fact, referred to in early documents as the Court of Conscience, and the Chancellor as "the Keeper of the King's Conscience". Conscience played an equally crucial role in the divine law, since sin was defined in subjective terms as what violated the dictates of one's conscience.[11] (This "kynde" law-giver within a man, who can be ignored but never wrong, is given an increasingly important role in the poem: he becomes the dominant guide and instructor in the final Do-Best section (XIX-XX), and in the C-text is present from the start, figuring even in the Prologue as an instructing and interpreting voice). The legal connotations of the meed/truth antithesis are, in short, of primary relevance to Langland's use of it in Passūs I-IV.

The perversion of justice attendant on Mede is at once evident in the identification of the persons most intimate with her. "The route that ran about Mede" contains men of all kinds and degrees, but most prominent in her *entourage* are the corrupters of secular and sacred justice, Symonie and Cyvylle, those who sell the laws of God and man:

> Ac Symonie and Cyvylle and sisours of courtes
> Were moost pryvee with Mede of any men, me thoughte.

> (63-4)

Marriage is both a sacrament and a legal act, and
so must be sanctioned by divine and positive law.
So it is here, though the sanction is a bought one.
"Cyvile" is a reference to the Canon Law of the
ecclesiastical courts. The term strictly refers to
Roman Law as codified by Justinian, which on the
continent provided the basis of legal principle
and procedure in the secular as well as the church
courts. But the Civil or Roman system never
became established in the secular law-courts of
England, where, owing to its great influence on
Canon Law, it became associated exclusively with the
ecclesiastical courts.[12] Since matters matrimonial
fell under their jurisdiction, it is they which
constitute the relevant department of law in the
present instance. These courts were as notoriously
and as extensively corrupt as their secular counterparts. Here, Civil is coupled with Simony, a sin
defined as trafficking in "the 3yftys of holy
cherche",[13] under which the sale of church law
would certainly fall. The two terms taken together
suggest the corruption of both positive and divine
law in the courts where the two most significantly
converged: the courts of the church, which part-
icipated at once in both the ecclesiastical and
the judicial governance of the nation. Their
corruptibility with regard to matrimonial affairs
was well known, and Langland refers to it elsewhere.
Annulments were easily procured from them for a
price (*cf*.XX 138-9). Here, it is the wrongful
making rather than unmaking of a marriage that is
at issue, the marriage being that of Mede and False
- an allegorical representation of the pernicious
union of wrong-doing and gain, wrong-doing rewarded
with wrongful gain that is itself used to obtain
immunity from legal penalty by the doer; the
connivance of law itself at this is accordingly
represented (in the allegory) by the courts whose
profiteering in the administration of matrimonial
law was so notorious.

The connivance of law at this match is, in
fact, more dangerous than the match itself, since it
tends towards the weakening of the 'authoritative'
distinction between right and wrong. All the forms
and ceremonies of the law are pressed into service
to legitimate this wrongful union. The deed pro-
claiming Mede's dowry is the prime example: both
because it is itself a legal document, a conveyance,
enfeoffing Mede and False in certain lands and
tenements, complete with legal formulae (*Sciant presentes & futuri*; "feffeth by this chartre"; "to have and to

holde, and hire heires after", . 74*a*,79,102), and
observant of procedural form, since witnesses, seal,
and date are not neglected (108-14); and because
dowry was an important element of the marriage
transaction in Langland's day, and evidence of the
legality of the proceedings.[14]

The deed is, of course, a grotesque parody of
law, for what it legitimates is illegality. It
grants licence from the law. False and Mede are to
be free to disobey the laws of the land and of the
Church (by engaging, for instance, in false witness,
usury, and fast-breaking) - and of God Himself.
They are to be licenced by it to be "Unbuxome and
bolde to breke the ten hestes" (83), to violate
that truth which is obedience to law, and especially
to God's, the working "as his word telleth". The
lands they are seised in are the realms of the seven
deadly sins, the capital   offences against those
"hestes". They are to be "Princes of Pride",
possessing the "erldom of Envye and Wrathe" and the
"countee of Coveitise"; the sins of the spirit
then lead into those of the flesh, as the "lordshipe
of Leccherie" is added to the list, followed by
"Glotonye", and culminating in "Sleuthe". - Sloth is
always represented as the final degree of sin
whenever Langland uses the *schema* of the seven
deadly sins:[15] a spiritual slough whose depths are
"wanhope", despair, where even the moral energy to
repent and ask mercy is lacking. - Wealth enables
False freely to break the law - for he can buy it
off. It grants him that dangerous liberty that is
licence, lack of constraint on his will.[16]

There is, however, a price to be paid for these
freedoms, as there is for everything in Langland's
world. Typically, the document turns back on the
grantees, proving at last to be not a deed of gift
but a contract, not seisin but rental. The documentary 'pardons' of Passūs VII and XIX are likewise
to turn out to be not, after all, free grants, but
contracts of exchange, demanding something in
return for what they bestow. - And the full sum of
the debt Mede and False will incur on their tenure,
on the expiry of the traditional contractual term
of one year,[17] is stated with legal exactness at
the end of the "feffement":

> 'Yeldynge for this thyng at one yeres ende
> Hire soules to Sathan, to suffre with hym peynes,
> And with hym to wonye with wo while God is in
>   hevene'.

(105-7)

There will be a reckoning, then, at which debts
due at law will be paid. And as Holy Church had
warned, where the treasure of truth proves good
coin at trial, that of Mede and False proves
treacherous, and those who trust on it "bitrayed arn
sonnest". For the lands the liberties of which are
granted, the "erldoms", "chastilets", "countees",
and so on, extend themselves almost imperceptibly
into Purgatory and Hell, and False is discovered
to have been endowed with true title to a
"dwellynge" in Hell, where his liberties 'lead':

> 'And thei to have and to holde, and hire heires after,
> A dwellynge with the devel, and dampned be for evere,
> With alle the appurtinaunces of Purgatorie into the
>   pyne of helle'.

(102-4)

It is after Theology has objected 'just cause
and impediment' to Cyvylle, and cursed the corrupt
law by which he connives at the match ("fy on thi
lawe!", 124), that the decision is taken to make a
test-case of it at the law-courts of Westminster:

> '... to loken if the lawe wolde
> Juggen (them) joyntly in joie for evere'.

(156-7)

The test-case for the poem is: can false, through
meed and bribery, win over the highest courts of
the land to connive at his misdoing, and to refrain
from enforcing the law against him? To 'carry' an
unlawful cause many corrupt minor officials in the
secular and ecclesiastical courts are necessary:
men willing to be bribed out of enforcing the law.
These are the pack-horses of Cyvylle and Symonie,
on the backs of whom the corruption of both laws is
sustained, and they are now listed: "Fals-witnesse",
"sherreves", "sisours", "notaries", "somonours",
"registrers" (145-74). What Langland is talking
about is failure to enforce the penalties of the
law, the relaxing of it through interest. This is
plainest in his account of the Church courts where
such offences against Canon Law as adultery and
usury were tried; the sin is 'suffered' in return
for remuneration from the offenders:

> 'Erchedekenes and officials and alle youre
>   registrers,
> Lat sadle hem with silver oure synne to suffre –
> As devoutrye and divorses and derne usurie –
> To bere bisshopes aboute abrood in visitynge.
> Paulynes pryvees for pleintes in consistorie
> Shul serven myself that Cyvyle is nempned.
> And cartsadle the commissarie – oure cart shal he
>   drawe,
> And fecchen us vitailles at *fornicatores*'.

                                        (174-81)

A vivid acount of corruption in the Archdeacon's court, and how *fornicatores* could be rather blackmailed than punished by its officials, may be found in the Tale Chaucer's Friar tells against the Summoner. Langland claims that the corruption extends to the bishop himself, who (in the periodical investigatory visitations of his diocese he was obliged to undertake) is prepared to wink at transgressions; and to his court, the consistory, and that of his legate, the commissary.

The king, the 'head of law', makes a determined effort to resist the evasion of law being attempted. The miscreants, he vows, will not escape,

> 'But right as the lawe loketh, lat falle on hem
>   alle!'
>
>   (198)

The formal machinery of the law is activated to perform its true function: "constables and sergeaunts" are dispatched to "attachen" the wrongdoers (199-208). And the various kinds of legal penalties at his disposal the King orders to be enforced in all their rigour, and not to be waived for pity or interest:

> 'Fettreth Falsnesse faste, for any kynnes yiftes,
> And girdeth of Gyles heed – lat hym go no ferther;
> And bringeth Mede to me maugree hem alle!
> And if ye lacche Lyere, lat hym noght ascapen
> Er he be put on the pillory, for any preyere, I
>   hote'.
>
>   (201-5)

The King, like Reason and Repentance after him, knows that law loses its reality if its penalties are not enforced, and his commitment to those penalties is here portrayed as energetic and total.

On realizing that the law is to be enforced,
the miscreants scatter, and the personifications of
wrong-doing (Falseness, Guile, and Liar) go underground. They find refuge among friars, pardoners,
merchants, and physicians, whose frauds represent
the continued existence of these forces even in a
society where the law is active in pursuit of them.
Langland is realistic: rigorous enforcement of the
law does not eliminate crime: it merely denies it
free and open action. Even societies with an
unimpeachable judiciary and police have their
underground. Most of us, however, would prefer
to live in communities where criminals escape
punishment by fleeing rather than by bribing the
law. So it would be wrong to regard the close of
this passus as totally cynical in significance - as
implying that, the very characters threatened with
punishment having escaped, nothing has therefore
been gained. The integrity of the law has been
vindicated, and the "drede" that puts the criminals
to flight is surely a healthy and proper fear of
the law. And, although the King can punish
individual transgressors, the law can never hope to
eliminate what he had sought to shackle and
exterminate: falseness and guile themselves.
However, the unholy diaspora that thus terminates
this passus does temper the note of confident
satisfaction on which it would otherwise have
closed, and its implications are worth considering.
What happens is that Falseness finds refuge
with the friars, and Guile with merchants; Liar
is taken up by the pardoners, though courted also
by physicians and others, and is finally domiciled
with the friars, though, like the friars themselves
(to whose unrestricted 'liberty' of movement
Langland attaches a sinister significance), not
confined to quarters (232-3); for even the ill-will
of a Langland toward this brotherhood could not
maintain that lying was an activity exclusive to
them. He satisfies himself, therefore, with
implying that the friary provides a safe home-base
from which the friars can conduct their lying
excursions into the outer world, the lie safely
concealed under the seemingly pious roof of the
institution to which they belong.
The list thus begins and ends with the friars.
After them, the sect given most attention is that
of the pardoners. These two groups are doing
precisely the same thing, and for that reason had

been juxtaposed also in the Prologue: they are
selling pardons, giving "pardoun for pens" (223).
The relaxing of penalties for money, of "penaunce"
for "pitaunce" (to adopt Chaucer's memorable
rhyme),[18] the sale of the law, thus continues in a
disguised form, the more dangerous because it is
disguised. The more flagrant forms of it can be
prevented by the state, but the sale of God's law
by these clerks is a more insidious evil. For to
buy one's way out of the penalty of sin is an
aggravated form of bribing the law.

   The venality of the friars in this respect is,
of course, to become ever more important as the poem
progresses. One may ask why Langland's desperate
anger does not fall equally on the Pardoners, since
both here and in the Prologue they are revealed to
be doing precisely the same thing: facilitating
the evasion of their debts by sinners, enabling
them to buy themselves off the penitential penalties
of God's law. Yet, except for one brief passage at
the end of Passus V, the pardoners do not re-appear.
Langland evidently regarded them as less dangerous.
Unlike the sophisticated and scholarly friars, they
were mostly men of mean birth, pretending to rather
than possessing the authority of learning, of
"clergye": Chaucer's Pardoner stands not "*as* a
clerk", but "*lyk* a clerk" in his pulpit (*CT* VI.391).
Moreover, the falsity of their claims to knock
years off Purgatory in exchange for a few pence was
gross enough to be unable to impose on any but the
simplest of intellects. Chaucer's Pardoner,
describing how he cheats "lewed peple" (*CT* VI.392,
437), knows he cannot put one across on the relatively intelligent company in which he finds
himself, and therefore does not attempt at first to
do so; when, in a heady moment, under the influence of drink and half in jest, he tries it, even
a tavern-keeper is capable of administering to him
a very downright rebuff. Langland's pardoner, too,
can impose only on the "lewed" ("Lewed men leved
hym wel", *Prol*.72), and cannot draw from Langland
that apocalyptic note of impending doom heard when
his eye falls on the friars ("The mooste mischief
on molde is mountynge up faste", *Prol*.67). Nor
were the Pardoners in orders, so they did not
appear to speak with the whole authority of the
Church, the guardian of the divine law, behind them,
as did the friars. The friars were different. They
were sophisticated, educated men, confessors to the
rich and powerful ("chief to shryve lordes", *Prol*.
64), who sold the law in a manner less gross and

more artful. People were not invited to buy pardon
from penance and penalty: they were urged to
demonstrate their penance - give sign that they were
"wel yshrive" through alms, donations to a "povre
ordre" - of friars (*CT* I.225-6): a charitable and
pious deed, surely. By such means the precise
nature of the friars' actions could be prevented
from impressing itself fully on the minds of the
community.

This passage gives some support to such a view
of the situation. It will be noticed from the
lines quoted above that Liar seems to be visualized
as a more vulgar kind of criminal than Falseness and
Guile. It is the common pillory, the stocks, for
him, not prison or execution. He escapes to lead a
ragged, hole-in-the-corner, back-street existence,
"Lurkynge thorugh lanes, to-lugged of manye" (217),
obviously recognizable as a dishonest tramp by all,
as he seems to be beaten from village to village.
It is this character that the Pardoners take up,
which would seem to indicate the grossness and
cheapness of the frauds they perpetrate. They can
give him but a shabby, threadbare respectability:

> They wesshen hym and wiped hym and wounden hym
> in cloutes.
>
> (221)

The physicians also patronize him, but the friars
give him a dress that more effectually conceals his
disreputable origins:

> And for knowynge of comeres coped hym as a frere.
>
> (231)

This suggests that any comer with half an eye would
have recognized the cheap lie that peeped pathet-
ically through the rags and bones of the Pardoner's
'relics'; but in the friar's cope it may not be
recognizable as the same lie. The implication is
that the friars have taken up the lie of the
pardoners (the pretence that God's justice can be
bought off) in such a manner as to make it less
palpable.

The passage, then, has somewhat sinister
implications. Though the King appears to have
enforced the law, and put a stop to the buying of
pardon from its penalties in its most obvious forms,
the same malpractice has infected the officers of
God's law, and the same evil remains in the back-

ground - to be rediscovered in Passus XX, when there
is no King to halt the marriage between Mede and
the falseness that is sin to which the friars are
giving the sanction of divine law, as accredited
members of the church. Behind the cope lies
Cyvylle's lie; but, although Langland demonstrates
this habited lie in action at the beginning of the
very next passus (III.35-63), it is a lie disguised
so well that the relevance of the episode has often
been questioned. It is to become patent only at
the close of the poem.

II: *Passus III*

Mede is herself now brought before the King,
the head of law, and the highest court of appeal
in the land. He is himself the presiding judge in
the case of Mede v Conscience that is argued before
him; but before that dispute begins, the reader is
twice given yet more proof of her corrupting
influence on the law, secular and sacred, first in
general, and then in particular. On her arrival,
she is courted by justices, for "That wonyeth at
Westmynstre worshipeth hire alle" (12). They pledge
themselves to work in her interest, and in return
she dispenses among them "Coupes ... richesses
manye", as a lord to his "meynee" (22-4). The scene
in fact is an allegorical representation of that
vicious perversion of feudal 'maintenance' whereby
the officials of any given district were often in
the pay of the local magnate, retained or 'maintained' by him, and thus unofficial members of his
"meynee",[19] a situation that, as here, produced a
perverted parody of feudal loyalties, the munifi-
cence of the overlord providing a due return for
loyal service. Those who 'maintain truth' and 'hold
with the rightful' (II.37,III.242) are, in fact,
throughout contrasted with those who 'maintain'
misdoers (III.167,247) for meed, and so are themselves 'maintained' by her in her "retenaunce" (II.
54): the two parties of truth and false thus being
conceived of in feudal terms as rival powers of
patronage. - These officials of the secular law
are succeded by those of the sacred law, the
"clerkes", who similarly swear to her an oath of
feudal fealty: "For we beth thyn owene For to
werche thi wille the while thou myght laste" (27-8)
- not, interestingly, as long as their own lives
last, the more usual formula (*cf* I.78,VI.36); the
faith of the venal lasts only till the money runs
out. In return, Mede promises to advance them, "And

in the consistorie at the court do callen hire
names" (31), whether they are fit to sit there or
no:[20] she will be a 'good lord' to them. The law
and the clergy are thus discovered to be in her pay,
to have betrayed their true duties to their true
lords to enter her service.

What this means in more specific terms is then
made clear. It means the relaxation of *pena*,
punishment legal and penitential, and non-payment
of debts of sin and at law, which remain unrendered
to God and to Caesar, disturbance of the equilibrium
of justice that is preserved by punishment. First
comes Mede's confession (35-75), a passage in which
the sale of God's law is coped as a friar "for
knowynge of comeres". "I shal assoille thee myself
for a seem of whete" (40), the friar promises, and
Mede, proceeding to make a "shamelees" confession,

> Tolde hym a tale and took hym a noble
> For to ben hire bedeman and hire brocour als.

(45-6)

The alliterative and syntactic conjunction of
"bedeman" and "brocour" provides its own pungent
analysis of the situation. The friars offered the
prayers of their fraternity to penitents whose
spiritual re-habilitation manifested itself in
donations to the brotherhood. This friar, in
becoming such a "bedeman", becomes in effect the
"brocour" of Mede; "brocour" had highly derogatory
connotations,[21] referring to the activities of an
intermediary in corrupt transactions. Mede is
trying to buy off heaven, and the friar is her go-
between - and at the same time her 'agent' in the
wider sense that he carries her gospel of 'buy
yourself off' among his clients and associates,
"knyghtes and clerkes, Conscience to torne" (42).
He, like the justices who likewise promise to work
for her against conscience (19), seeks to corrupt
and beguile the true judgment of that inner faculty
by providing exemption from penalties for wrong-
doing. For the friar mentions neither penance nor
satisfaction, but only monetary 'amends'.

The nature of the friar's confessional conduct
is made yet clearer by the juxtaposition of this
passage with that on Mede's dealings with the mayor
and other municipal officials whose business it is
to administer and execute the laws of the land,

> that menes ben bitwene
> The kyng and the comune to kepe the lawes,
> To punysshe on pillories and on pynynge stooles
> Brewesters and baksters, bochiers and cokes -

(76-9)

Other offenders against the laws controlling weights, measures, and quality that governed the retail trade are then listed. These officials, however, like the friar, allow the sins to go unpunished in return for meed:

> Ac Mede the mayde the mair heo bisoughte
> Of alle swiche selleris silver to take,
> Or presents withouten pens - as pieces of silver,
> Rynges or oother richesse the regratiers to mayntene.

(87-90)

The conjunction of the two passages is highly significant.[22] It emphasizes and develops the implications of the juxtaposition of the justices and the clerics that immediately precedes, and pursues the logic of the joint investigation into church and state, clergy and lawyers, begun in the Prologue, and found also in the pairing of Cyvylle and Symonie as the twin leader's of Mede's train. It is such pairings that help to point the real significance of the friars' action in Passus XX, and give to their malpractice its juristic definition.

In the present instance, the analogy between the confessional and the municipal misconduct of the friar and the mayor is emphasized by other parallels. In each case, Mede abuses two of the key terms of Holy Church's sermon - mercy and love - in her attempts to persuade to pardon of offenders. Of lechery, she coaxes the friar to "Have mercy ... of men that it haunteth" (59). It is a "freletee of flessh", she explains, the least of the seven deadly sins (55-8): an example, presumably, of precisely that 'glosing' flattery the friars themselves would have used to soothe the consciences of their clients out of the real penitence that would urge satisfaction in other than monetary terms.[23] She similarly urges charitable 'suffrance' on the mayor:

> 'For my love', quod that lady, 'love hem echone,
> And suffre hem to selle somdel ayeins reson'.

(91-2)

"Reson" might well here be a semi-personification, since it is against 'mercy' of this sort that Reason is loudly to object in the following Passus. The poem is beginning to distinguish between different kinds of pardon, forgiveness, mercy: between the mercy that is divine commanded by the angel, and the mercy that is a corrupt relaxation of the penalties imposed by the rules the goliard defends. Mercy may in one sense be the consummate perfection of justice, the performance of the highest law, the *Lex Christi*, the New Law, but in another it is its overthrow, and thus less not greater than the Old Law.

The relation of both incidents is followed by a protesting interjection from the poem's narrative voice. Both protests take the form of *comminationes*. The first (64-75) is directed towards those who accept the friar's invitation and have their names advertised in religious institutions as benefactors of the order in question. The gratification this affords may constitute a reward for the charity shown which will disqualify the donor from further reward: "ye have youre hire here and youre hevene als" (72). This is the first development of the notion suggested by Holy Church that one cannot have two "medes". This would offend "egalitee". God's meed of mercy, heaven, is for those who have not taken the 'meed' represented by the lady in scarlet. Langland is here extending the principle to apply to any kind of reward for "wel dedes" received on earth. The text adduced as authority is from the New Testament (Mt.6:3). When it turns to address the "mayres and maceres" (93-100), this voice takes its "teme" from Solomon: *Ignis devorabit tabernacula eorum qui libenter accipiunt munera*. And it warns that Hell-fire awaits those who take

> Yiftes or yeresyeves because of hire offices.
>
> (100)

The acceptance of these types of *munera* even more decidedly excludes the remuneration of heaven. Both homiletic codas, then, warn, in different ways, of the danger of accepting 'hire' that may annull one's claim to meed in the hereafter.

When Conscience delivers his emphatic denunc-iation of Mede, it is her corruption of the laws of church and state, of heaven and earth, that he

insists on (120-69). His opening words include
the charge of the murder of kings and popes:

> 'Youre fader she felled thorugh fals beheste,
> And hath apoisoned popes and peired Holy Chirche'.

> (127-8)

Whatever specific reference Langland may or may not
intend, the accusation that she destroys the very
sources of rule, social and spiritual, heralds in
forceful terms the nature of Conscience's case
against Mede. Using the imagery of sexual licence
frequently associated with her to convey the breach
of rules she provokes and sanctions, he claims that
she is a "baude" (desire of gain being often the
instrumental cause in coupling men to crime and
sin). She causes justice, the equilibrium between
reward and desert, to miscarry; under her
influence *nullum malum* is no longer *impunitum*,
for she

> '... taketh the trewe bi the top and tieth hym faste,
> And hangeth hym for hatrede that harmede nevere'.

> (140-1)

- and, more importantly, she gives *nullum bonum*
licence, liberty from the law and its penalties:

> 'She leteth passe prisoners and paieth for hem ofte,
> And giveth the gailers gold and grotes togidres
> To unfettre the Fals - fle where hym liketh'.

> (137-9) [24]

The lines are followed by a significant passage in
which Conscience claims her power over the laws of
church and state to be such that the seal of her
approval legitimates more effectually than the
seals which are the authenticating tokens of the
decrees of state and church, and, again in the
sexual metaphor, they do not enjoin laws, but
licence illegitimacy:

> 'She may neigh as muche do in a monthe ones
> As youre secret seel in sixe score dayes!
> She is pryvee with the Pope - provisors it knoweth,
> For Sire Symonie and hirselve seleth hire bulles.
> She blesseth thise bisshopes, theigh thei be lewed;
> Provendreth persones and preestes she maynteneth

> To holde lemmans and lotebies alle hir lif daies
> - And bryngen forth barnes ayein forbode lawes'.

(145-52)

She not only destroys kings and popes; she usurps
their function, producing a new and perverted law
of her own that chokes the functioning of true law.
It is this strangulation of law that forms the
climax of Conscience's denunciation:

> 'For she is favorable to Fals and defouleth truthe
>   ofte.
> Be Jesus! with hire jeweles youre justice she
>   shendeth
> And lith ayein the lawe and letteth hym the gate,
> That feith may noght have his forth, hire floryns
>   go so thikke.
> She ledeth the lawe as hire list and lovedaies
>   maketh,
> And doth men lese thorugh hire love that lawe
>   myghte wynne -
> The maze for a mene man, though he mote evere!'

(154-60)

The defence duly has its say after the
prosecution has completed its case. Mede begins by
asserting the integrity of her motives:

> 'And thow knowest, Conscience, I kam noght to chide,
> Ne to deprave thi persone with a proud herte'.

(178-9)

Pleaders in medieval courts were obliged to take an
oath that they would not procede in malice.[25] Mede
is slyly asserting the propriety of her own pleading
methods, and covertly impugning those of Conscience,
who, she implies (with some justice) has improperly
taken refuge in malicious insult. Mede's disin-
genuity here, however, is comically revealed by her
immediate change of tone from injured self-
righteousness to the very abusive ill-will she has
just foresworn:

> 'Wel thow woost, wernard, but if thow wolt gabbe', *etc.*

(180)

But her answer is by no means utterly devoid of
reason. Her peroration is particularly important.
All men take "mede" for the services or goods they
render, and,

'No wight, as I wene, withouten Mede may libbe!'

(227)

She is here articulating an objection that must have
been uneasily forming itself in the mind of the
reader as he listens to the harangue of Conscience,
whose verdict may well have come to appear rather
too absolute. Surely all forms of remuneration
cannot be so unholy? As Mede points out, the
smooth and equitable functioning of society depends
on the circulation of money given in exchange for
services so that men may come honestly by the
necessities of life that money buys.

To appreciate the significance of the reply
given by Conscience, it is necessary briefly to
review the course of the allegory as it relates to
Mede; for that reply is in essence a fuller restatement of the position taken up by Holy Church on
Mede's first appearance, and thus constitutes
another instance of the poem's working its way
through to a truth adumbrated, but not fully understood, in advance. The most striking example of
this occurs in the confirmation given by Passus XIV
to the decision taken by Piers at the end of Passus
VII,[26] a sudden decision (to abandon his life of
labour for a life of prayer and penance) which at
the time the dreamer scarcely notices, and which
surprises most readers. These prophetic conclusions
and subsequent verifications perhaps afford some
evidence that the confusion of Langland's poem is
not entirely an unwilled confusion; he knows where
he is going, but works in every sense to 'take the
reader with him' on his journey.

The Mede episode has been examined in detail
by others,[27] and it is unnecessary to do more here
than briefly to summarize the nature of the problems
arising from it. These stem essentially from the
ambiguity of the word "mede" itself, three distinct
senses of which are to be found in Langland's
treatment of the subject.

(1)   The word could be used in a neutral sense,
      without any derogatory implications, simply to
      mean 'reward'. In this sense, it could be
      quite compatible with virtue, and the word

119

could thus properly be used of the 'reward'
of heaven God gives to the true, and is so
used by Theology and Conscience ("God graunted
to give Mede to Truthe", II.120;   "That oon
(meed) God of his grace graunteth in his blisse
To tho that wel werchen while thei ben here",
III.232-3).   Expressions such as 'meed of
heaven', 'heavenly meed', were, in fact, very
common.[28]

(2)   In certain contexts, the word had a narrower
and pejorative sense, referring to *munera*,
gifts or money, corruptly taken, especially by
officials and especially legal ones, to the
end that they should not exercise their office
with proper impartiality, but should show
favour to the donors (more loosely, the word
could refer simply to the materialistic
orientation of those whose actions are motivated more by desire for profit than by
principle[29]).   In this sense, the word very
nearly translates the modern 'bribery'.   And it
is this sense of the word that is to the forefront in the "meeds" of Spenser's Lady Munera
in Book V of *The Faery Queene* (The Book of
Justice), the lady whom the champion Knight
of Justice, Artegall, must overcome;   and it is
this sense, too, that is largely uppermost in
the Mede sequence of Langland's poem, which
likewise presents this seductive female as the
enemy of justice.

(3)   The word could also denote the agreed price of
goods or services rendered, and thus a
contractual debt due in law or equity (which
a 'reward' need not be).   In this sense it was
equivalent to modern terms like 'pay', 'wages',
'hire', 'salary', 'fee'.   Thus Theology can
speak of it being proper to give "meed" to
truth on the principle of "*Dignus est operarius*
his hire to have" (II.123).   And it is this
sense of the word Mede is drawing on when she
claims that   "mede" is the fundamental
principle on which the whole process of earning
a living depends.   In this sense, it is quite
unreasonable to expect even officers of the
law, sacred and secular, not to claim their
"mede" from society in return for performing
a service to it, as all other trades and
professions do:

'The Pope and alle prelates presents underfongen
And medeth men hemselven to mayntene hir lawes,
Servaunts for hire servyce, we seeth wel the sothe,
Taken mede of hir maistres, as thei mowe accorde.
Beggeres for hir biddynge bidden men mede.
Mynstrales for hir myrthe mede thei aske.
The Kyng hath mede of his men to make pees in londe.
Men that kenne clerkes craven of hem mede.
Preestes that prechen the peple to goode
Asken mede and massepens and hire mete also.
Alle kyn crafty men craven mede for hir prentices.
Marchaundise and mede mote nede go togideres:
No wight, as I wene, withouten Mede may libbe!'

(215-27)

Langland has thus complicated his allegory by
reminding us (through Theology, through Mede herself,
and by other means) of the unexceptionable senses
of the word whose derogatory sense only is personified by the character of that name.

For when Mede is first introduced to us through
the description of her by Holy Church it is sense
(2) we are forced, consciously or unconsciously, to
adopt. Mede is contrary to "leaute" and subverts
law; those who "caccheth Mede" and those who
"maynteneth truthe" are placed in antithesis (II.
36-7), and the reward of heaven and the reward of
"mede" are therefore mutually exclusive ("And what
man taketh Mede ... shal lese for hire love a lappe
of *Caritatis*", II.34-5). The Psalm that itself
polarizes the nature of the two activities and the
rewards due them is then cited by Holy Church as her
"auctoritee", though she does not recite the relevant
verses. Unless Holy Church means that anyone who
takes money for anything is debarred from heaven
(an interpretation which does not naturally suggest
itself), this must be Mede (2): the replacement of
truth by interest as the movivation of conduct,
especially as it shows itself in the actions of those
who are bribed to pervert the course of justice.
This, of course, makes of Mede a character intrinsically and unambiguously evil.

However, the allegory itself procedes to suggest
the more neutral senses of the word, according to
which Mede would not be herself evil, but evil only
if wrongly joined to *nullum bonum*, leaving *nullum
malum irremuneratum*. This is the effect of making
the point at issue her marriage rather than herself.
It is thus implied that it is the union of meed and
false that is the central evil, not meed itself.

121

Mede is deplorable only when given to and for False.
It is the marriage that Theology and the King object
to ("And thou hast fest hire to Fals; fy on thi
lawe!" II.124; "Ac worse wroghtest thow nevere
than tho thow Fals toke", III.107). They desire to
marry her to Truth and Conscience; that is, their
goal is not the extermination of Mede, but that
rewards should be distributed with justice and
equity, according to the dictates of conscience, to
those who truly deserve them. This is to remind us
of the neutral sense of the word, and of the fact
that all kinds of reward and returns are not in
themselves evil. That Mede in itself is something
neutral, partaking of good or evil only as it is
joined with true or false deeds, is the central
implication of making the character a woman whose
marriage hangs in the balance. For by medieval
law, a married woman had no identity of her own;
she assumed the name and status of her husband,
becoming 'one flesh' with him, and (legally) an
extension of himself.30 Until, therefore, it is
settled "whos wif" (18) she is, Mede's whole identity
hangs in the balance. The allegory, then, is
encouraging us to interpret her according to sense
(1) - something which can be good or bad, according
to the truth or false it is wed to. That is, it
performs an insidious move toward Mede (1) and (3),
away from the Mede (2) initially suggested by the
scarlet clothing of the whole of Babylon, and by
Holy Church's words.

What also contributes to this shift is the
characterization of Mede herself right up until III.
180, when she rounds on Conscience to take the
initiative. Up until then she has been essentially
rather a passive creature, has spoken scarcely at
all, and has been but obediently responsive to any
overtures that are made to her - from False, Guile,
Liar, justices, friars, or kings. She is quite
happy to comply with the marriage with False that is
arranged for her, but equally happy to accept
Conscience instead when the King suggests it (III.
112). Contrary to first appearances, Mede, in
effect, had showed as yet *no* moral character; any
she does have derives from the courses others
devise for her.

The first specific indication that a sense of
the word other than that indicated by Holy Church
is under review comes with the interjection of
Theology, who objects, not, like Holy Church, to
her, but to abuse of her, the mis-marriage of her.
This leads him to give an account of her genealogy

startlingly different from that outlined by Holy
Church:

> 'For Mede is muliere, of Amendes engendred;
> And God graunted to gyve Mede to truthe,
> And thow hast gyven hire to a gilour - now God gyve
>   thee sorwe!
> The text telleth thee noght so, Truthe woot the
>   sothe,
> For *Dignus est operarius* his hire to have -
> And thow hast fest hire to Fals; fy on thi lawe!...
> And Mede is muliere, a maiden of goode'.

(II.119-32)

Mede is a "muliere", and the offspring of "Amendes".
Since we were given to understand not one hundred
lines previously that she was a bastard and the
daughter of Fals, we can no longer allow the shift
in interpretation of the word to go unnoticed. It
is rather disturbing to find characters called
Holy Church and Theology in such apparent radical
disagreement,[31] but the difference is one of
semantics, not of principle. He is interpreting
Mede in senses (1) and (3). Mede should be
distributed according to justice and equity to those
who have earned it (*Dignus est operarius*), not to
the false, who merit not reward, but punishment.
The marriage represents a perversion of the equilibrium between desert and reward that justice
requires. The affirmation of 119 Schmidt glosses:
"Meed is ideally, *ought* to be, the offspring of
Amends (= satisfaction for sin, which God will
reward in heaven)". This is quite possible, would
accord with the insistence by Reason and Repentance
that debts and penalties must be paid, and contrast
with the evasion of penalties Mede is shown to
facilitate (III.137ff, IV.175ff). But the line
would then be totally unrelated to what follows,
which can scarcely refer to the meed of heaven. It
may be that Theology is asserting Mede to be
legitimate, related to law and justice, because a
product of the equitable principle of "Amendes" =
due recompense, compensatory recognition of labour
done, to which 'hire' is thus due. Theology is,
at any rate, clearly arguing that rewards should be
equitably distributed on the basis of desert, and
at least at 123 using "mede" in sense (3), which
puts him at odds not only with Holy Church, but also
with Conscience, who specifically excludes it from
the word's field of reference - a melancholy

position for theology to be in. He is, in any case,
forcing on our notice the favourable senses of the
word the allegory is also hinting at.

Mede, furthermore, does not flee before the
law, as the other criminals do. She remains, albeit
in fear and trembling. Nor had the King threatened
her with punishment. This, again, is because the
allegory has not yet settled that meed *per se* is
illicit. Nor does the king treat her as a criminal,
but as someone abused and ill-advised. She has
sought to make an improper match against his will,
and if she will now be guided by his election, all
will be well (104-111). Interestingly enough,
Mede seems to be conceived allegorically as a
wealthy heiress with the legal status of ward of the
crown.[32] Wardships were coveted perquisites in the
Middle Ages. Where the ward was female, the
guardian's liberty to dispose of her in marriage was
virtually total, so long as he did not 'disparage'
her - that is, marry her beneath her status. It is
just such a 'disparagement' Theology claims to have
been perpetrated.[33] Mede is a "muliere, a maiden
of goode, And myghte kisse the Kyng for cosyn and
she wolde", who is being unlawfully married to "a
bastarde ybore of Belsabubbes kynne" (II.131-3), and
the sanction of the courts must therefore be sought
before the marriage can proceed. The King orders
Mede to be brought to him, not for punishment, but
apparently because he conceives of her as belonging
to him; and he treats her as if her only crime had
been in contracting a marriage without his consent,
it being his right to choose the groom, which right
he now intends to exercise. Again, the effect is
to encourage a neutral interpretation of the word
"mede": meed is something that it is in the law's
gift to bestow (as a wealthy heiress is in her
guardian's), which may be unlawfully disparaged by
being falsely given, or lawfully dispensed according
to conscience.

The King's decision to marry Mede to Conscience
is entirely in accord, therefore, with the logic of
the allegory. It is Mede's marriage to False which
has been presented as the evil to be averted; the
logical counterbalance would be the marriage to some
quality such as conscience which would ensure that
rewards were justly distributed. Conscience's
energetic refusal, "Crist it me forbede!" (120), and
his following speech in which he denounces her as an
arch-perverter of law and justice, the reader thus
hears with some surprise, and not a little exas-
peration, realizing that the allegory is returning

to the Holy Church sense (2) of "mede", and therefore to the notion of Mede as intrinsically evil;
whereas we have been led away from that viewpoint
by events, and by Theology and the King, to an
interpretation of the word that suggests a morally
neutral quality that can operate for good or ill
according as she is given in marriage. Again,
Conscience dissents from the King not on principle,
but on semantics. The perversion of justice he
describes is just what the King is trying to avert
by ensuring Mede be joined to a power capable of
standing by the discrimination between right and
wrong to which the law seeks to give authoritative
status. All this is very confusing for the reader,
since it results in some dislocation between
allegory and sense. We have a situation in which a
woman branded as the whore of Babylon by a *persona*
of unimpeachable credentials seems to charm the King
and Theology over to her side, and cause a rift
between Holy Church and Theology, and between the
King and Conscience: whereas in fact all four
characters agree that rewards can be good or evil,
and merely disagree as to whether Mede, the
character before them, represents that ambiguous
potential or realized evil. The resultant strain
on the reader is an effect highly typical of
Langland's allegory, which his admirers term fluid
and many-layered and his detractors muddled and
confused. The line is certainly a thin one, and to
those of his critics who argue that this is more
like brain-teasing than poetry, his enthusiasts
can probably only answer that the beauty of Langland
is that he is one of the few poets who give one as
much pleasure as a good brain-teaser.

However, the reader is made some amends in the
present instance. When Mede defends herself by
drawing on sense (3) of the word, Conscience feels,
not before time, the need to define one's terms. In
his reply, therefore, he in effect separates the
word out into those three consitituent meanings of
it which have been the source of the confusion and
disagreement: true or good meed; false meed; and
hire, or wages.

"Mede" Conscience defines as something given in
consideration of something else, but not strictly
due to the latter. Since no-one should take what
is not due him, there is only one 'good' meed, and
that is the reward of heaven God gives "of his
grace" to those who "wel werchen" in this life, in
consideration of their truth and righteousness.
This is not strictly due them, because no-one can

really earn heaven, and because 'Virtue is its own
reward', and should be exercised for its own sake
"withouten mede", which God yet in His magnanimity
gives (230-46). The only other kind of meed is
that bestowed in consideration of connivance at
crime (246-54). Wages and fees do not fall within
the referential compass of the word, but within that
of *mutuum* being the exact measure of an amount due
in amends or recompense of time, energy, or goods
expended: the "mesurable hire" which makes good a
loss, pays a debt due (255-8).

Conscience thus in effect restates the teaching
of Holy Church in a more detailed way. You may
take the mercy of God, or you may take "mede", and
the two are mutually exclusive: the former is
given only to those who have performed the works
of justice "withouten mede". The clearest signal
that the analysis of Holy Church is regained its
ground is Conscience's use of the very Psalm she
had cited in her own support: Psalm 14. Holy
Church had, however, cited only one phrase from it,
Domine, quis habitabit in tabernaculo tuo, leaving
its bearing on her argument unexplained. Its
relevance had constituted something of an enigma,
which Conscience 'solves', glossing the significance
of the verses that follow (in which the Psalmist
answers his own question - "And David *assoileth*
it hymself", 237), in a manner which supports his
own and Holy Church's assertion about the incompatibility of the two types of reward: the mercy
of God is extended to the righteous only; the
corollary is drawn from the same Psalm - it is not
given to those who have unjustly taken gifts
super innocentem.

The curious fact emerges, then, that meed is
received both for upholding and for perverting
justice. It is a term associated with the reward
of the works of justice, as 'hire' is for the reward
of other works. For the Psalm in question promises
God's "mede" primarily to him *qui operatur
iusticiam*, which Conscience glosses thus:

> 'Tho that entren of o colour and of one wille,
> And han ywroght werkes with right and with reson ...
> And alle that helpen the innocent and holden with
>   the rightfulle,
> Withouten mede doth hem good and the truthe helpeth -
> Such manere men, my lord, shul have this firste mede
> Of God at a gret nede, whan thei gon hennes'.

(238-45)

And the texts chosen to illustrate the taking of
illegitimate meed refer to *munera super innocentem*,
munera from those *In quorum manibus iniquitates
sunt*, which Conscience takes as referring to those
who "To mayntene mysdoers mede thei take". But the
line negates 242-5 not only through the antithesis
"holden with the rightfulle" (which Holy Church had
rendered "maynteneth truthe")/"mayntene mysdoers";
but also through that of "withouten mede"/"mede
thei take". For the law should be both obeyed and
administered "withouten mede"; justice is corrupted
as soon as it is served for profit or meed. So
God's meed to *iusticia* excludes any other kind of
meed. Here again Langland is exploring further the
principle of singularity of "mede" per head: no-one
is eligible for double payment. God's meed and meed
of other kinds cancel each other out. This applies
in particular to "lordes that lawes han to kepe", for
justice is incompatible with meed;[34] and also to
the keepers of God's Law to whom Conscience now
turns: priests (252-5).[35] They, too, cannot take
reward for their services, because it is of the
essence of those duties too that they be not
subject to sale; if they do, they, too, have
forfeited the right to meed in the herafter:

'Amen, amen, receperunt mercedem suam'.

(254*a*)

God will recompense only such deeds whose re-
imbursement is yet outstanding. This is a re-iter-
ation of the principle ennunciated at 72: "On
aventure ye have youre hire here and youre hevene
als". And in fact the text then quoted - *Nesciat
sinistra quod faciat dextra* - occurs only three
verses priot to the *dictum* Langland adopts above
as the epitaph on priests who "Taken mede and
moneie for masses that thei syngeth" (253). One and
only one reward may be taken - here, or hereafter.
    The reasoning by which Conscience excludes
from the above scheme the hire or wages by reference
to which Mede had sought to defend her legitimacy
is not wholly convincing. The *distinctio* is neat:
that is "mesurable hire", whereas "mede" is
"mesureless". But in other ways it is quite clear
that Langland wishes to present God's meed as being
distinct from false meed through its equity and
proportion, and to be given according to the rule
Theology had referred to as governing God's law on
meed: "*Dignum est operarius* his hire to have".

Heaven is the wages of the works of justice, paid at
the evening of life, but not paid if hire has
already been received (*Amen, Amen, receperunt
mercedem suam*), in which case it would have ceased
to be a work of justice, to which reward is anti-
pathetic. All other works can honestly take hire,
but justice cannot - not in this life - for then it
ceases to be justice and becomes *mutuum*; its hire
is heaven. Both the verses from Matthew quoted in
the Passus assume that heaven is "hire"/*mercede* for
the works of piety, to be paid as, but not how and
when, other works are; and Piers is himself first
presented as a labourer in the service of Truth
whose "hire" is promptly paid by his master. And
in the C text, in fact, Langland distinguishes
illegitimate 'meed' both from the reward of heaven
and from fair wages precisely on the principle of
"relacyon right": the latter have a fit relation
to the works they reward, and are therefore "no
mede but a mercede, a manere dewe dette"; only
where there is no such logical concord or proportion is the payment 'meed', and therefore unjust
(C.III.290-339).
   And the line in which Langland here attributes
the "mesurelees" quality to meed is actually rather
ambiguous:

> 'Ther is another mede mesurelees, that maistres
>   desireth';

(246)

The line can be read in two ways, according to
whether "mesureless" is interpreted as predicative
or attributive: 'There is another kind of meed,
which is measureless (*ie* distinct from the first
by being measureless)'; or, 'There is another kind
of measureless meed (*ie* like the first in being
measureless)'. After one has heard that wages are
no meed but "mesurable hire", one realizes that the
argument requires the second reading. But, in
context, one rather reads it with the former
emphasis: God's reward is fair and equitable, given
to the *dignus operarius* who *operatur iusticiam*, to
workers who "wel werchen "; the second kind bears no
correspondence with the desert of its recipients.
The grammatical ambiguity allows Langland really
rather to have his cake and eat it.
   There is a further point, however, to be made
about the 'fair wages' that Conscience excludes from
the definition of meed. Meed applies only to the

works of justice and piety, for which 'hire' in this
life is forbidden. Their payment is termed 'meed' -
false if taken here, just if taken in the hereafter
- as the equivalent of the wages other kinds of
'work' claim. Work that is done for hire is not the
work that sustains truth "withouten mede" that God
will pay, but the pay taken for it does not
disqualify one from the reward of heaven the way
meed (payment for the works of justice) would.
Equally, however, 'a fair day's work for a fair
day's pay' would not itself qualify for meed in
heaven. Observing that principle means that one
has properly taken only what is one's due; but to
receive the meed of heaven one has to have laboured
in the works of justice "withouten mede", and thus
have hire outstanding. This is a point relevant
to the sudden disclosure in Passus VII that the
'honest labourers' may not actually, after all,
yet have proved their claim to the meed of God's
mercy; they have simply attained to a state whereby
they are not automatically disqualified from it.
The Wel they must Do for *that* 'hire' is something
quite apart from the honest labour for which they
fairly take their wages - and for which they have
already, therefore, been rewarded.

The poem, then, has argued its way through to
a verification of the proposition from which the
sequence began: there are two meeds, mutually
exclusive, God's and that of Mede the Mayde, which
is intrinsically evil, and which is a corrupter of
law and justice. The Psalm Holy Church began
Conscience completes. In the interval, Langland
has had to discriminate between different kinds of
reward, just as he will have to discriminate
between true and false mercy, between the begging
that is pious and the begging that is unlawful.
His poem forces him often to discriminate, for he
can be just neither morally nor intellectually
unless he does so.
The question of false meed is, in fact,
intimately related to that of false mercy, and hence
the relevance of the character to the problem posed
by the exchange between the angel and the goliard.
We have heard Mede urge mercy on friars and mayors
for the offenders against the laws of God and man:
to pardom them the penalties. In the following
Passus, she is likewise to urge that Wrong be
forgiven the penalties he has incurred. Conscience
therefore follows up the elaborate *distinctio* that
distinguishes true from false meed with an *exemplum*

against false mercy: the mercy given in consideration of meed. The *exemplum* chosen is the Old Testament story of Saul and Agag; it is one of that not inconsiderable number of Old Testament anecdotes which make distinctly unattractive reading, but it does come in very apt. Saul has been appointed executor of a penalty decreed by divine justice:

> 'God sente to Saul by Samuel the prophete
> That Agag of Amalec and al his peple after
> Sholden deye for a dede that doon hadde hire eldres'.

(261-3)

Whatever we may judge to be Agag's liability for the crime of 'his elders', whatever may be our opinion of the degree of the punishment to be inflicted (the total extermination of the tribe), the justice of the sentence, decreed as it is by God, is not in context open to question. Samuel warns Saul not to mitigate its severity "for mede ne for monee" (271). Saul, however, refrains from inflicting the penalties due:

> 'And for he coveited hir catel and the kyng spared,
> Forbar hym and his beestes bothe as the Bible
>   witnesseth
> Otherwise than he was warned of the prophete,
> God seide to Samuel that Saul sholde deye,
> And al his seed for that synne shenfulliche ende'.

(273-7)

What would have been Saul's position in the eyes of God had he spared the nation because his heart had been touched by compassion rather than by "coveitise" we do not know, for the Bible and Conscience are silent on this point.[36] But they are loudly positive on the facts as they stand: the mercy that comes of meed is a capital and damnable offence, constituting a corrupt relaxation of the penalties justice decrees, and Saul is to die for it, together with 'all his seed': he becomes liable to the very penalty he had corruptly forborne from enforcing. The relevance of the story to the mercy given by friars and mayors under the persuasions of Mede, to Reason's adamant refusal in the next Passus to relax penalties at her intercession, and to the later insistence on the payment of debts divine justice demands, is

130

clear. The poem is beginning to make the discriminations about mercy necessary for deciding when and
whether the angel's command or the goliard's
prohibition should prevail. And one type of mercy
definitely falls in the latter category.

Conscience ends his speech by an apocalyptic
prophecy of some perfect future time after the
Second Coming, when the corruption of justice by
Mede represented by Saul will be succeeded by Mede
rule of David, the type of the ideal earthly king,[37]
and in this *regnum davidicum* absolute justice will
reign:

> 'Shal na moore Mede be maister as she is nouthe,
> Ac love and lowenesse and leautee togideres -
> Thise shul ben maistres on moolde truthe to save.
> And whoso trespaseth ayein truthe or taketh ayein
>   his wille,
> Leaute shal don hym lawe, and no lif ellis.
> Shal no sergeant for his service were a silk howve,
> Ne no pelure in his paviloun for pledynge at the
>   barre'.

                                                    (290-6)

Absolute equity between doom and desert will then
prevail, and mercy will be dispensed according to
the dictates not of meed but of true justice
itself, for true mercy can never run counter to true
justice:

> 'But after the dede that is doon oon doom shal
>   rewarde
> Mercy or no mercy as Truthe moste accorde'.

                                                    (318-19)

The truth, like Spenser's Una, is single and
indivisible. The true church is "Unite", permitting
no deviation from its simplex rule, but demanding
that single-minded adherence to itself that is
sancta simplicitas.[38] So the ideal state on earth
and the justice it will administer is single. There
will be but one kingdom, and one king, -

> 'And David shal be diademed and daunten hem alle,
> And oon Cristene kyng kepen us echone' -

                                                    (288-9)

one court, and one judge:

> 'Kynges court and commune court, consistorie and
> chapitle –
> Al shal be but oon court, and oon burn be justice:
> That worth Trewe-tonge, a tidy man that tened me
> nevere'.

(320-2)

This, of course, will not occur in the real world
as we know it, but is expressly set in some
apocalyptic future, replete with the riddling
symbolic signs traditionally associated with the
apocalyptic mode (325-30), when Jews will believe
"That Moyses or Messie be come inmyddes this erthe"
(303), and when the Antichrist typified by Mahomet
will be overcome. The apocalyptic mode here acts
as a vent by which Langland's fierce idealism can
be asserted without prejudice to the realization
that told him such things belonged not in our time
but to that safely dateless era of the prophesied
golden age. Till then, we live in the reign of the
undefeated Antichrist, and in that condition of
multiplicity which is a legacy of the Fall, and
which, in the realm of justice, obscures that
absolute simplicity of true justice: the "oon
doom" according to "the dede that is doon".
Similarly, the ideal "Unite" of the Church is later
revealed to be unable to survive in the age of
Antichrist in which it actually exists, and unable
to defend its single integrity against those subtle
modifications to the stern and absolute simplicity
of its one rule of justice (*Redde quod debes*) the
friars introduce into it.

"Latyn", and the construing it requires, is
once again used to signal precisely the problem
that had arisen in the Prologue through the
conflicting tenors of the Latin texts of the angel
and the goliard. Mede is confident of her Latin
("'I kan no Latyn?' quod she. 'Clerkes wite the
sothe!'" 332); she knows that the Bible says
Honorem adquiret qui dat munera. And Conscience
acknowledges her "Latyn" to be "trewe" (337).
'Giving' is that act that 'works the word' of the
New Law of love and mercy: "love and lene", *Date
et dabitur vobis*. But she lacked the "konnynge
clerk" (347) who could have added the goliardic
rider: *Animam autem aufert accipientium*. To give,
mercy or *munera*, may be divine; to receive the
gift of either, that is, as something unearned,

unpaid for, is to fall into debt to justice and
equity by precisely that amount: "The soule that
the soude taketh by so muche is bounde" (352).

And here Passus III closes. With the truth of
a single text thus divided between the disputants,
the case is referred at the beginning of Passus IV
to Reason, the power that judges of right and wrong,
and is "the mother of all laws". When he appears,
however, it is a different case he is asked to
pronounce upon. A petitioner appears to present
a Bill at the court, which is thus now seen more
distinctly in its legal function as a court of law.
What has happened, however, is that the allegory has
in effect translated itself into the very issues it
had figured: the relationship between meed, mercy,
and justice. The scene is therefore now precisely
the Court as a court of law, and the dispute one at
law: a formal petition issued by Peace against
Wrong. And the decision referred to Reason at IV.
112 is one that combines the two related issues of
meed and mercy: can Wrong be released from the
penalties of the law through the intercession of
'meed', that is, by offering money to his accuser
and to the court? Nor is this really an issue
separate from the one on which his advice had
originally been sought. He had been sent for to
decide whether or not Mede could be reconciled with
and married to Conscience. The case with which he
is confronted raises precisely this issue: for it
is one in which the giving of 'meed' might be judged
as conformable with conscience - when conscience
might pronounce the 'meed' offered Peace as constituting a sufficient recompense for the wrongs
he had suffered, and so a sufficient repayment of
the debt owed him by Wrong. The compatibility of
meed and conscience is thus exactly what Reason
does give a judgment on. The issue raised
allegorically is merely reformulated by posing a
non-figurative example. The climax of the Mede
sequence is thus very precisely related to the
problem of the conflicting claims of rule and mercy
raised in the Prologue: it takes place in a court
of law, in which the question of whether Wrong may
be pardoned the penalties of the law is specifically
raised - and categorically answered.

NOTES

1. Eg, V.ii.9,23.
2. *The Book of Margery Kempe*, p.59; Skelton's *Ware the Hauke*, 11.149-155; Scattergood, *Politics*, pp.321, 301, 282,303.
3. *Policraticus* V.ix,x (pp.112,114); *Libro de Buen Amor*, st.218.
4. Augustine, *De Doctrina Christiana*, iii.10,n.15 (*PL* 34, 71).
5. Bastards were, in the Middle Ages, thought to have contracted corruption in their very conception, to be inherently indisposed to knowledge or virtue, could not succeed to patrimony, and were excluded from ordination (see *De Laudibus*, pp.94,98,100,192).
6. *cf* VII.88-91; IX.108ff; XX.156-62.
7. On Leute, see further Kean, *art.cit*; E.T. Donaldson, *Piers Plowman: The C-Text and its Poet* (New Haven, 1949), pp.65-6.
8. "(bribes) against the innocent": a key phrase in the psalm verse quoted against Mede (Ps.14:5) at III.241*a*.
9. "Synderesis (conscience) dicitur lex intellectus nostri, inquantum est habitus continens praecepta legis naturalis, quae sunt prima principia operum humanorum" (Aquinas, *ST* I-II.xciv.1).
10. See Bennett, n. to III.1; *cf* previous note, and n.62 to ch.I *supra*.
11. *Potter's Outlines*, pp.84,248-9; Luscombe, *Ethics*, p.xvii.
12. For a full explanation of the term 'Civil' in this passus, and of the church courts represented by him, see B.B. Gilbert,''Civil' and the Notaries in *Piers Plowman*', *Medium Aevum* 1 (1981), 49-63.
13. *OED sv* Simony (1).
14. See Chrimes, in *De Laudibus*, pp.190-1.
15. *cf* V.386ff; XIII.406ff; XX.156ff. Sloth denoted spiritual apathy, and was quite consonant with energetic physical activity (*cf*V.417-20). Repugnance to any "gastely gode" was its chief characteristic (*Lay Folks' Catechism*, 11.525-6). Juan Ruiz calls it "the most subtle and deceitful" of the seven sins (st. 1600), and also places it last. See further S. Wenzel, *The Sin of Sloth: Acidia in Medieval Thought and Literature* (Chapel Hill, North Carolina, 1967).
16. Though freedom was desirable, unconstrained liberty was dangerous and much distrusted: see Skelton's *Magnificence*, 11.37-239; *Policraticus*, VII.xvii (p.282); and Spenser's cautions in his Legend of Justice against the desire for 'uncontrolled freedom' and 'licentious liberty' (*FQ* V.ii 33; v.25); and *cf* n.21 to ch II *supra*.
17. *cf* VI.43, and *Gawain and the Green Knight*, 11.297-8; here merged with the notion of yearly rental (Bennett compares

the legal formula, *reddendo annuatum*).

18. *CT* I.223-4.
19. See Scattergood, *Politics*, p.316ff; and *cf* A. Baldwin, p.26ff.
20. *cf* Juan Ruiz's account of the power of Money (sts 490-514): "on many ignorant clerics he conferred high honours" (st 494).
21. The word came to be "simply a euphemism for corrupt influence or bribery" (Plummer, in *Governance*, p.337).
22. Juan Ruiz also conjoins legal and penitential venality in his account of the power of Money (st 496).
23. For other complaints that the friars condoned lechery in the rich and absolved them for cash, see *Lay Folks' Catechism*, 11.767ff (Wycliffite version); *Jack Upland*, p.70.
24. *cf* Juan Ruiz on the power of Money: it can "free you from stocks and fetters and dangerous prisons; they put handcuffs on the man who has no money" (st 497).
25. See *Policraticus* V.xiii (p.136).
26. See ch.V. p.245ff.
27. See, for instance, Dunning, p.69ff; and J.A. Yunck, *The Lineage of Lady Meed: The Development of Medieval Venality Satire* (Notre Dame, 1963).
28. See, for instance, Chaucer's 'Balade de Bon Conseyl', 1.27; Hoccleve, *The Story of the Monk who Clad the Virgin*, 1.100; *The Book of Margery Kempe*, pp.130,134, 161,186,203,204.
29. As, for instance, in the short verse debate, 'Mede and Muche Thank', where service for reward is contrasted with service out of loyal duty (*Twenty-Six Political and Other Poems*, ed. J. Kail, E.E.T.S. O.S. 124 (1904), no.II).
30. See Fortescue, *De Laudibus*, p. 101ff.
31. In the C text, the contradiction is smoothed over somewhat, as Theology distinguishes (II.121-2) Mede's *father* (False) from her *mother* (Amends), which mixed parentage heightens the moral ambiguity of the principle of 'meed' at this point of the poem.
32. As Bennett points out (n. to III.1).
33. On disparagement, see J.W. Baldwin, i.248; Plummer, in *Governance*, p.271. Anna Baldwin also sees the question of disparagement as relevant to the Mede episode (p. 32ff).
34. See n.3 *supra*.
35. It was common to link the professions of the law and the church, as Langland does here, as falling equally under the ban of selling their services. For to sell these 'moral arts', as opposed to the mechanical or liberal arts, constituted simony (J.W. Baldwin, i.126). This applied equally to priests (*ibid* i.108; *Policraticus*, VII.xix (p.295)), and to judges (J.W. Baldwin, i.128,191;

ii.122,130) - justice being "everywhere an obligation or indebtedness in such a sense that no price may be charged for it without committing a crime" (*Policraticus*, V.xi, xvi (pp.125,148)).

36. In the Bible, however, Saul's motives for retaining the "catel" are not quite as Langland represents them (see I Kings 15-16).

37. See Bennett's note, and *cf* Bolton, p.82.

38. On this quality of persevering loyalty to a single absolute, see Leclercq, *passim*, esp. p.205.

CHAPTER IV

REASON, REPENTANCE, AND MERCY

I: *Passus IV*

Passus IV pronounces what is to prove a crucial judgment, and Langland begins it by himself drawing a *distinctio* between different kinds of wisdom that may be brought to bear in matters legal and judicial. Reason, appealed to as the properly competent arbitrator, is a morally discriminating intelligence. He is pursued, however, to the scene of trial by two characters who represent rather different aspects of the human 'wit':

> Oon Waryn Wisdom and Witty his fere
> Folwed hem faste, for thei hadde to doone
> In th'Escheker and in the Chauncerye, to ben
>   descharged of thynges,
> And riden faste for Reson sholde rede hem the beste
> For to save hem for silver from shame and from
>   harmes.
>
> (27-31)

Wisdom and Witty clearly denote that type of shrewdness and cunning whose orientation is expediency and self-preservation rather than principle. They are here represented as attempting to evade their debts at law: as seeking ways of delivering themselves from the unpleasant consequences of their misdoings. They are later to perform the same service for Wrong. They are the characters which show him the most likely way out (compensation of Peace, and bribery of the court). They judge of good and ill according to the expediency or otherwise of the results of any course of action; thus they are capable of condemning that lawless will in Wrong which led him to the present *impasse* ("'Whoso wercheth by wille, wrathe maketh ofte'", 70). They tend to speak in a rather gnomic style, for their wisdom is the wisdom of proverbs: practical, amoral rather than immoral, concerned with self-preservation rather than with salvation, with ways to avoid discomfort or danger (as in such proverbs as 'look before you leap', 'more haste, less speed', *etc*). It is best exemplified in the following couplet from Wit, with its persuasive, pithy, punning logic:

'Bettre is that boote bale adoun brynge
Than bale be ybet, and boote nevere the bettre!'

(92-3)

It is only in retrospect that one realizes that
'better' here is used in the sense of more expedient,
more profitable, less painful to all concerned,
which may or may not be the same thing as morally
'better'. It is this kind of wisdom that Reason
must rigorously dissociate himself from if his
judgments are to retain their purely moral character:
in the allegory, Witty and Wisdom stand to him as a
couple of clever and unscrupulous Q.C.s,[1] bearers
of gifts and persuasive arguments designed to win
over the judge. Conscience counsels complete
detachment from them: Reason must not even stop
and argue with them, but must ride fast straight
ahead (33).

The shunning by Reason of the pursuit made upon
him here turns out to be an allegorical presage of
the course of events that ensues on his arrival.
The pursuit is conducted by those eager to attempt
an evasion through meed, by 'silver', of penalties
incurred through a breach of the law at present
sub judice. When Reason arrives at his destination,
the conflict he was summoned to settle has translated itself precisely into a law-suit at present
pending, where the offender likewise attempts to
evade the due penalties of his crimes, and Reason
has resolutely to turn a deaf ear to the strong
persuasions of the money and arguments advanced on
his behalf by Wisdom and Wit.

Peace's complaint is given a strictly legal
context: it is a 'bill' presented to Parliament,
the King in Parliament being the highest court of
appeal in the land. Wrong has been guilty in a
multitude of ways of not paying his debts, and not
paying them at Peace's expense: he "taketh me but
a taille for ten quarters otes" (58). He is the
archetypal offender against that justice that gives
to every man his due, and the antithesis of the
true or just man who 'takes but his own'. Wrong
has helped himself to his neighbour's - materially,
sexually, commercially (48-60). He is "bold for to
borw ac baddelyche he payeth" (C.IV.55). As a
consequence he owes the law a debt, a *debitum* (the
formal term for the legal penalty due a crime),
which he is likewise set on not paying.

The offences of Wrong, then, are of the
essence of injustice. Peace in the land is what

laws and justice aim to establish (it is the King's
function "to make pees in londe", III.221), and the
man who does not offend against them keeps the
peace. Spenser took over from Langland (or
arrived independently at) the same formulation of
that essential task justice must address itself to:
for the climax of his Book of Justice, as of the
Mede sequence, concerns the deliverance by the hero
knight, Artegall, of the princess *Irena* from the
wrongful oppression of the giant *Grantorto*.[2] The
Latinized names are a good indication of the
difference in the allegorical mode of the two poets.
Spenser chose a higher, more romantic register,
and his treatment of the conflict has nothing
beyond the nomenclature of the *personae* in common
with Langland's. The comparison is, in this case,
all to Langland's advantage. Even taking into
account the difference in Spenser's style and
intention (the last two Cantos of the Book are meant
also as an allegorical reference to the Irish
question), his *Irena*, a typical damsel-in-distress
princess, languishing under the heinous tyranny of
the monster-usurper, *Grantorto*, a three-bodied
giant, has none of the expressive force of Langland's
earthier picture of a peasant Pees, miserably
proffering his bleeding head, "his panne blody"
(78), as crude evidence of what he has suffered at
the hands of that jumped-up thug and bully-boy
whose name is Wrong.
    Pees's name relates to the action in several
different ways. In part, it signifies his
innocence as a peaceful, law-abiding citizen who
has done nothing to provoke the outrages committed
against him and against the King's peace. It also
refers to the instinct that leads him to urge the
forgiveness of Wrong once the latter has offered
him compensation. He is not, like Reason, concerned
primarily with vindicating the integrity of the law.
He wants the whole thing settled as peaceably as
possible. There is also the issue of how and
whether Wrong can 'make his peace', atone for his
offence against the King's peace. For the guilt of
Wrong is not at issue in the Passus: no-one denies,
no-one questions it, not even the defendant. The
issue is how and whether he should be punished,
"Mercy or no mercy as Truthe moste acorde". Wrong
attempts to 'make his peace', that is, compensate
for the injury he has done Pees, by offering him
money. He seeks out Wisdom "To maken pees with his
pens" (64), repeating at 74-5 this attempt through
Wisdom "To maken his pees with his pens, handy dandy

payed".
     The denomination 'Peace' also refers import-
antly to the nature of the offences committed by
Wrong.   These latter constitute a classic case of
Trespass, the action brought when the plaintiff
alleged assault on his person, property, or land
by the defendant (all which types of violation
figure in Peace's Bill here, 48-60).   Now the writ
issued under Trespass alleged that the offence had
been committed "against the King's peace" (*contra
pacem regis*).   Trespass thus differed from other
civil actions in being a Plea of the Crown: that
is, it involved a criminal element.   The State, the
Crown, was an interested party, and the defendant
was held to have committed a crime not just against
his neighbour, but also against the King as the
guardian of "commune profit".[3]   The name Langland
gives to his plaintiff alludes to this fact, which
bears significantly on the issue of what penalties
Wrong should be made to undergo.   In ordinary civil
actions, compensation of the plaintiff would
constitute adequate redress.   But this solution is
rejected here (104 ff):   for Trespass being a Plea
of the crown, the defendant (as in criminal law)
is held to have committed an offence against the
common interest of society (represented by the
crown) for which he cannot atone simply by compen-
sating the party he has injured, any more than can
a robber or murderer.   The name Pees given to the
'injured' party here thus indicates an important
factor in Langland's disinclination to accept the
money offered by Wrong to the plaintiff as adequate
amends for his offence.

     All this bears upon the question crucial to
this Passus and the next of what appeasement,
atonement, amends, for an offence may properly be
said to justify mercy: render the exercise of it
not discordant with the justice that demands
payment of *debita*, balancing of accounts.   For,
properly, "pardon is granted only to him who amends
... or to him who is resolved upon amendment".[4]
Meed has from the first been associated with a type
of amends, and a type of mercy given in consideration of it, that Reason is to reject as illegitimate.   Theology had claimed that Mede was "of
Amendes engendred".   But he had been referring to
the mercy that "God graunted to give ... to truthe"
- Conscience's Mede (1).   The lady in the poem is
actually his Mede (2), and represents a perversion
of the principles of mercy and amends.   For the

giving and the mercy Holy Church· commends as the
essence of love both find their impious antitypes
in her activities.   The two words 'mercy' (which
Holy Church had claimed as *her* dowry) and 'amends',
which are to become insidiously associated with
Mede, are first used by the lady herself in the
treatment of those "that lecherie haunten" she
urges on the friars:

> 'Who may scape the sclaundre, the scathe is soone
>   amended;
> It is synne of the sevene sonnest relessed.
> Have mercy', quod Mede, 'of men that it haunteth'.

> (III.57-9)

It is to "lordes" and "ladies" (III.53-4) only that
she counsels such mercy be extended, it may be
noted: *ie*, those wealthy enough to pay the friar's
type of 'amends' for the 'release' of the sin.   She
gives the same counsel to mayors, at which point
the narrator interrupts to point out that her
advice conflicts with that of "Salamon the sage";
in rehearsing which he uses the word 'amend' in
such a way as to demonstrate that it has another
important sense - the reformation of one's ways,
something not taken into account in Mede's use of
the term:

> ... a sermon he made
> For to amenden maires and men that kepen lawes.

> (III.93-4)

In Passus IV, the appeals for 'mercy' on
Wrong's behalf because of the 'amends' he offers
through meed (that is, through offering money to
the court and to the plaintiff) become ever louder
and more insistent.   On his instructions, Wisdom
and Wit "wenten togidres, And token Mede myd hem
mercy to wynne" (76-7).   The King resists the
persuasive eloquence of "catel" (82), declares that
Wrong shall be treated according as his deeds have
deserved (that the doom should be "after the deed
that is done"), and prepares to activate the legal
machinery designed to execute that rule of justice:

> The Kyng swor by Crist and by his crowne bothe
> That Wrong for hise werkes sholde wo tholie,
> And comaundede a constable to casten hym in irens.
> (83-5)

141

But thereafter the arguments for mercy in view of
the amends Wrong offers gather force and volume.
Wisdom and Wit speak first:

> 'And he amendes mowe make, lat Maynprise hym have
> And be borgh for his bale, and buggen hym boote,
> And so amenden that is mysdo, and evermoore the
>   bettre',

> (88-90)

argues Wisdom: let him 'buy' mercy through
monetary amends.   The term "boote" (remedy) is here
used in the semi-legalistic sense (redress, compensation) illustrated by the term *'botleas* wrongs',
which were those which, in the earliest days of
the English law (when redress for personal injuries
was left largely to the injured party and his kin
to exact), the community took as offences to its
collective being and exacted communal vengeance
for;   in time, these *botleas* offences developed
into the basis of the criminal law: offences for
which the defendant was answerable to the law of
the land, to the King's Judges, and not merely to
the party he had injured.[5]   Wisdom is arguing that
surely "boote" (of mercy) can be purchased in the
present instance by Wrong's willingness himself to
offer monetary 'remedy' to Pees.
     Wit takes up the "boote/bale" antithesis his
confrere has introduced in the witty aphorism he
now subjoins:

> 'Bettre is that boote bale adoun brynge
> Than bale be ybet, and boote nevere the bettre!'

> (92-3)

It is surely better that Peace find from Wrong a
'remedy' for the injuries he has suffered than
that Wrong be duly punished and Peace never the
better off.   Another covert plea for mercy is
contained within the lines, for "bote of bale" was
a common periphrasis for the passion of Christ,
the act by which mercy for their sins was obtained
by mankind collectively through the "bote" or
'amends' He offered for their original "bale".   This
restoration of the phrase to its original legal
context is important evidence that Langland's
present investigations into legal pardon are
relevant to his later theological reasoning on the
availability of Christ's mercy;   and the allusion

also lends a spurious air of New Testament piety
to the arguments of Wisdom and Wit. Wit's argument,
in fact, appears to make very good sense; and
these pleas for mercy are, after all, presented as
the arguments of wisdom and wit: of common sense,
of reason in the modern sense of the word.
Langland elsewhere refers to 'wisdom and wit' in an
approving manner,[6] and the usually non-derogatory
connotations of the collocation seem here to
sanction the logic of the course they suggest. In
fact, Langland is adopting with Wrong's case much
the same procedure as he had in his presentation of
Mede: an initially unfavourable view, which the
reader is lulled into relaxing, only to be treated
to a surprise re-assertion of the hard line.
Reason's adamant "no ruthe", when it comes, goes
as much against the prevailing logic as had
Conscience's "Christ it me forbede!"
    Mede now adds her voice to the calls for mercy,
accompanying her plea with a gesture that gives the
glitter and solidity of 'pure gold' to the argument of 'amends' on which it is based:

> Thanne gan Mede to meken hire, and mercy bisoughte,
> And profrede Pees a present al of pure golde.
> 'Have this, man, of me', quod she, 'to amenden thi
>   scathe,
> For I wol wage for Wrong, he wol do so na moore'.

> (94-7)

Wisdom, Wit, and Mede are, of course, suspect
characters, however persuasive. But Pees himself
now (literally) feels that their is substance to
their arguments, and when the voice of the injured
peace itself urges pity, mercy, forgiveness, for
the offender, declaring itself satisfied at the
'amends' offered -

> Pitousley Pees thanne preyde to the Kynge
> To have mercy on that man that mysdide hym so ofte.
> 'For he hath waged me wel, as Wisdom hym taughte,
> And I forgyve hym that gilt with a good wille.
> So that the Kyng assente, I kan seye no bettre,
> For Mede hath maad myne amendes - I may na moore axe'.

> (98-103)

- the reader himself is almost persuaded that an
obstinate insistence on the penalties laid down by
the law would in this case be unreasonable - in the

modern, not in the medieval sense of the word -
that is, contrary to that kind of practical
intelligence here represented more by Wisdom and
Wit than by Reason. And, once again, Peace uses
the word Wisdom here in a sense and in a context
calculated to make us forget the amorality of the
character earlier revealed to us.

But Langland's concern here is not with what
Wisdom but with what Reason (justice) counsels.
Moreover, his concern with injustice is now revealed
to arise not simply from compassion for the wrongs
suffered by the poor and oppressed, but also from
a hard conviction that those wrongs should be
punished. Peace gets the chance of redress, but
Langland denies it him. Significantly for the
final stages of the poem, what he is here concerned
to emphasize is that the *debitum* of wrong must be
paid as laid down by the law, and not commuted to
a fine; no monetary payment must be allowed to
absolve Wrong from his present debt to the law.
Most importantly, though the pity and forgiveness
to which Peace is moved may be in him, as the party
injured, a Christian virtue of the kind enjoined by
Holy Church and the angel, in the upholders of the
law such mercy could be nothing but a refusal to
enforce justice and rule. It would be a mercy
unjustified by real amends from Wrong.

For the King now shows himself unconvinced by
the amends offered on Wrong's behalf. His objection
is twofold:

> 'Lope he so lightly, laughen he wolde'
>
> (106)

- if offenders escape with monetary penalties, they
lose respect for the law, and for the distinction
between right and wrong to which it gives authority.
For men need that kind of evidence of the reality
of ethical rules which law and punishment provide.
The King's words here are a prophetic foreshadowing
of the results of the commuted penalties for transgression offered to sinners by the friars, who are
discovered to have "plastred hem so esily that hii
drede no synne" (XX.380).   Contemptuous laughter
is the antithesis of dread, and "when man dredys
not he sone forgetys þat he schulde do".[7] Moreover, there is one feature of true amends the King
sees as lacking: the commitment to an amended
future course of life, an amendment of his ways by
Wrong, who, he thinks, will in fact "eft the bolder
be to bete myne hewen" (107). Those who trust on

Mede's treasure "bitrayed arn sonnest", and the
King is unwilling to rely on her promise that she
will guarantee or "wage" that Wrong "wol do so na
moore", or that, what is 'misdone' having been so
'amended', all will really be, as Wisdom claims,
"evermoore the bettre". Monetary amends, he
rightly suspects, offer *no* guarantee or assurance
of reformed, amended habits on the part of the
offender thenceforward.

But thus beset by pleas for mercy, the King
refers the question to Reason, for it is in accord
with that natural justice discerned by the power
of the mind that judges of right and wrong that the
law should always be determined:

> 'But Reson have ruthe on hym, he shal reste in my
> stokkes'.
>
> (108)

Reason was sent for to judge of the compatibility
between Mede and Conscience. The allegory has now
completed its translation of the terms of the
question and reputs it. Can meed, in the present
instance, be legitimately, conscientiously,
accepted, as the satisfaction that can reconcile
justice and mercy, justify mercy?
Reason is as adamant as was Conscience that
mercy and meed are mutually exclusive. Conscience
had distinguished it from the mercy of God;
Reason excludes it as a claim on the legal pardon
of the crown in earthly law. Mercy cannot be
bought, and penalties must be paid. His emphatic
verdict of "no ruthe" is twice decisively
affirmed:

> 'Reed me noght', quod Reson, 'no ruthe to have ...'
>
> (113)

> 'And yet', quod Reson, 'by the Rode! I shal no
> ruthe have ...'
>
> (134)

Each affirmation introduces a passage in which
reasons for the verdict are given, the two passages
together constituting a *distinctio* between legitimate and illegitimate mercy and amends, that in
some ways recalls that drawn by Conscience. For
in the first, Reason describes the circumstances in

which he could sanction "ruthe"; and, in the
second, the circumstances that at present prevail
and under which he will not sanction it.
     The conditions in which he could allow mercy
are described in a prolonged temporal clause,
sustained by repeated "Till"s -

> 'Til lordes and ladies loven alle truthe ...
> Til Pernelles purfill be put in hire hucche
> And childrene cherissynge be chastised with yerdes ...
> Til clerkene coveitise be to clothe the povere and
>   fede', *etc.*

                                        (113-33)

-which is also in effect a conditional clause:
"Dont's ask for mercy unless and until ...". Those
"Til" clauses define an ideal state of society in
which that integrity or truth in conduct, which in
medieval Latin fell under the term *iustitia*, is
observed by all, and in which each truly 'knows his
own', performing his function in society to the
"commune profit", and not for personal interest: a
society, in short, from which wrong-doing has been
eradicated. This might appear to be an anticipatory
version of the later paradox on which Langland makes
God's mercy conditional: forgiving the debt of sin
only for those who have paid their debts. For
Reason appears to be saying mercy will only be given
where there are no offences to extend it to. But
Reason may not actually intend here to be so
awkward as to be impossible. He wishes to see an
amendment of their present ways by society, is
pointing to the nature of the amends on which a claim
to mercy must rest. Evidence of real amends shows
itself in an amended way of life, not in the
increased 'boldness' in crime which pecuniary amends
encourages. The passage, moreover, repeats
Conscience's ruling that mercy is the reward of deeds
of truth and piety, and provides further evidence of
Langland's concern that doom, reward ot punishment,
mercy or no mercy, should match deeds.
     When he repeats his refusal at 134, Reason
follows it with another temporal clause, also in
effect a conditional clause, relating to the
conditions in which mercy cannot be given:

> 'While Mede heth the maistrie in this moot-halle'.

                                        (135)

He will not give it 'while and if' it is at the persuasion of meed. Grace cannot arise from gifts, nor mercy from meed:

> 'Ne get my grace thorugh giftes, so me God save!
> No for no mede have mercy'.

(141-2)

Mercy cannot be given in consideration of money, which should not have the power to relax the penalties of the law. The poem is beginning to grapple with the apparent conflict between *ius* and *pietas* posed in the Prologue. It is doing so through *distinctiones*, through discriminating between different kinds of mercy, and different kinds of that amends on which mercy must depend: for amends restores the equilibrium of justice, and so allows mercy to be consonant with it. One type of invalid amends, and consequently of invalid mercy, has not been identified: the type that rests on money, on meed. Nor can the mercy the angel had urged run counter to that supreme rule upon which even the New Law depends, which the angel himself had pronounced: *Qualia vis metere talia grana sere*. This means that sentence must faithfully reflect deeds, and that wrong, unless satisfied by amends, must be punished. Reason now proceeds to pronounce his own version of that rule. For, he says, he can "shewe ensamples as I se outher" (136). He is probably here referring to Wit's glibly aphoristic argument for mercy:

> 'Bettre is that boote bale adoun brynge
> Than bale be ybet, and boote nevere the bettre!'

(92-3)

If the defence can produce that maxim, the prosecution can match it with another, one that actually does take the form of a tiny narrative "ensample", and one that strictly apportions sentence to desert:

> 'For *nullum malum* the man mette with *inpunitum*
> And bad *nullum bonum* be *irremuneratum*'.

(143-4)

No wrong should go "unpunysshed" if Reason, true justice, reigned (138-40). In fact, the source

from which the maxim is quoted uses it to define
true justice: *Ipse est iudex iustus ... qui nullum
malum praeterit impunitum, nullum bonum irremuneratum.*[8] Langland is asserting through Reason the
sanctity of strict equity, which even the mercy
enjoined by the New Law cannot violate. More
pertinently, he is asserting the sanctity of
penalties (as Conscience has already done through
his "ensample" of Agag and Solomon), their importance to the moral health of a community, in a way
that bears directly on the spiritual malaise he is
later to see as the result of the relaxation of
penitential penalties by the friars. His is a hard
logic that at once repels and appeals: what is hard
is rigid, but also firm; rules that are absolute
both alarm and yet satisfy.

Reason challenges the assembled "clerkes" to
construe his maxim (145): yet another invitation
carefully to consider the plain English sense of a
Latin *sententia* with implications for the administration of justice. The effect of this one would
be to place important constraints on the relaxation
of penalties, and what is particularly interesting
in the present context is that legal and confessional judges are briefly brought together as
equally bound by it - and equally desirous of evading it. For it is to "confessours" that Reason
delivers the text for interpretation -

> 'Lat thi confessour, sire Kyng, construe this
>   Englyssed'.

(145)

and confessors who respond to it:

> Clerkes that were confessours coupled hem togideres
> Al to construe this clause.

(149-50)

This is directly to point the relevance of the
present issues to the rules of the penitential
court of confession, and the obligation on spiritual
judges to ensure that God's justice is satisfied
by the due payment of penalties for sin before
granting their mercy of absolution. Like the
digressory confession conducted by the friar at the
beginning of Passus III, it reminds the reader that
there was a second dimension of justice with a
problematic power to absolve introduced to us in the

Prologue, that of the Church, the guardian of the
law of God, and that it too is implicated in the
present investigation into the legitimacy of mercy.
Both these allusions to confessional practice
prepare for the transition to the confession scene
that is to follow in Passus V, and explain the
bearing of these early passūs of the poem on the
crucial relaxation of confessional penalties
presided over by the friars at the end of it.

For the space of half a dozen lines or so,
then, there are in fact two layers of allegory
present at this point of Passus IV. When Reason
invites the "clerkes" to construe his text, he is
on one level addressing himself to the legal
experts and advisers of the court (who would often
be members of the clergy) so that a legal maxim can
be interpreted and applied to the present case; and
on another to confessors, to the clergy *qua* clergy,
challenging them to define what this text would
imply as to the imposing of penances and the granting of absolution. Similarly, there are two levels
of reference present in the account of the response
Reason's challenge meets, since the word "confessours" figures here too:

> Clerkes that were confessours coupled hem togideres
> Al to construe this clause, and for the Kynges profit,
> Ac noght for confort of the commune, ne for the
> Kynges soule,
> For I seigh Mede in the moot-halle on men of lawe
> wynke,
> And thei laughynge lope to hire and lefte Reson manye.
>
> (149-53) [9]

On one level, the passage describes venal "men of
lawe" who give a false 'gloss' to the law to
persuade the court, here the King, in his own
financial interest, that a monetary fine can be
interpreted as punitive 'amends'; on another, it
refers to confessors who 'glose' the Church law on
satisfaction to flatter a penitent into believing
that donations to their own institutions can
constitute the payment of his spiritual debt
required by the rules of shrift - so showing less
regard for his soul than for what is to their mutual
profit. The lines provide a prophetic foreglimpse
of the glosing friars of Passus XX, the effect of
the two levels of allegory being directly to equate
venal lawyers, twisting the law for their clients
at the instance of meed, with confessors who like-

wise in their own interests misrepresent God's
justice to penitents.

One legal concept that Langland has made use of
in his inquiry into what sort of mercy is, and what
sort is not, consonant with law and justice, is
that of 'bail'. In medieval law, an accused person
could in certain circumstances be set at liberty
providing he could find adequate sureties, persons
willing to stand bail for him, and deposit pledges
for his future good conduct and answerability to
the law. Such a person was called a "borgh" (a
guarantor, surety), or a "maynpernour" (one who
'takes the hand' of the offender, to deliver him
from prison). What, in abstract terms, can act as
a viable "maynpernour" for Wrong to justify his
release? The defence is represented as offering
Mede as a "maynpernour", since they are trying to
secure that release through gifts and bribery. The
prosecution is from the first, however, unwilling to
accept her. As early as II.197, the King had, in
despatching officers for the arrest of False and
his accomplices, declared that there would be no
bail, that the offenders could not be allowed under
any guise to buy themselves off: "Shal nevere man
of this molde meynprise the leeste". During the
trial of Wrong, however, Wisdom asks that he may be
granted bail, since he can make (monetary) amends:
"And he amendes mowe make, lat Maynprise hym have
And be borgh for his bale" (88-9). This is, in
effect, to propose that Wrong's money be permitted
to bail him out. It is to offer Mede as a
"maynpernour", and Mede confirms at 97 that she is
the surety referred to:

> 'For I wol wage for Wrong he wol do so na moore'.

Public opinion seems to approve the arrangement,
and many present petition the court "That Mede moste
be maynpernour" (112). This solution is, as we
know, firmly rejected by Reason, and at the end of
the Passus the King utters a general threat that in
future Mede will not be accepted as a "maynpernour":

> 'Mede shal noght maynprise yow, by the Marie of
>   hevene!'

> (179)

The release from penalties that money procures, the
commuting of penalties to fines, offers, as the King

has already realised, no respectable or reliable
guarantee of future good conduct. It in fact
encourages contempt for a law so easily appeased.

Can there then be no mercy, or, to use the
terms of the allegory, is there no "maynpernour"
the law would accept as sufficient? Although the
thrust of this Passus is mainly negative, there are
some hints given on this question. Just before the
public request to Reason that "Mede moste be
maynpernour" (112), the King indicates the possibility of a different "borw" he might be induced to
accept:

> 'But Reson have ruthe on hym, he shal reste in my
> stokkes
> As longe as I lyve, but lowenesse hym borwe'.

(108-9)

'Lowness': the King is indicating a quality that
connotes humility and obedience, and one which
would therefore guarantee that outer and inner
submission to the law and its authority, that
penitent acknowledgement of one's answerability to
it and guilt before it, which is the very opposite
of the laugh of scorn the King has just seen would
be produced by the office of "borw" being executed
by Mede. This might indeed make amends for the
insult offered the law by offence, and guarantee
future amendment.

The antithesis thus set up between the two
abstractions, by this representation of them as
alternative "borwes" or "maynpernours", recurs at
142 ("Ne for no mede have mercy, but mekenesse it
made"), and at 160, when, Reason's verdict having
been accepted as accordant with 'truth', those
present "leten Mekenesse a maister and Mede a
mansed sherewe". The emphasis is perfectly in
accord with Langland's stress on the importance of
authority, and thus of obedience and submission to
rule and rules. Holy Church's definition of truth
as the acknowledgement that one has a lord and his
word to be true to, the definition of Do-Wel as
obedience to the law, the introductory sketch of
Piers as the obedient servant of a master, the
route to truth through obedience he describes, all
bear this out. The will must accept and respect
constraints on its liberty, and acknowledge it is
not its own master. In a manner typical of Christian paradox, meekness will thus be exalted to the
"maistrie" it has renounced. Meekness can sway the

law, command its mercy, because the law does not
need to assert its authority over those who accept
its "maistrie". The rule of law is not threatened
by those whose spirit is meekened before it. The
acclamation of "mekenesse" as a "maister" of the
law completes the antithesis with Mede, whose
assumed 'mastery' over it has led to the necessity
of humbling her to it. Conscience had earlier
complained that the law had become perverted,
"Swich a maister is Mede among men of goode" (III.
169). Reason had refused mercy, "While Mede hath
the maistrie in this moot-halle" (IV.135). Through
Reason, the King comes to realize that "Mede
*over*maistreth Lawe and muche truthe letteth" (176).
Law is denatured, loses its proper authority or
"maistrie", when it is subjected to the arrogant
contempt of those who treat it not as their master,
but as the servant of their money, and thus subject
to their will, and not *vice-versa*.

The Passus ends with the declared determination by the King to act henceforth in accordance
with the principles of justice Reason has laid
down. He realizes, for a start, that he loses
"manye chetes" (175) through the corrupt relaxation
of the law by his representatives. This is partly
a dryly realistic acknowledgement by Langland that
the King has, after all, a personal stake in seeing
that the law is enforced against offenders, since
many of the penalties it imposed took the form of
forfeitures to the Crown. In the case of a felon,
his property reverted (or 'escheated') to the King.
Such fines and escheats made a significant contribution to royal income, and were part of 'the King's
debts', as moneys due the Crown were called.[10] But
there may be more important points of law and
justice hinted at. Firstly, the King's solvency
was agreed to be a good desirable by all, not just
by the sovereign himself; the King must be able to
'live of his own'; otherwise his needs would
force him to impose oppressive burdens of taxation
on his people, and to other undesirable measures
"to perversion of Justice and perturbacion of the
peas and quiete of the reaume".[11] Any illegitimate
diminution of his proper revenues would therefore
prejudice "commune profit", and conduce to just
that inequitable distribution of money the dreamer
had angrily observed in the Prologue.

But upon the logic of the poem as a whole
the fact that 'the King's debts' are not paid when
the law is falsely relaxed has a bearing that

scarcely needs to be stressed. For *debitum*, as
explained above, was also the term for the penalty,
the legal liability, incurred by an offender. So
that the relaxation of the penal law resulted in a
double manner in non-payment of debts. It violated
the justice that "gives to each his due", which
commanded payment of debts, and most of all to the
two laws one is subject to: "Render unto Caesar
the things that are Caesar's, render unto God the
things that are God's". Where penalties are
relaxed, the coin of Caesar is not rendered to
Caesar, just as the debts due the King of Heaven
from offenders against His laws are later to be
corruptly withheld by those responsible for
collecting them.

In fact, the one check of realism on the
prevailing idealism of the close of this Passus is
to be found, I think, not here, but a little earlier.
While the King is declaring his laudable intention
to ensure that henceforward Reason will judge all,
and so deem all as they have deserved (177-8), and
no-one shall be able to buy themselves mercy, and
while the "commune" are loudly decrying Mede as a
whore (166), one or two officials of both laws
yet remain faithful to the Lady who has just been
so decisively disgraced:

> Ac a sisour and a somonour sued hir faste,
> And a sherreves clerk bisherewed al the route:
> 'For ofte have I', quod he, 'holpen yow at the barre,
> And yet yeve ye me nevere the worth of a risshe!'

(167-70)

That embittered curse has a truth of its own not
utterly obliterated in the euphoria produced by the
victory of that other 'truth' at present being
celebrated. It is all very well for those of the
"commune" with nothing to lose and all to gain from
the law's being freed from the control of the rich
to denounce the Mede whose blessings are never
likely to come their way. This sheriff's clerk is
a poor man, and probably could not subsist without
her;[12] and now, even with his eyes opened as to her
infamy, defiantly sides with her. Something more
than honesty and determination on the part of the
King is needed to reform the law. As other contemporary writers on government and justice pointed
out, its officials must not be so ill-paid as to
be driven by their needs to corruption.[13] Though
Langland briefly hears the voice of such dangerous

indigence at this point, it is not until later that
the arguments of poverty and needs which only
dishonesty can relieve really claim his undivided
attention.[14] But Conscience's sober warning that
the co-operation of all the "commune" will be
necessary to make a reality of the true law of
payment of debts (182-4) strikes with more force
on our ears after we have heard this angry dissent
from at least one rather relevant member of that
commonalty.

It is impossible to overstate the importance of
this Passus and the principles it establishes for
the poem as a whole. With it, the first dream ends,
and Langland returns to the abandoned field of
miscreant folk with a new decisiveness. Reason has
pronounced that sovereign rule of like for like,
nullum malum inpunitum, and *nullum bonum irremuneratum,* the doom that answers the deed and will "deme
yow ... as ye han deserved" (178); it is the basis
of all law, which even the New Law of mercy cannot
subvert. The mercy that comes of Mede is an
illegitimate mercy because it violates justice,
allowing debts to go unpaid under cover of the
monetary 'amends' that is no satisfaction at all.
Penalties must be exacted, and cannot be commuted
to money payments, or the law falls into disrespect.
It is this Passus above all that condemns the friars,
who, in their service of the law of God, dispense
His mercy in prejudice to His justice, allowing the
satisfaction on which absolution depends to be
commuted to monetary fines. And this court-room
scene in which human justice is administered is
now followed by a confession in which it is divine
justice which is at issue. For in shrift, the
sinner is an offender upon whom the priest must
pronounce the sentence of God's law.
Langland was not alone in stressing that mercy
must square with justice, not supersede it, as he
does here in the context of human law, and as he is
to do later in the context of the divine law, whose
debita must also be paid. We tend now to regard
mercy as a higher principle on which to act than
justice, as showing a generosity superior to
strictly 'legalistic' procedure. The Middle Ages
and the Renaissance did not, having a greater
respect for law and justice, and perhaps taking more
seriously the claim of Christ, the founder of the
New Law, that He·came not to destroy the law but to
fulfil it (Mt.5:17). Mercy that overrides justice
was often seen not as a virtue but as a vice. And

though mercy in a ruler was invariably commended,
there were those ready to qualify their commend-
ation by warning that it must not be indiscriminate.
For instance, John of Salisbury, urging this divine
attribute on the rulers he addresses in his
Policraticus, is quick to add that it does not
amount to a rule that Kings should pardon all
offenders. That would be silly, and worse than
silly, it would be sinful, because it would err on
the side of excess against that just mean or
"mesure" in which all virtue subsists. And he
comments of Job: "that you may not suppose he lent
encouragement to vice by showing mercy too
leniently, he says, 'I was clothed in justice, and
with my judgment as with a diadem'".[15] Mercy, in
short, could not properly be dispensed by a king to
the prejudice of his primary responsibility to
justice. Indiscriminate mercy was an offence against
equity, and no king who indulged in it (the King of
Heaven included) could be called just: "A God all
mercy is a God unjust".[16]

Again, towards the end of his Book of Justice,
Spenser leads Sir Artegall to the court of Mercilla,
a lady renowned for her beneficence and clemency.
There he is to witness her holding court and
passing judgment. The reader is led to expect some
striking instance of merciful magnanimity, but the
case chosen to illustrate the great selflessness
and charity of Mercilla is in fact one in which she
does not grant mercy to the accused (Duessa).
Though moved by her plight, and more in sorrow than
in anger, she condemns her to the penalty prescribed
by the law.[17] Spenser, too, then, has chosen to
emphasize that the greatness of mercy is constrained
by justice, and that is part of its greatness.

Langland differs only in the urgency and
complexity of his approach to the problem. John of
Salisbury contents himself with vague and indefinite
formulations: the king must temper justice with
mercy, must be now just, now merciful, must not err
in either excessive strictness or in excessive
leniency, and so on. He never attempts to define
when mercy is and when it is not consonant with
justice. That penal justice need not be counter to
charity he shows by insisting that punishments
should never be inflicted in a spirit of anger or
vengeableness, but in that of loving regret. The
King's heart must bleed for the offender he is
constrained to punish.[18] Mercilla's charity, too,
is shown, when it comes to the point, not in her
forgiveness, as one is expecting, but in the sorrow

with which she refrains from forgiving: the climax
to the sequence is a highly moving one, when, in
utter silence, having heard the pleas on both sides,
Mercilla merely lets fall "in stead of vengeance" a
"few perling drops" of tears upon the prisoner;
and it is only later that one hears that she had in
fact not spared Duessa, but punished her, after
Spenser has explained that, though mercy piously
"seeks to save", it "Yet never doth from doome of
right depart".[19]

Such approaches to the problem of the place of
mercy in justice must seem vague and sentimental
beside Langland, who worries chaotically at the
problem till he wrings from it a partial solution.
No mercy that allows wrongs to go unpunished, which
ignores debts and penalties, is legitimate, and the
mercy granted in consideration of Mede rather than
in consideration of Mekenesse is a mercy corruptly
granted.   It is what is called in the C text
"Vnsittynge soffraunce" (improper or inappropriate
forbearance[20]). His king, moreover, has no "few
perling drops" to waste upon Wrong.   Wrong has no
tears for himself, for tears in Langland are
generally penitential tears;   and the punishment
of the impenitent, since both words derive
ultimately from the same root, merely restores "the
equilibrium of justice", and is not for Langland
a fit subject of pity.

II: *Passus V*

With Passus V, a new dream begins.   Conscience
had declared that the co-operation of the "commune"
was necessary if the realm was to be set on a just
footing, and it is to them that attention is now
turned.   The initial presence of Reason provides
a further link with what has gone before, and
indicates the essential connection between Passus IV
and V.   His sermon is both a new beginning and a
continuation: a return to the field of folk last
seen in the Prologue, to subject that erring
community to the authority of Reason, whose judgments have been established to be founded in
justice and truth, and who has clear ideas on what
they should do to reform their ways.   Accordingly,
his hortatory sermon begins by recalling the scheme
of the Prologue, in order to redress the wrongs
there discerned.   It begins thus:

> He bad Wastour go werche what he best kouthe
> And wynnen his wastyng with som maner crafte.

> (24-5)

His next command is addressed to those guilty of excessive love of finery:

> He preide Pernele hir purfil to lete,
> And kepe it in hire cofre for catel at hire nede.

> (26-7)

This exactly recalls the opening items in the list of the Prologue, which had begun with ploughmen who "wonnen that thise wastours with glotonye destroyeth" (22), and had continued with those who "putten hem to pride, apparailed hem therafter, In contenaunce of clothynge comen disgised". But Reason's commands here not only refer back to the Prologue, but also to his own description at IV.113-33 of an amended society. "Pernele" had figured second in that list, too, which had also included the line

> 'And childrene cherissynge be chastised with yerdes'

> (IV.117)

here recalled by 34ff: "And thanne he chargede chapmen to chastisen hir children", etc. This emphasis on the healthy effects of corporal punishment on those of tender years falls rather harshly on modern ears, but the Middle Ages had stricter and more specific ideas on the responsibility of governance than we have. They did not undervalue true parental love, but they regarded indulgence of children as a betrayal of their trust by those placed in authority over them,[21] and as a subtle form of pride and selfishness, to be contrasted unfavourably with the devotion to parents, which is pious and disinterested.[22] Devotion to parents preserves the hierarchy of authority, indulgence of children subverts it. Reason also adjures husbands to keep their wives in better order. Such assertion of domestic authority was, for the Middle Ages, a subject related to that of law, justice, and proper rule generally. Spenser's Legend of Justice in fact includes several references to the misrule that results when women forget their proper subordination to men.[23] Filial dis-

obedience was likewise seen as a symbol or symptom
of lawless revolt from rule in the community at
large: "Lords ben owtyn lawe & chylderen ben with-
owtyn awe"; "*adulescens sine obedentia ... plebs
sine disciplina, populus sine lege, Sic soffocatur
iustitia*".[24] And in the C text, "unboxomnes" to her
parents is confessed by Pride, the first sin, to
have been the first beginnings of a life fundamentally
"inobedient" to God and the church (C.VI.14ff).

So it is significant that Reason, having in the
previous Passus vindicated the authority of the law,
and the proper subjection of all to it, here
includes among his primary commands the re-exertion
of the proper authority of husbands over wives (28-
31), and parents over children (32-40). In fact,
Reason addresses himself primarily to governors
and rulers, for his words to these husbands and
fathers who are domestic governors, heads of household, are followed by rules of conduct for the
guides and governors of the community as a whole:
the clergy (41-7); the King (48-9); the Pope
(50-1); and the administrators of the law (52-5).
He is concerned with how they may best and most
effectively discharge their offices. In three
cases, the governors themselves are urged to conform
themselves to law and rule: priests must realize
("preven") in their own works the precepts they
preach; those in religion are advised "hir rule to
holde"; and the Pope must "governe" himself as he
governs others. The King must love his commons,
and those who have laws in their keeping must
dispense them according to 'truth' and not to meed.
That truth which it is the business of law and
authority to uphold through *ius* and *iura* it is likewise the duty of the people to observe: they should
seek Truth rather than far-away shrines, 'truth'
being here as elsewhere the equivalent of the
Biblical *iustitia*: that is, they must walk in the
paths of the just.

Reason's strictures on the proper observance
of justice, rule, and authority are accompanied by
remarks aimed at correct economic balance, good
husbandry, literally and metaphorically. Pernell
is adjured to keep her finery "in hire cofre for
catel at hire nede" (27). Wat is reproached that
his wife's "heed was worth half marc and his hood
noght worth a grote" (31). The monks are warned
that the moral prodigality of their rule-less
conduct may result in the King's appropriating the
stewardship of their estates, if they continue to
show themselves so unable to 'keep their houses in

order' (45-7). The King is warned not to squander
the 'treasure' of his people's love (48-9). Like
Holy Church, Reason associates moral order with good
husbandry, and again one notes the coincidence in
Langland's thought between moral and financial
regulation, which shows itself supremely in his
pre-occupation with that financial definition of
justice that equates it with the paying of debts,
giving to each his due.

In this 'sermon', Reason has exchanged the
secular authority of judge he enjoyed in the
previous Passus for the spiritual authority of
priest, in token of the translation of the issues of
that Passus from secular to sacred terms that is
about to occur. The transition is completed when
he is replaced as both judge and priest by
Repentance, who now "reherce(s) *his* teme" (60), and
the hearing of the case of Wrong at secular law is
now repeated in the hearing by Repentance of the
sins of the offenders against God's law.

Pride begins, promising, from her position
prostrate on the earth, that she will 'hold herself
low' (67), and declaring: "Now wole I meke me and
mercy biseche" (69). Meekness was the virtue
contrary to the sin of pride, but it here refers
back also to the 'lowness' and 'meekness' indicated
in the previous Passus as a possibly acceptable
"maynpernour" for release, or 'absolution'. For
these offenders likewise ask for mercy, as had the
party of Wrong. But they do not ask it through
Mede; Lechour, the second sin, has a different
mediatrix in mind. He

> on Our Lady cryde,
> To maken mercy for his mysdedes bitwene God and his
>   soule.

                                         (71-2)

They, too, are attempting to 'make their peace',
but not with pence. They too stand before the
court acknowledgedly guilty ("I, Glotoun, ... gilty
me yelde"), this time by their own confession, and
are therefore, as had been Wrong, *in misericordia
regis*, the king being the King of Kings Himself.
The judge in this spiritual court is Repentance,
who in the allegory represents the priest who
hears the shrift. It is in his power, as it had
been in Reason's, to grant mercy and forgiveness
(absolution) and to impose penalties (penances).

With respect to the availability of God's
mercy, penitential theory, considerably influenced
as it was by legal and judicial procedure and
principles, laid it down as a definite rule that
that mercy could not be extended to offenders in the
form of absolution unless His justice were satisfied - by amends, by some kind of payment of the
debt of sin. "þe riȝtwisnes of God askes þat a
trespas don be not forgifen bot if amendes be maad
for it if it may be don".[25] The sacrament of shrift
itself was always defined as the opportunity to
commute to temporal punishment the penalties that
would otherwise be paid in Purgatory; punishment
for sins God's justice would always have, and those
who did not pay the penalties here would pay them
hereafter.[26] Shrift, therefore, was traditionally
conceived of as comprising three distinct and
equally vital phases: contrition; confession;
and satisfaction, by which the 'equilibrium of
justice' was restored.[27] This last could take any
or all of several forms. Where the sin involved
wrongful appropriation, the money or goods would
have literally to be restored; one cannot "be
pardon'd and retain th'offence". Restitution could
not, however, be so literal and specific in the
case of all sins, and in the majority of cases
satisfaction was made, as at law, by the undergoing
of some penalty or punishment. Justice must be
satisfied by the punishment of Wrong, as Reason has
emphasized. In law, this punishment, the statutary
penalty to which the offender was liable, went by
the name of *pena*; in shrift, its derivative
equivalents were penance, and penitence - the inner
and outer 'pain' the offender underwent as *pena* for
his wrongs, and which thus satisfied the requirement
that wrong must never go "unpunysshed" that justice
Reason-ably makes, and so renders the offender
eligible for the mercy that does not contravene
justice - or, more strictly, for 'absolution',
'release' from debt in formal recognition that
'payment' of it has been received.
It is this inner and outer pain/*pena* which
justifies mercy by paying a penalty for offence
that the Pearl-maiden refers to when she declares
that the sinner cannot have grace by right, as can
the 'innocent'. That *nullum malum* be *inpunitum* is
a principle of justice, and the innocent has no sin
to atone for before the grace of deliverance from
punishment be granted ("Hit is a dom þat never
God gave, þat ever þe gyltleȝ schulde be schente",
Pearl, 667-8). This grace is also available to

sinners, but at the price of atonement:

> 'Bot wyth sor₃ and syt he mot hit crave,
> And byde þe payne þerto is bent'.

(663-4)

The first line refers to the inner pain (penitence)
that is the most important part of the *pena*
demanded by God's justice; the second to the formal
penance imposed by the confessor as a condition of
absolution, an answering outer "payne".[28] Another
important element of amends or satisfaction was the
spiritual renunciation of his offence by the
sinner: he must, to receive mercy, be in true will
to desist from his sin henceforth (which is why
Shakespeare's Claudius knows his own prayer for
mercy is quite hollow).[29]
    All these four elements of satisfaction or
amends (literal restitution, pledge to future
reform, outer and inner *pena*) are dealt with in the
present confession scene. Restitution Langland
made the subject of a passage specially added for
the purpose at the time of the B revision, and that
will be considered later. The pledge to renounce
their respective wrong-doings henceforth is also
made by all the personified sins, most expressly by
Envy. He has been ever envious, he admits, but,

> 'I wil amende this if I may, thorugh myght of God
>   Almyghty'

(132)

he concludes. His promised amends is significantly
different from that offered by Wrong, which, as the
King had seen, offered no guarantee at all of
amended ways. Though less tangible, it is therefore
more real.
    External "payne", formal penances, are not
neglected by the penitents here. All promise to
perform such typical acts of penance as a priest
might impose at shrift, such as fasts or pilgrimages. And they regard their mercy or absolution as
conditional on the performance of these penances.
Lechour asks for God's mercy

> *With that* he sholde the Saterday seven yer therafter
> Drynke but myd the doke and dyne but ones.

(73-4; my italics)

161

It is to be mercy given in consideration of "payne", penal payment of the debt.

But there is no doubt that in Langland's view (and most theologians then and now would concur in it) it is that inner pain of penitence which constitutes the most vital and efficacious payment of the *pena* which can justify mercy. This is implied in his representing the confessor in whose power absolution or its refusal lies as Repentance. The root element *pena* contained in the word signifies the punishment, the penalty, the payment of the debt, on which absolution must depend. But the word as a whole indicates the sort of *pena* that most effectually pays that debt, and from which alone can come absolution from it. In this connection, too, the word 'amends' is used, again in a context that offers a significant contrast with the type of amends offered by Wrong:

> And (Repentance) bad me wilne to wepe my wikkednesse
> to amende.
>
> (185)

It is a line that suddenly brings the central abstraction of the will, personified by the dreamer himself, into play. The most effective *pena*, the most effective amends, is that pain the will voluntarily enjoins on itself. Though Langland places a special emphasis on the importance of literal restitution, he is prepared to admit, through the Samaritan, that in extreme (though rare) cases, justice can regard *pena* as paid by repentance alone, and so extend its mercy:

> 'Yis', seide the Samaritan, 'so thow myghte repente
> That rightwisnesse thorugh repentaunce to ruthe
> myghte turne'.
>
> (XVII. 300-1)

And, at the end of the poem, it is the fact that the penitents are led to forgive themselves that inner *pena* as much as the forgiveness of the outer *pena* granted by the friars that causes Langland to despair at the false absolutions given by the latter, the mercy bought by "mede" on the basis of false, because monetary, amends. That vital compensatory penitence has been stupified:

> Contricion hadde clene foryeten to crye and to
> wepe,
> And to wake for his wikked werkes as he was wont to
> doone.

$$(XX.370-1)^{30}$$

And, though Repentance respects all four forms of
satisfaction, he shows least interest in the formal
outer *penae* (these are imposed on the sinners by
themselves, not by Repentance), and grants absolute
power to the inner:

> 'Sorwe for synnes is savacioun of soules'.

(125)

Repentance, however, has some rather prophetic
difficulty in making his sinners understand the
true principles of shrift. For there are two
passages in which there occurs a rather comic
misunderstanding between Repentance and his penitents, who reveal that they quite literally do not
know what words like "sorwe", "repent", and
"restitucion" really mean. To the words of
Repentance quoted above, Envy replies somewhat
impatiently that "sorwe" (a spirit made miserable
by the good of others) he has in plenty and is
precisely what he is confessing to:

> 'I am evere sory', quod Envye, 'I am but selde
> oother,
> And that maketh me thus meagre, for I ne may me
> venge'.

(126-7)

More famously, Avarice totally misinterprets the
question,

> 'Repentedstow evere?' quod Repentaunce, 'or
> restitucion madest?'

(228)

Avarice seems quite incapable of applying the 're-'
element in these words to himself, and recalls with
grim enjoyment how he once robbed a pack of
merchants (famous for their extortion and avarice)
while they slept. It is "sport to have the
enginer Hoist with his own petar" (robbers robbed),
and this was indeed a kind of restitution; but it

is scarcely what Repentance had in mind. The
incidents are humorous, and the difficulties are
not allowed here, ultimately, to stand in the way
of absolution, but they are a foretaste of that
dreadful isolation of Conscience at the end of the
poem; when he alone is conscious of the infraction
of the true principles of "sorwe" and "restitucion"
committed by the confessional practice of the friars,
and whose voice is quite unable to penetrate the
comatosed complacency of his fellow Christians.

Langland's allegorical mode does not remain
constant through the confessions here. Pride,
Lechery, and Envy are dealt with through 'exemplary'
personification: that is, they speak as examples
of proud, luxurious, or envious people. Wrath
(133-79), however, is treated differently, as a kind
of dissociated force working insidiously through
certain environmental conditions to produce a final
explosion of angry ill-will. It is the persons on
whom the speaker acts, not the speaker himself, who
are wrathful. He is the convent gardener responsible for the 'growth' of ill-will between friars
and priests, the convent cook who 'brews' the
bitchiness that breaks out in the claustrophobic
confines of the nunnery. This is the type of
allegory that realizes the metaphors of ordinary
speech, and one thinks at once of such idioms as
'to sow the seeds of discord' and 'to stir things
up'.[31] The change in mode makes for an interesting
perspective on wrath: it is a force working
latently in the very conditions of social living,
and particularly in the peculiar conditions of the
religious life. Like one of their domestics, it
remains out of sight in the grounds or beneath
stairs, but its effects are imperceptibly imbibed,
until it 'blossoms abroad' or 'leaps out' (139, 161)
in sudden flashes of anger.

Significantly, there is one religious institution where Wrath finds the conditions less
favourable to his unimpeded operation: monasteries
which observe their 'rule', where discipline is
strict, and penalties rigorously imposed. Here, the
mode changes, and Wrath becomes briefly an examplary
personification, speaking in the person of an angry
monk duly corrected, and using an image important
to this Passus - that of the child reduced to
obedience (picked up from Reason's "Til childrene
cherissynge be chastised with yerdes" (IV.31));
repeated in his elaboration of the text *Qui parcit
virge odit filium* (V.34-41); and due to recur at

the climax of the Passus in Piers's definition of
the truth in the heart):

> 'And am chalanged in the Chapitrehous as I a child
>   were,
> And baleised on the bare ers - and no brech bitwene!'

(172-3)

    With avarice, Langland returns to exemplary
allegory, but this time the sin is represented not
through personal but through professional vices.
Avarice is revealed through the fraudulent practices
of a certain trade: the retail trade. In particular, he and his wife[32] are guilty of falsifying
weights and measures. This 'wicked weighing' and
"wikke chaffare" (225) is in central contravention
of the virtue of justice that gives to each his due
and takes but its own. It is the same sin to
which the Brewer of Passus XIX is dedicated, and by
which he refuses to cultivate the 'seed of justice'.
Fraud was the vice contrary to the virtue of
iustitia, and the false exchange described here
violates not only the principles of 'the just price'
as re-inforced by law positive (for there were
regulations governing weights and measures in
Langland's day), but the essential principle of
justice itself, which is true and exact exchange or
retribution (the punishment of wrong, the payment
of debts, hire for the *operarius* "labour for
lyflod"). All debts must be paid, and all for
which a just price has not been paid, be it mercy
or money or goods, is a sin against justice.
Avarice has given false measure for all he has
received, and is thus in debt to all those he has
defrauded. The commercial nature of his offences
makes of him an epitome of Langland's financial
concept of sin as a debt, a liability incurred, and
of the financial logic he rigorously applies to
justice and to penitential theory.
    It is not surprising, therefore, that at the
time of the B revision Langland decided to give
added emphasis to the significance of Avarice's
debts and the literal repayment required from him
before absolution or mercy can be given. In the
A text, Avarice's confession had closed, according
to the pattern established, with a pledge to desist
from the sin henceforth, and a vow of penance:

> 'Ac I swere now (so thee Ik!) that synne wol I lete,
> And nevere wikkedly weye ne wikke chaffare use,
> But wenden to Walsyngham, and my wif als,
> And bidde the Roode of Bromholm brynge me out of
>   dette'.

(224-7)

But on re-reading the poem, that word "dette" seems
to have arrested Langland's attention, and prompted
him to look closer into Avarice's case, and explore
more narrowly the logic implied in the conception
of sin as a 'debt', so peculiarly applicable to the
nature of the offences described here. The material
he added leads to an angry insistence by Repentance
on restitution, repayment of debts, satisfaction
for justice. This both prepares for the crucial
condition later attached to Piers's pardon (*Redde
quod debes*), and emphasizes the link between this
Passus and the last: Repentance, like Reason,
refuses mercy where the price of wrong has not been
paid, will give no mercy that contravenes justice
by being granted where amends, satisfaction for the
sin, is deficient:

> 'Thow art an unkynde creature - I kan thee noght
>   assoille
> Til thow make restitucion' quod Repentaunce, 'and
>   rekene with hem alle.
> And sithen that Reson rolle it in the Registre of
>   hevene
> That thow hast maad ech man good, I may thee noght
>   assoille.
> *Non dimittitur peccatum donec restituatur ablatum'.*

(269-72a)

In the logic of penitential justice, restitution
(the restoration of dishonesly obtained gains to the
persons wronged, the repayment of one's debts to them)
occupied a central place; where this most obvious
form of amends was neglected, where so specific an
imbalance remained unrectified, the satisfaction of
offended justice through the sacrament of penance
could not take place: *Si res aliena cum reddi
possit non redditur, non agitur penitentia sed
fingitur.*[33] In the case of the penitents here,
the opportunity to insist on this most tangible and
literal form of amends, or satisfaction, has not
really arisen hitherto. All have been contrite,
have imposed penances on themselves, and committed

themselves to amend their ways, and the fourth
element of satisfaction, literal restitution, is not
really relevant in their cases. But it is here.
And Repentance, at the word "dette", decides to
avail himself of the right and duty of the confessor
to "appose" the penitent to ascertain the exact
nature and extent of his sins and his present state
of grace (228-58); his findings appal him - Avarice
is clearly a hardened sinner - and turns out,
furthermore, to have practised covert usury, the
arch sin against commutative justice and the
principle of 'the just price', and forbidden by
Canon Law.[34] Repentance - after searching in vain
for some redeeming evidence of contrition, or of the
love or charity that gives freely to compensate for
his career of wrongful taking - decides to get tough.
And he becomes remorselessly literal in his interpretation of Avarice's obligation to restore his
wrongful gains. It will not do, for instance, for
him to make his peace by donating or bequeathing
them all to religious institutions; for no house
should consent to profit by gifts from such a
source (259-68). For if wrong could earn mercy thus,
it would be in effect the mercy through meed
rejected in the previous Passus: mercy cannot be
bought through gifts to the law, but must be earned
by amends. Furthermore, all who take Avarice's
money connive at his sin and take on a share of the
debt it represents:

> 'For alle that han of thi good, have God my trouthe,
> Ben holden at the Heighe Doom to helpe thee to
>   restitue;
> And who so leveth nought this be sooth, loke in the
>   Sauter glose,
> In *Miserere mei, Deus*, where I mene truthe:
> *Ecce enim veriatem dilexisti*, &c'.

(273-76a)

Repentance is, in fact, affirming the official hard
line on the receipt of moneys properly owed by the
giver in restitution: the church was not supposed
to accept contributions or bequests of such a
nature - most particularly from usurers - since they
represented debts due to those he had wronged; and
the obligation to restore was in fact, as Repentance
says, held to extend indefinitely, *etiam in manu
centesima*, so that anyone who received what had been
wrongfully gained was also bound by it.[35]
    In stating his refusal to absolve Avarice at

269-272, Repentance expresses himself in the
financial terms appropriate to Avarice's career,
substituting, however, for the principles of false
measure he has lived by, a commercial ethic of true
measure: full and exact repayment of all that is
owing.   His reference to Reason draws attention to
the link between this Passus and the last, as does
his use of the verb 'reckon', recalling the King's
"'Reson shal rekene with yow'" (IV.177).   Justice,
in the commercial metaphor, demands a fair reckoning.
Avarice had better observe this principle himself,
because Reason, the true judge of right and wrong,
will ensure that justice is satisfied by drawing
him to a reckoning, as he had done Wrong in the
previous Passus;   and until Reason (justice) is
satisfied that accounts have been settled mercy will
not be given.   In the words "rolle" and "registre"
financial and legal images interconnect;   the
metaphor evokes both the notion of an entering of
receipts in a kind of heavenly debt-register of sins,
and a judgment in a law-court, for a 'registrar' was
an official who kept the records of the court in
which its judgments were 'enrolled'.[36]
      The kind of exact justice best epitomized in
the commercial logic of price and debt, then, must
be done before mercy can be given.   Repentance
emphasizes the point by referring to that passage of
the "Sauter Glose" which, referring to *veritatem*,
'truth' or justice, interprets Ps 50:8 as a declaration that God will not "contravene His own truth by
allowing sin to pass unpunished", but demands
satisfaction from the sinner (*sic et misericordias
dat us servet veritatem*).[37]   Repentance, then,
repeats Reason's avowal that justice must not be
compromised by a mercy that exempts wrong from its
due punishment.   And, as is becoming a habit with
Langland's abstract mentors, he too follows on by
setting us a text to construe:

> 'Shal nevere werkmen in this world thryve with that
>   thow wynnest.
> *Cum sancto sanctus eris*:   construwe me this on
>   Englissh'.

(277-8)

In context, it must be the converse of this *dictum*
that applies: the just man cannot take money that
comes from an unjust source without implicating
himself in the injustice whereby it was obtained.[38]
Avarice cannot hope, therefore, as Wrong could not,

that justice will accept his money as the price of
pardon.

At this, Avarice understandably falls into
"wanhope" (279), for it does indeed seem he must
despair of mercy unless he can repay personally
each and every man he has ever defrauded, which,
given his long and varied criminal career, would be
an impossible task. Repentance now backs off a
little, and tells him there is nothing impossible to
God's mercy, which is the greatest of all His works.
But there are conditions attached in this case.
Firstly, Avarice must abandon "marchaundise" (285).
This is not because Repentance regards it as an
inherently vicious employment, but because of the
literalness and rigour with which Langland applies
the logic of 'debt' to the definition of unjust
practices. Avarice's present capital, which would
form the basis of any further "marchaundise", was
unjustly got, and is so 'owed'; so he cannot use it
as the just *quid* for any future *quo* , for that would
simply compound his debt to God and society, by
increasing the number of receipts paid for in
unjust measure:

> 'For the good that thow hast geten bigan al with
> falshede,
> And as longe as thow lyvest therwith, thow yeldest
> noght but borwest'.

(288-9)

Secondly, restitution is not to be pardoned him,
but is to be made vicariously to the appropriate
spiritual authority, the bishop. This does not
contradict the interdiction Repentance had earlier
imposed on the receipt of ill-gotten gains by
religious. For there the donation would have been
invested in the institutions themselves, which
would thus have been in a sense taking *munera super
innocentem*. The bishop, however, is to distribute
the money in good works to make vicarious
restitution for its unlawful gain. Other moralists
who had dealt with the question of restitution had
likewise concluded that when (and only when) it
could not be made to those to whom it was really
due, then it could be distributed in alms - but (to
prevent abuse) under the supervision of a prelate,
not of a religious house.[39] So here, too, the
bishop is to be requested to

> 'Bisette it hymself as best is for (Avarice's) soule'
>
> (292)

- and if he does not, then the debt will be his to
answer for on the great Day of Reckoning, for the
liability will have been transferred to him. And,
in a figurative extension of the prevailing notions
of debt and settlement of accounts, the bishop is
expressively defined as a steward-treasurer of the
wealth of God, charged with dispensing it in the
form of guidance and instruction to penitents
(especially in Lent, the period above all others
when - in a play on the word that turns it into an
accounts period - such coin should be "lente" to
sinners), and due eventually to have his accounts
subjected to the audit of his lord:

> 'For he shal answere for thee at the heighe dome,
> For thee and for many mo that man shal yeve a
>   rekenynge:
> What he lerned yow in Lente, leve thow noon oother,
> And what he lente yow of Oure Lordes good, to lette
>   yow fro synne'.

> (293-6)

With Gluttony, the allegorical mode changes yet
again, giving way to narrative allegory. For
Gluttony's sin is not reported through his own mouth
alone, but first given narrative and dramatic
representation (297-364). He is pictured as being
actually on his way to church "to here masse, And
sithen ... be shryven, and synne na moore" (301-2).
A pious resolve; but he turns aside from this
straight and narrow path when a friendly tapstress
invites him in for a quick one, and all his good
intentions come to nought. The altered approach is
beautifully calculated to convey the essential
weakness rather than perverseness of the will from
which gluttony arises: the poor man means well, is
actually 'on the right road', but so easily and so
comically diverted from it by the alluring aroma of
good ale and spices. In this respect, gluttony
contrasts with the hardened misdirection of will
toward money that characterizes the sin of avarice
with which it is juxtaposed. The same contrast is
observable in the account of Gluttony's doings in
the tavern, which take a mercantile turn that
recalls the career of Avarice. But here, the true

commercial principle of fair exchange, a pennyworth
for another, emerges as a parody rather than a
perversion of itself. "Bargaynes and beverages"
make their appearance (338), and two of the
customers decide to engage in the game of 'the new
fair' (321), offering the one a cloak and the
other a hood. "Chapmen" (324) are chosen to evalu-
ate the items, and, in fact, every care is taken to
ensure a fair *mutuum*, and that,

> Whoso hadde the hood sholde han amendes of the
> cloke.

> (325)

The principle of amends is respected, and, where
Avarice had given short measure, the characters
here are determined that the unequal value of the
articles to be exchanged be made good. They choose
a "nounpere" (331), who declares that the difference in value should be made up by the relevant
party standing a round, which sounds like an equitable solution:

> Hikke the Hostiler hadde the cloke
> In covenaunt that Clement sholde the cuppe fille
> And have Hikkes hood the Hostiler, and holden hym
> yserved.

> (332-4)

But unless 333 means that Clement should fill his
own cup at Hick's expense, things seem to have been
got the wrong way round, since the cloak was
presumably the more valuable item (cf 325). But the
error would be the result of drunken fuddledness and
not intention, since great efforts have been made
to be scrupulously fair. This is perhaps another
instance of laudable intentions going awry. At any
rate, it is the *levitas* of the context in which
these serious principles of equity are applied, and
the clouding of the judgment by drink in the
application of them, that alone convict Gluttony of
any offence against them. The contrast with the
deliberate cunning of Avarice in the devising of
false measures is marked; and the different nature
and cause of their respective offences against the
straight road and strict equity of justice is
nicely brought out in the juxtaposition. The prevailing comedy of the Gluttony sequencè, as compared
with the anger elicited by Avarice, also indicates
a difference in the response the two sins evoke.

When Gluttony eventually gets to the confession he had been distracted from (368), one notes in Langland's definition of the sin the same concern with good husbandry and economic equity that marks the Passus as a whole. Glutton is guilty primarily of waste; he has unjustly encroached on the needs of others by flouting "mesure" (as, in a different way, had Avarice), taking more than what he needs (or can even retain) of what God gave "in commune" to all; and so

> '... yspilt that myghte be spared and spended on som hungry'.
>
> (374)

As in the case of all the sins, however, Langland is careful to emphasize that due measure of satisfaction for God's justice is not waived in the mercy eventually extended to him. Glutton makes "great doel" (380), and vows "to faste" (382) and (in another recurrence of the notion of the child submitting to rule and correction) to subject himself to the discipline of Abstinence his "aunte", eating only when 'given leave' by this elder relative whose austere authority he admits to having always hitherto found uncongenial (384-5). Glutton thus performs satisfaction under the three heads relevant to his offence: commitment to reform, and inner and outer *pena*, penitence and penance. The fourth requirement of literal restitution is not applicable - unless the regurgitation of his excesses be taken as representing it, in accord with that element of grotesque parody of 'fair return' that characterizes the passage as a whole. Poor Glutton is apparently in the habit of making such involuntary restitution fairly regularly (373).[40]

Sloth Langland always presents as the last and most desperate phase in the descending journey of the sinful soul. The last manifestation of this sin is precisely "wanhope", despair of God's grace: it is a spiritual lethargy that in the end finds despair easier than the mental agitation of hope, repentance, and resolve the amend. Accordingly, it is Sloth who brings up the rear in the present survey. And in his treatment of this sin, too, Langland gives further evidence of his conception of vice as essentially an offence against the justice that gives to all their due, that pays its debts, and observes the principle of fair 'measure',

in every sense. Sloth finds such 'truth' too much
effort, and his lack of truth shows itself primarily
in his neglecting the debts he owes God in satisfaction for his sins:

> 'I have maad avowes fourty, and foryete hem on the
> morwe;
> I parfournede nevere penaunce as the preest me
> highte,
> Ne right sory for my synnes, yet seye I was I
> nevere'.

> (398-400)

The first of the above lines accuses Sloth of that
most central violation of truth that is bad faith:
non-fulfilment of the obligations one owes as the
result of a specific and voluntary pledge. It is
immediately followed by his neglect of the greatest
due and duty he owes: his debts to God. He shirks
both the outer and inner *pena* he owes justice in
payment of the debt of sin. His neglect of the very
sacrament of shrift itself has the significant
result that he "most to the Freres" (412): that
notorious resort of those who find debt-paying too
painful to bear. And even then his reckoning is not
a true one, but made "up gesse" (415).
  The unjust withholding of debts that this
constitutes manifests itself in other features of
Sloth's habits:

> 'If I bygge and borwe aught, but if it be ytailed,
> I foryete it as yerne, and yif men me it axe
> Sixe sithes or sevene, I forsake it with othes ...
> And my servaunts som tyme, hir salarie is bihynde:
> Ruthe is to here the rekenyng whan we shal rede
> acountes,
> So with wikked wil and wrathe my werkmen I paye!'

> (423-9)

In more general terms, he does not repay the kindness shown him by others, choosing to forget it
rather than be mindful of what is due them in
return from him:

> 'If any man dooth me a bienfait or helpeth me at
> nede,
> I am unkynde ayeins his curteisie 'and kan nought
> understonden it ...
> The kyndenesse that myn evencristene kidde me fernyere

> Sixty sithes I, Sleuthe, have foryete it sitthe
> In speche and in sparyng of speche'.

(430-6)

Sloth is, in all ways - spiritually, financially, socially - mentally lazy in remembering what he owes. In fact, the general injustice of his ways is epitomized in his neglect of his literal debts.

Sloth, like Gluttony, has also been guilty of the economic sin of waste, and so again of injustice to others, since thereby that store of what God gave "in commune" to meet collective needs is depleted, and others thus defrauded. He, too, confesses that his habits have been not only morally but also economically anti-social, in contributing to remove from circulation what should be available to 'serve' the needs of life; he has

> '... yspilt many a time
> Bothe flessh and fissh and many othere vitailles,
> Bothe bred and ale, buttre, melk and chese
> Forsleuthed in my service til it myghte serve no
> man'.

(436-9)

He has, in fact, ever since childhood, "be beggere be my foule sleuthe" (441). This is a significant charge, for the beggar is to become for Langland (in the *Visio*) the very type of that social injustice which does not pay its way, lives at the expense of others, in perpetual debt to society, refusing to pay the price of labour for "lyflod". Sloth, in short, is a man in spiritual, literal, moral, and social debt.

He, too, however, bows to the payment of the penal debts due from sin according to the law of the confessional. And, though no true king can extend "grace thorugh giftes" (IV.141) to wrong-doing, the grace of the King of Heaven, Repentance again affirms, is available at the request of the guilt that offers more literally heartfelt amends for its offence:

> '"I am sory for my synnes", seye to thiselve,
> And beet thiself on the brest, and bidde Hym of grace,
> For is no gilt here so gret that his goodnesse nys
> moore'.

(446-8)

That amends takes the familiar form: the inner
pena of penitence, which is the one stressed by
Repentance (bidding him accompany his request for
grace with words and gestures designed to kindle
and fan penitential grief in his own breast); the
outer *pena* of formal penance (strict observance of
all the Sunday church services, and a metaphorical
pilgrimage to truth, 450-5, 461), which Sloth
imposes on himself; and a pledge to future reform.
And this payment of the penitential debt (which had
occupied first place in the long list of those he
had confessed to leaving unpaid, 399-400) Sloth
realizes commits him to pay also those other
neglected debts:

> 'And yet wole I yelde ayein, yif I so muche have,
> Al that I wikkedly wan sithen I wit hadde;
> And though my liflode lakke, leten I nelle
> That ech man shal have his er I hennes wende'.

(456-9)

The confession of Sloth, then, is such as to
foreground the centrality of the whole notion of
debt to Langland's concept of sin as an offence
against justice. It is brought even more to the
fore by the passage on Robert the Robber which he
added as a coda to the confession sequence (462-
477). In the C text, this passage was transposed
to follow the confession of Avarice, for obvious
reasons: both episodes are crucially concerned
with restitution. In fact, all sins which carried
with them such an obligation were, in penitential
theory, referred to as types of 'robbery', and the
antithesis between robbery and restitution drama-
tized in Robert's speech has already occurred semi-
comically in the confession of Avarice (228-35).
For the robbery that all wrongful appropriation thus
amounted to could be by force or fraud.[41] All that
was gained by fraud, *sub dole*, was in effect
stolen, and so must be restored. Under robbery by
fraud fell such falsification of measures and
offences against 'the just price' as Avarice
confesses to.[42] Usury, however, which he has also
been guilty of, was the prime type of robbery by
fraud, and usurers were equated with thieves in
penitential literature.[43] Usury and robbery were,
in fact, used as catch-all categories for all gains
to which the obligation of restitution applied. So
it was the moneys of usurers and thieves (*feneratorum*

175

et raptorum), gained from *usuris et rapinis*, which were always specified in references to those types of moneys it was forbidden to anyone knowingly to receive, and which could not properly even be tithed or distributed in alms, for such coin must be always unjustly used as long as it remained a debt withheld from its true owners.[44] Avarice, the fraudulent merchant and usurer, and Robert the Robber therefore typify the two types of extortion in which restitution is essential: for justice is satisfied by payment of debts, and money or goods wrongfully taken are plainly owed (*debentur*) to their rightful owners (*illis qui ius habuerunt in re debita*), and must therefore be restored (*reddenda*).[45]

The juxtaposition of Robert and Avarice in C is, therefore, logical. But, all kinds of wrongful gain being viewed as robbery,[46] Robert is actually the more comprehensive type of the sinner bound to restore, and his position in B has more dramatic expressiveness. For, though strictly redundant (as there can be no sin that does not fall under one or more of the seven heads already dealt with), his unexpected appearance as a postscript to the other trespasses seems to make him representative of the nature of all sin (not simply of a sub-division of avarice), and of all guilty men who ask for mercy - a plight more powerfully expressed through his prayer, in fact, than through any of the preceding personifications. The passage is worth quoting in full:

> Roberd the Robbere on *Reddite* loked,
> And for ther was noght wherwith, he wepte swithe soore.
> And yet the synfulle sherewe seide to hymselve:
> 'Crist, that on Calvarie upon the cros deidest,
> Tho Dysmas my brother bisoughte thee of grace,
> And haddest mercy on that man for *Memento* sake;
> So rewe on this Robbere that *Reddere* ne have,
> Ne nevere wene to wynne with craft that I knowe;
> But for thi muchel mercy mitigacion I beseche:
> Dampne me noght at Domesday for that I dide so ille!'
> What bifel of this feloun I kan noght faire shewe.
> Wel I woot he wepte faste water with hise eighen,
> And knoweliched his coupe to Crist yet eftsoones,
> That *Penitencia* his pik he sholde polshe newe
> And lepe with hym over lond al his lif tyme,
> For he hadde leyen by *Latro*, luciferes Aunte.

The passage raises with real urgency the whole
question of satisfaction, the payment of the debt to
justice the offender owes, and the place of literal
restitution in it. How can that sinner be said to
make the restitution demanded by justice if what was
literally taken is not literally restored? What is
the position in the eyes of divine justice of the
offender who cannot restore? Can he make good the
debt through the other forms of *pena*? It is a
question Langland is to put to the Good Samaritan,
but it is at present put as a question from the
heart of Robert the Robber himself with an alliterative energy and force of expression that makes the
passage one of the most memorable in the entire poem.
Its power derives partly from the precise and
economic significance of its word-play. The nature
of sin in its entirety suddenly comes sharply into
focus in the single person of a common "robbere",
robbery being the complete contrary of debt-paying
justica. And in one incisive alliterative antithesis, the "robbere" is confronted with the key-
word of justice expressed in imperative and
infinitive form, *reddite* and *reddere*; the latter
being the most effective in context, since the
common English noun "robbere" and the Latin verb
reddere are thereby made to appear as if they
belonged to the same part of speech, thus heightening
the contrast between the two words.[47] The latter
epitomizes both that justice Robert has flouted,
and also, more crucially, the justice that demands
he pay the debts incurred through his sins before he
is absolved from them. This he can never hope
literally to do. And the energy of his appeal for
mercy makes us consider the human as well as the
abstract ethical implications of Langland's regard
for strict equity in justice. The cryptic shorthand
references to Biblical texts by single Latin words
(*Reddite*, *reddere*, *Memento*) give the prayer an
elliptic urgency and a concentrated force of
expression that make it both intellectually and
emotionally powerful.
     Robert begs for "mitigacion" (a legal term),[48]
since he cannot hope honestly to earn enough to
repay all he has dishonestly taken. But, although
the sympathy of the poem is surely with this
distraught and penitent sinner at this moment,
Langland is not prepared to commit himself as to his
fate: "What bifel of this feloun I kan noght faire
shewe"(472). He cannot pay his debt to justice, and
his fate must therefore remain doubtful. And the
word "feloun", following on the reference to

Judgment Day (471), is ominous: theft was a felony,
and to felony was due 'the penalty of blood'.[49]
Robert's mortal and eternal life both stand forfeit
for his crimes. However, the reader is left not
unhopeful, despite the fact that the poet's own
respect for justice will not allow him to confirm
the hope he suggests to us. Robert's reference to
the salvation of the penitent thief establishes a
precedent for mercy in circumstances such as his,
and English law has always respected precedent.
Moreover, though the poet cannot tell what would be
Robert's fate at the hands of that justice which
cannot err, there are things he does know ("wel I
woot ..."): he knows that Robert offered apparently
genuine inner and outer *penae* - that he "wepte
faste water with hise eighen", and, veritably
offering 'lowness' as his "borgh", acknowledged his
guilt repeatedly, and promised to lead a life of
penance henceforward as a pilgrim. Both forms of
pena are significantly brought together in the line
"That *Penitencia* his pik he sholde polshe newe".
The pike-staff was one of the badges of the pilgrim,
but the staff of the pilgrimages Robert vows as
penance is to be true inner penitence. And the use
of the Latin word reminds us that it contains the
element *poena/pena*: it may be, then, that Robert
can pay the penalty through it. What, however,
most encourages hope that his case is not desperate
is the extended account of the Passion that now
follows. Christ then and for all time paid that
part of the penalty humanity could never hope to
repay of itself: He can surely be appealed to to
make up the difference in Robert's case.

For the climax of this judgment scene is
significantly different from that of the last.
Whereas Reason had emphatically twice refused to
have "ruthe", and had counselled his king to give
no mercy, Repentance does have ruth, and petitions
the King of Heaven to show His mercy:

> And thanne hadde Repentaunce ruthe and redde hem
>   alle to knele.
> 'For I shal biseche for alle synfulle Oure Saveour
>   of grace
> To amenden us of oure mysdedes and do mercy to us
>   alle'.

(478-80)

This mercy is not, however, to be given in return

for the 'amends' offered by Mede, but in return for
the more real amends of penance, penitence, and all
restitution possible. Moreover, there is one factor
operative in divine justice that has no counterpart
in human: the Passion. Through it, Christ
vicariously paid all that part of their debt, their
amends, humanity could not pay. His grace may
therefore be called upon to make amends good and so
give that satisfaction to justice that legitimates
mercy. And it is in an exultant celebration of the
Passion by Repentance, as the grounds for his
request for mercy, that the sequence closes. It
is a celebration marked by that peculiarly compelling use of non-naturalistic images that Langland
often reserves for the sublime mysteries. He is
one of the few poets able to use them with a vividness and fervour that at once animates them and
preserves the thrill of their exotic strangeness
- witness his description of the Christ who

> 'Feddest tho with Thi fresshe blood our forefadres
>   in derknesse ...
> And the light that lepe out of Thee, Lucifer it
>   blente,
> And blewe alle Thi blessed into the blisse of
>   Paradys!'

> (493-5)

With his imagination thus fired by the mystical
amends of Christ, by the vision of a thirst so
supernaturally but abundantly slaked, and a salvation so extraordinarily and effortlessly beyond
human reason, Repentance is emboldened to repeat
his plea for "ruthe" at the end of his prayer, as
Reason had repeated his denial of it:

> '... be merciable to us,
> And have ruthe on thise ribaudes that repenten
>   hem soore
> That evere thei wrathed Thee in this world, in
>   word, thought, or dede!'

> (504-6)

The alliterative link forged between "ruthe" and
"repenten" is significant. This is to be a ruth
given in consideration of a *pena* truly paid by the
will itself for its offences. This, conjoined with
the overflowing grace of Christ, constitutes the
true amends that can release the mercy of divine

justice.

The amends is, however, as yet incomplete. The penitents have yet to fulfil their pledge to amend the falseness of their ways and be true henceforward. In the allegory, the penance they have imposed on themselves, a pilgrimage to the shrine of St. Truth (to "seken truthe", in the words of Sloth) has yet to be performed. Their absolution is to that extent conditional on their paying this part of their debt to justice. But for Truth, they soon discover, they need guidance and governance, they need laws and a ruler to be true to. Without these, as the rats and mice of the Prologue had discovered, confusion reigns. The folk of the field set off with all the enthusiasm of new brooms, but it immediately becomes apparent that none knows the way, and that they present the very image of a straying herd of sheep without a shepherd:

> Ac there was wight noon so wys, the weye thider kouthe,
> But blustreden forth as beestes over baches and hilles.
>
> (513-4)

And even after the route has been mapped out for them, the folk are only too aware that "This were a wikkede wey but whoso hadde a gyde" (VI.1). "Who so desireth to gete and conquere The blisse of hevene needful is a guyde".[50] It is specifically in the role of a guide that Piers now enters the poem, and the figure is therefore essentially relevant to Langland's preoccupation with the need for authority and submission to it in the pursuit of truth. In Piers he finds an authority nearer home than the King of England or the King of Heaven; his is the authority of the good-living man that is accessible to all, can be taken by all as a guide, and one which adds, moreover, the more powerfully persuasive authority of example to that of precept. His works can be imitated as well as his word obeyed.

His authority as guide is stressed in several different ways. In the allegorical context, he, in contradistinction from the pilgrim who has visited all shrines but never heard of a St. Truth, 'knows the place' well: has, in fact, as he explains, lived and laboured in the estate of truth all his life. His consequent competence to guide others to it is underlined by an emphasis on the verb "wisse"

(which also suggests the guidance that comes from
the provision of trustworthy rules - as in the
Ancrene Wisse, a work designed to provide a *"riwle"*
of life for anchoresses):

> 'Koudestow wissen us the wey wher that wye
>   dwelleth?'

(533)

The pilgrim to whom the question is addressed cannot,
but Piers's first speech ends with the assertion
that he can:

> 'I wol wisse yow wel right to his place'.

(555)

And he repeats at the beginning of Passus VI his
assurance that he can "the wey teche" (6).
        Piers is also from the first associated with
that official body of guides specifically instituted
as 'shepherds' and guides in the way of truth: the
priesthood. The very first word he utters, "Peter!"
(537)- cf. "By Seint Peter of Rome" (VI.3) - is an
asseveration by that first priest and head of the
Church, St. Peter, with whom he is to become more
intimately associated as the poem proceeds: the
Saint charged with the duty of founding the
institution that should provide the authoritative
and administrative repository of the laws of Christ.
And Piers at once adds to his oath by Peter that he
knows Truth "as kyndely as clerc doth hise bokes"
(538). He is as intimate with the subject as the
clergy should be with the books from which they
teach the laiety. He therefore possesses also
intellectual authority, *auctoritas*. He proceeds to
describe himself, furthermore, as a veritable *servus
Dei*, the dutiful servant-labourer of Truth/God. The
denomination *servus Dei* was one regularly bestowed
on a priest, who was likewise often described as a
harvester in the fields of God.[51] Piers, then, is,
in one way, nature's priest: a man fitted by
nature, by "kynde knowynge", to fill the role of
pastor, and guide men in the way of truth. He is
the priest or guide nature provides in the person of
every just man as an authority on truth until the
seekers after it shall have internalized the "kynde
knowynge" observable in him, and so require no other
guide but their own consciences. Chaucer represents
his ploughman, in fact, as the brother of his parish
priest, implying that their functions are analogous,

181

and that the ploughman (who "wolde thresshe, and
therto dyke and delve For Cristes sake, for every
povre wight, Withouten hire") is the secular
counterpart of the priest who is so zealous in
providing spiritual food for his flock.[52]
    What qualifies Piers to be an authority is the
absoluteness of his own submission to what he
recognizes to have lawful authority over him: his
feudal lord. True feudal loyalties had been
preached by Holy Church, perverted by Mede, and
those who 'maintain' truth have been consistently
contrasted with those who, in a corrupt version of
the lord-retainer relationship, 'maintain' False.
The lord-servant relationship between Piers and
Truth exemplifies the feudal ideal of the true
duties of maintainer and retainer. For in the
account of that relationship he now gives, the
feudal interpretation of the word 'truth' suggested
by Holy Church recurs: it is that good faith and
unquestioning obedience to the word and will of one's
'lord', that acceptance of being not one's own man,
but the man of a master. Piers's truth is to Truth
itself. His own conscience and natural moral
sensibility have pointed out to him who and what he
ought to pledge himself to, and to that he has
given an oath of fealty he is now bound in good
faith, or truth, to observe:

> 'Conscience and Kynde Wit kenned me to his place
> And diden me suren hym siththen to serven hym for
>   evere'.

> (539-40)

The lines thus restore one of its primary meanings
to the word 'truth': fulfilment of one's pledged
word. The life of the just man is the observance
of an implicit pledge to truth, and consists in
doing always "what Truthe' hoteth" (545, 548): that
is, in obedience to its dictates. Piers withholds
nothing of the service he owes his master:

> 'For though I seye it myselve, I serve hym to paye'.
> (549)

This being so, the eternal rule of 'measure for
measure' operates to reward him. If he serves "to
paye" (to the 'satisfaction' of his master), he
deserves his pay, and the following lines confirm
the pun in asserting that the payment thus due comes
fully and promptly:

> 'I have myn hire of hym wel and outherwhiles moore.
> He is the presteste paiere that povere men knoweth:
> He withhalt noon hewe his hire that he ne hath it at
> even '.

(550-2)

There are no debts in this relationship. Piers has given his life to the service of justice, that which pays its debts and gives to all their due. And as he shirks nothing of the service he owes, so the wages owed him (unlike those owed to the servants of Sloth) never fall into arrears. The account confirms all Holy Church had said. Truth has a reciprocal action, and by those who 'work as his word telleth' He will be found a "Fader of feith", returning measure for measure in accord with truth. Truth is for the true, and its treasure the truest on earth: it never fails of its debts to those to whom it is owed.

But Piers, prompted by Conscience (whose teaching on "mede" has been rehearsed in Passus III), energetically refuses the "huyre" proferred him now for his assistance in directing the penitents to Truth, knowing that by whatever amount he takes he will stand so much the less in credit with Truth:

> 'I nolde fange a ferthyng, for Seint Thomas shryne!
> Truthe wolde love me the lasse a long tyme after'.

(558-9)

And so he maps out the route free of charge, helping the seekers after truth "withouten mede", *gratis* - as Conscience had declared all works of justice must be to qualify for the "mede" of heaven, which is the 'hire' of those works.

As Piers describes it, the way to truth lies through obedience and submission to authority, acceptance of rule and rules, in conformity with an emphasis already evident in the poem, and especially in his own account of the nature of his intimacy with Truth. The journey begins in the "Mekenesse" that Passus IV had indicated as the only "maynpernour" the law could accept as a guarantor of submission to itself:

> 'Ye moten go thorugh Mekenesse, bothe men and wyves'.

(561)

This submission of the self will lead to a state of
mind in which the conscience may testify

> 'That ye loven Oure Lord God levest of alle thynges,
> And thanne youre neghebores next in none wise apeire
> Other wise than thow woldest hii wroughte to
>   thiselve'.

(563-5)

- that is, one will be in the spiritual state that
disposes towards obedience of "all the law and all
the prophets". For in these two commandments
Christ declared the whole of God's law to be
contained (Mt.22:37-40). They therefore stand
before the ten commandments of the Old Testament
that now follow as the New Testament summary of them,
so enjoining simultaneous obedience to both the Old
and the New Law (for the New Law Christ had
affirmed to be the fulfilment of the Old). They
also stand as the internal state which informs that
outer conformity to the law; for the truth that
pays its debts to God and man is in essence, as Holy
Church had said, a "kyndely" instinct to love the
one better and the other equally with oneself.
    The remainder of the route follows straight on
from this, lying through obedience to the divine
law - the ten commandments (to observe which is to
work "as (God's) word hoteth"), reversing the
journey mapped out in Mede's dowry, which had lain
through the breach of "the ten hestes". The conformity to law and authority thus stressed is
further emphasized by subsidiary pointers at the
start of this journey of obedience on that very
quality. The meakness that generates love first
follows the course marked out by a brook called
"Beth-boxom-of-speche" (566), and the commandments
are re-arranged to allow *Honora patrem et matrem*
to stand first (567-9): parental authority being
the first kind of authority a man encounters on his
journey through life, and his duty to respect it
the first manifestation of a continuing obligation
to observe larger kinds of rule and rules. And its
position here at the head of the ten commandments
recalls other references in this Passus to the
corrected child, particularly in Reason's sermon,
which had likewise begun by urging the restoration
of domestic authority. The journey continues
through the prohibitions of the tablets of the law,
allegorized as places to be avoided and their
fruits left untouched, in a way that restores to the

word 'trespass' its legal force, and underlines the
concept of the just man as him who 'takes but his
own' (cf 575).

The entrance to the heavenly city is through
Grace, in recognition of the fact that salvation
comes of the gracious mercy of God, not of merit.
But once again, Langland stresses that mercy does
not contravene justice, that it "never doth from
doom of right depart", and can be given only - as
even Mede had recognized - where justice is satisfied by 'amends'. That important word now recurs as
the name of the "man" of the porter, Grace; and it
is through addressing oneself to the injunction
"Amende-yow" that the gate of grace is actually
opened. To him must be given the password that
testifies to one's eligibility for grace: the
password that is a "token" (597) that the debt owed
by sin has been paid, the penalty due from wrong
has been performed, according to the dictate of
justice as Reason perceives it: *nullum malum
inpunitum*. That debt is paid by the outer and
inner *pena* of penance and penitence, and the
continuing resolve to amend one's ways, all of which
together constitute the only real amends acceptable
to justice. The password thus is:

> "Truthe woot the sothe -
> I parfourned the penaunce that the preest me enjoyned
> And am sory for my synnes and so I shal evere
> Whan I thykne theron, theigh I were a Pope".

(597-600)

As the Pearl-maiden says, grace man may have, but
only when the debt of *pena* owed to justice is paid:
"With sorghe and syt he mot hit crave/And bide þe
payne þerto is bent".

What 'unlocks' the gates of heaven is a problem
that preoccupies Langland. In the Prologue, he had
seen those gates as hinging on the 'cardinal'
virtues. In Passus I, it had been the 'lock of love'
that "letteth out" God's grace. Here, it is amends
for acual sin that releases the lock on the gate
closed by the Fall, and allows the atonement for
that original sin given by Christ to become
operative - "Amende-you" has the power to request
grace

> 'To wayven up the wiket that the womman shette
> Tho Adam and Eve eten apples unrosted:
> *Per Evam cunctis clausa est et per Mariam virginem*
> *   iterum patefacta est'.*

The combination for Langland's locks, in short, becomes an ever more complex equipoise of the justice of the Old Law of 'measure for measure' and the mercy of the New.

In paying these debts to justice, the justice that pays to all their due and is perfect truth is discovered reigning supreme in the heart itself:

> 'And if Grace graunte thee to go in in this wise
> Thow shalt see in thiselve Truthe sitte in thyn herte
> In a cheyne of charite, as thow a child were,
> To suffren hym and segge noght ayein thi sires wille'.

> (605-8)

The journey through obedience that began with "Your-fadres-honoureth", submission to the will of the physical father of the flesh, ends in a total submission to the will of a mystical presence in the heart itself, whose word is accepted as having the same authority over one as has a father over his child. The climax of the journey is thus an internalization of the law. What had begun as obedience to constraints seen as imposed by exter-nally locatable authorities and rules has become a "kyndely knowynge" of the law that guides one from within. Observance of the external letter has led to the presence of the spirit of the law as a guiding force within, engraved now on the tablets not of Sinai but of the heart. "For the first (law) could be inscribed on tablets of stone; but the second is imprinted only on the purer intelli-gence of the mind",[53] as John of Salisbury put it, referring to a spiritual assimilation of the law similar to that Langland here alludes to.

The lines describe a victory for spiritual truth quite as profound as that visualized in Passus IV for truth in the conduct of secular justice. Let truth preside over the heart, as Reason over the courts. In both cases, however, the goal remains a future and a conditional one, with much yet to be accomplished before it can be reached. The King's exultant determination that all law shall be administered henceforth with the same uncorrupted truth, free of the meed that "muche truthe letteth" (IV.176), is checked by Conscience's sober reminder

that people must change before that can be brought
to pass. Truth as an authoritative presence in the
heart, as in the court, is similarly the destination
of a journey through obedience to law and justice
not yet even begun. And the voice of a sheriff's
clerk defiantly choosing meed in preference to the
truth which cannot pay his bills had provided a
counter to the prevalent note of idealistic resolve
in Passus IV; in the same way, at the end of
Passus V, while Piers earnestly encourages all to
hope and strive for entrance to the eternal City,
through establishing kinship with one of the eight
maidens who "serven Truthe evere" (618), a pardoner
and a prostitute agree in feeling more inclined to
try and buy their way in.

NOTES

1. The C text explicitly characterizes them as "men of lawe"
    (IV.66-73).
2. *FQ* V.xi.36ff.
3. On this distinctive feature of Trespass, see Jenks, pp.
    53,137,171; *Potter's Outlines*, pp.53,67,141-2,156-7.
4. William Lyndwood's *Provinciale*, quoted by Dunning (p.154).
5. On "bot" as a legal term, and "botleas" crimes, see
    Potter's Outlines, p.154; Jenks, p.11.
6. X.17; XV.29-30; XX.132-3.
7. *Lay Folks' Catechism*, 11.932-3 (Wycliffite version).
8. Pope Innocent, *De Contemptu Mundi*, lib.iii.c.15 (quoted
    by Skeat, n. to IV.143).
9. For the wink here given by Mede to the lawyers, *cf*
    Libro de Buen Amor (st 499): "Where Money is the judge,
    that is where the eye is winked meaningfully".
10. See, for instance, the text of the sheriff's oath given
    by Chrimes in *De Laudibus*, p.171.
11. See Fortescue, *Governance*, ch.V ("The Harme that Comyth
    off a Kynges Poverte"), pp.118-20.
12. On the very small pay enjoyed by sheriffs, see *Governance*,
    pp.147,314; for the extortions and corruptions practised
    by them, see *ibid*. pp.313-4; *De Laudibus*, pp.171-2.
13. See n.59 to ch.I *supra*.
14. XX.4ff.
15. *Policraticus*, IV.viii-ix (pp.37-44); V.vi (p.88).
16. Edward Young, *Night Thoughts*, Night 4, 1.233. In this
    connection, see further P.M. Kean, *The Pearl, An
    Interpretation* (London, 1967), for a discussion of the
    legal terms used in that poem to legitimize God's mercy
    within his justice (pp.185-96).
17. *FQ* V.ix.20-x.5. It is possible that Spenser is here also
    attempting to justify Elizabeth's execution of Mary Queen

of Scots.

18. He administers punishment "with reluctant right hand" (*Policraticus* IV.viii,p.37).

19. *FQ* V.ix.50; x.2.

20. In the C-text, the concept emerges as one sufficiently important to figure as a personification, referred to at III.207 as the sister of Mede, and at IV.189 as one whose 'seal' should not be found on royal dispensations.

21. *cf CT* VI.91-102; Skelton's *Magnificence*, ll.1920ff.

22. *Policraticus*, IV.xi (pp.50-51).

23. *FQ* V.v.25; vii.42.

24. Both quotations are from fifteenth-century pieces cited by Scattergood, *Politics*, pp.300-301.

25. *Scale of Perfection* II.ii (p.3); *cf* n.4 *supra*.

26. *cf* Abelard's *Ethics*, p.109.

27. "Tria itaque sunt in reconciliatione peccatoris ed Deum, penitentia scilicet, confessio, satisfactio" (*ibid*, p.76).

28. Some fairly typical forms of outer or formal *penae* are listed by Abelard: "these penalties (*penas*) ... with which we make satisfaction for sins, by fasting or praying, by keeping vigil, or by whatever means macerating the flesh, or by distributing to the needy what we forego ourselves ... "(*Ethics*, p. 109).

29. This was often added to contrition, confession, satisfaction, as a fourth element essential to true purgation through shrift: "This thre, with gode will to forsake our syn Clenses us" (*Lay Folks' Catechism*, ll.314-5); *cf The Book of Margery Kempe*, pp.175-6.

30. *cf* the warning given by Master Rypon to those who trust in papal indulgences that purport to absolve from penalty and guilt ("a pena et a culpa"): "O spes frivola atque vana, cum in hujusmodi litteris indulgentie scribatur, "vere" nedum "confessis" sed et "contritis", quibus predictus dolor secundus est omnino necessarius ad hoc quod per confessionem seu pena remittetur vel culpa" (quoted by Dunning, p.157).

31. "Sower of discorde" occurs, for instance, in a fifteenth-century verse (quoted by Scattergood, *Politics*, p.84; and a "*brewe*cheste" was one who stirred up strife (*cf* XVI.43).

32. Housewives frequently brewed ale to sell to their neighbours, and were often amersed for charging prices above those legally stipulated (see G.G. Coulton, *Medieval Panorama* (Cambridge, 1938), pp.368-9).

33. Augustine, *Epistola* 153 (*PL* 33.662), repeated by Abelard (*Ethics*, pp.79-80).

34. It could be lawful, however, to take interest where the money was not repaid by the date specified, as it was then regarded as compensation for the extra time 'lost' by the lender (J.W. Baldwin, i.282-3). This is how

Avarice has evaded the prohibition: he has profited by
his debtors 'breaking their day' and so falling into
'arrears' (241-2).

35. See J.W. Baldwin, i.69,307ff; ii.211; Abelard,
    Ethics, p.80n.
36. *cf* II.174; and *OED sv* Enrol *v*.5.
37. See the notes on the line given by Schmidt and Bennett.
38. *cf* Peter the Chanter: "Cavendum est ne ab his accipiamus
    quos scimus de lacrimis pauperum vivere, et in tobia
    legitur (2:18-21) ... Filii enim sanctorum sumus" (quoted
    by J.W. Baldwin, ii.210).
39. J.W. Baldwin, i.303,308.
40. Vomiting as restitution is actually an image used quite
    seriously on occasion: "a government which is corrupted
    by luxury ... will vomit forth under the pressure of
    God's judgment whatever it has drunk down with immoderate
    luxury" (*Policraticus*, IV.xiv (p.222)).
41. *cf* Frank, p.106.
42. See J.W. Baldwin, ii.189,141; i.266, ii.186.
43. *ibid*, i.301.
44. For the pairing of usurers and robbers as typifying the
    two kinds of unjust gain, see J.W. Baldwin, ii.49,88,
    94,206.
45. *Ibid*, ii.176.
46. Anyone who unjustly appropriated or withheld could be
    referred to as *fur et raptor* (*ibid*, i.222, ii.44); over-
    charging, usury, withholding tithes, imposing improper
    taxes, defrauding an heir, not returning what is found,
    extortion from the poor - all were characterized as forms
    of theft or *spoliatio* (*ibid*, i.222,236; 240,245; ii,
    178; *cf* Abelard *Ethics*, p. 80n, 84). Similarly, all who
    connived at, or consented to profit by, wrongful gains
    were said to 'run with the thief' (*currunt cum fure*), and
    so shared his obligation to restore (for examples, see
    J.W. Baldwin, i.306; ii.156,157).
47. Schmidt prints "Rober(d)" here, though "Robbere" is the
    reading of all B-MSS, and is accordingly the one I adopt.
48. See Bennett's note to the line.
49. The distinction between a felony and a misdemeanour was
    that the former carried a penalty of death (or maiming),
    which was referred to as the *pena sanguinis* (*Potter's
    Outlines*, p.159; *Policraticus*, VI.xi (pp.205-6)).
50. The opening lines of Hoccleve's third poem to the Virgin
    Mary in Huntingdon HM 744 (*ed.cit*. p.289).
51. For the agricultural metaphor as applied to priests
    (derived ultimately from the Bible), *cf Policraticus*,
    V.xvi, VIII.xvii (pp.153,345); and for other examples
    of associated figurative usages, see J.W. Baldwin i.110;
    Jack Upland, p.70; *Friar Daw's Reply*, 11.20,539.
52. *CT*.I.477-541. Bloomfield sees in Piers "the ideal or
    angelic Pope, or by extension, the ideal clergyman or

religious, the plower of souls and Christ Himself"
(p.148); *cf* Goldsmith, p.35.
53. *Policraticus* IV.vi (p.24). The difference between the
letter of the Old Law and the spirit of the New Law (of
Charity) was, in particular, often expressed in these
terms, and the C text adds the lines: "And charge
Charite a churche to make / In thyne hole herte" (VII.
257-8).

CHAPTER V

LABOUR AND PARDON

I: *Passus VI*

Other moralists who had interested themselves in the question of whether and how a livelihood is honestly earned had adopted the same criterion of labour as Langland now employs in Passus VI: earnings must be commensurate with labour. The labourer is worthy of his hire, but the idle or the extortionate, *non commensurans laborem et operam quantiti mercedis*, are merely thieves and plunderers. This was simply the social and vocational application of the principle of fair exchange on which commutative justice was based. Robert of Courson had even called for a general council of the church to decree that all men should work, physically or spiritually, for their bread.[1] Langland gives his own forceful logic to the respect for equity underlying such attitudes by representing society, labour, and livelihood in their most basic and primitive forms: a small peasant community, dependent for food on grain the land will not yield unless physically laboured upon by them. The plough thus becomes the central type of the tool that earns livelihood from labour, in confirmation of a status it already enjoyed in Middle English idiom (cf: "ye knowe it wel ynogh, Of chapmen, that hir moneie is hir plogh"; Kings "laboure on þe lawe as lewde men on plowes"[2]).

Having repented of their wrongful gains, then, the community is now to be taught what it is to gain an honest livelihood according to the precepts of Truth. They do not find it a "lovely lesson" (276), and rather resist applying themselves to it. And in attempting to enforce the rule of "labour for lyflod", Piers finds himself confronted with that idleness which had formed the first of the two vices discerned in the Prologue: again defined as the disposition to waste what one has not won (28,130, 133,161-2,201,302,320-2), to evade the debt of labour owed as the price of "lyflod", which, like mercy, requires in justice to be earned. In this sphere, too, 'measure for measure' is the principle that should prevail, and the angel's equitable maxim, *Qualia vis metere talia grana sere*, Langland applies now with a strictness and rigour most unpalatable to the seekers after truth, who had not counted upon having to pay or work for it. That is, only those who have contributed in some way to the labour involved in the cultivation of the land are to share in the harvest it yields (65-7). The ploughman is thus taken, as in the Prologue, as the very type of that truth which earns its "lyflod" by honest labour, since in the case of agriculture, the "lyflod" obtained from the land is, by the law of "kynde", very exactly proportionate to the labour expended upon it. The physical need to plough the land is therefore used in the present Passus as a metonymous illustration of the moral requirement that withdrawals from society should not exceed what has been paid in. This is also economic good sense, and until the rule is universally observed, there "worth nevere plentee among the peple" (163); a sound commonwealth, economically and morally, depends upon it. Through Piers, then, Langland explores the possibilities of establishing a truly equitable society, where out-take of "lyflod" balances in-put of labour, so eliminating the occupational iniquities of the Prologue, with their consequent inequity in the distribution of money and goods.

In the allegorical account of the state and the functions and duties of the various members of it that follows, the King is replaced as the ultimate guiding authority to whom all are answerable by Piers the Ploughman. In the Prologue, the emergence of a corporate state governed by a law that taught "ech lif to knowe his owene" (*Prol*.122) had been the result of a voluntary election of a ruler. Here it follows on the election of Piers as 'guide' to truth, and it is accordingly he who apportions duties, and describes how those who may not literally "tilie and travaille as trewe lif asketh" (*Prol*.120) may nevertheless contribute to the state: women should (in a fine example of that conjunction of secular with sacred needs characteristic of Langland) sew sacks and chasubles (9-12); knights, similarly, must defend the labouring commons and the Holy Church by whose truth they live. It is Piers, too, who decides what sections of the non-labouring community should, and what sections should not, be supported by the state: the genuinely incapacitated must be (136-8); idle wastrels should not be (70-78); those who forego manual labour to live in the spiritual labour of prayer and mortification of the flesh should be (145-51). The Passus, then, provides an allegorical framework in which to establish what are viable occupations, which roles

and functions are materially or spiritually productive for society, and who has a claim to be
sustained by the wealth produced essentially by its
labouring classes. It provides, in short, a social
theory of rights and duties erected on the rule of
"labour for lyflod" of which the Ploughman is the
authoritative exponent and interpreter.

Piers must 'decide' such matters, not because
Langland is advocating some communist doctrine of
peasant rulership and has at last seen that society's
true king is The Worker, but because, until the
authority of the principle Piers embodies is
accepted by the "commune", the King cannot rule
effectually. The King's task is to uphold justice
and law, and to this he had pledged himself at the
end of Passus IV: henceforth there would be "leaute
in lawe" (180), and all criminals would get their
just deserts. This, as Conscience tells him, he
cannot bring about unless his people themselves
accept the absoluteness of this just equilibrium
between desert and reward/penalty. In their own
domain, they must first obey the precept and example
of Piers the Ploughman, who teaches them what honest
gain is (gain paid for by labour), before they will
be ready to give their obedience to the laws of the
King aimed at the punishment of injustice.

So Piers in this Passus is in something of the
predicament of the King, attempting to reduce to his
rule a recalcitrant people who do not like paying
their debts, and facing the same problems of
enforcement of the law and the justice he represents.
Like the king, too, he must know to whom and when to
give 'mercy' from the natural law that those who do
not labour should starve. He consults the ruthless
Hunger on this question (as the King had consulted
the ruth-less Reason), who, like Reason, discriminates
between a lawful and an unlawful mercy: there are
some beggars to whom food should be given, some to
whom it should be all but totally denied until they
have learned to 'amend' their ways, and to work in
order to "soupe swetter". For Piers must know when
to invoke Hunger, when to 'bid him cease' (179,199).
Like the King, he does not spare to visit the
penalty due to disobedience of his law of "labour
for lyflod" upon those who incur it, and like him
realizes that his rule cannot retain its reality
for the ruled unless such penalties are enforced.
He, too, must discriminate between a mercy that is
just and one that is not. He must know who has,
and who has not, a claim on his "almesse" (146):
the 'alms' that derive from the Greek ἔλεος = pity,

compassion, 'ruth'. To the voluntary spiritual
beggars who are hermits and anchoresses he will
give his "almesse" freely, for they, he considers,
deserve it (as to other beggars, he must use
greater discretion in the distribution of the alms
they crave). For, in anticipation of the end of
the poem, he realizes that "it is an unreasonable
Religion that hath right noght of certain" (151).
Again, we must remind ourselves that "unreasonable"
does not here mean just 'unreasonable', but 'out of
accord with true judgment between right and wrong',
unjust: "*Dignum est operarius* his hire to have" is
God's own law; labourers of the spirit are entitled
to their "lyflod".

We are given, at the same time, some further
hints in the Passus as to the way the mercy and
"suffraunce" of God operate. The mercy and
suffrance born of meed have been discredited: her
suffrance is the connivance bought by wrong when it
bribes the law "oure synne to suffre" (II.175), and
when the law consequently listens to the voice that
bids, "suffre hem to selle somdel ayeins reson"
(III.92). What prompts God to suffer his justice
to be flouted on earth, as Piers indicates he
does? -

> 'And al is thorugh suffraunce that vengeaunce yow
> ne taketh!'
>
> (144)

How have such men escaped divine punishment thus
far? How is God's suffrance different from that of
the commissary and the mayor?

> 'Thei ben ascaped good aventure - now God hem
> amende!'
>
> (77)

There is suffrance and suffrance. God has suffered
not because He is prepared to wink at the sin of
injustice, but to give the sinners the chance to
make the amends that may earn His mercy. Similarly
Piers does not take the natural penalty of want of
food for those who will not work for it to its
logical conclusion of starvation, not does hunger
bid him to do so. He intercedes to prevent Hunger
from actually exterminating Waster and the Breton
("'Suffre hem lyve' he seide", 181). And Hunger
himself counsels Piers, not actually to starve such
troublesome rebels, but to give them only enough

food to keep them alive, so that they may learn from the penalty and not be destroyed by it: learn what it is that will bring them the food they require (213-7). A new element of limited "suffrance" has entered into Langland's thinking on the relationship between justice and mercy: suffrance gives the opportunity for amends, and so conduces to mercy without prejudicing justice, which is but delayed and not denied. It is "better to reforme, then to cutt off the ill", as Spenser puts it in his Legend of Justice (*FQ*.V.x.2). But by the end of the Passus, Langland is warning wasters (and God?) that this delay of just retribution cannot continue indefinitely, and that a time must very shortly come when there will be a "derthe" in real earnest, in which men really will "*deye* for hunger" (329). Langland's own powers of suffrance are not of divine proportions, and his patience is running out, even if God's is not.

The Passus is much concerned with the finer points of the law it lays down. What is the position before it of those who do not or cannot labour? Women and knights are the first groups dealt with, both, though in different ways, unfitted by birth and education for manual labour. The women do not interest Langland much: they can make themselves useful in various domestic ways, and may therefore be conceded to earn their keep (9-20). The Knight's case elicits a livelier attention (21-56). He and Piers come to a formal agreement, according to which Piers is to "fynde" the Knight in return for the armed defence against external and internal attack the knight provides for his farm. Langland is justifying a non-labouring aristocracy by positing a kind of implicit social contract, according to which they are sustained by the working classes in return for the military and policing services they provide, defending the community from "wastours and fro wikked men that this world destruyeth" (28). This view of the true role of knights being to exercise the functions of a law-enforcement agency, a police force, accords with similar ideas found elsewhere in the poem.[3] Langland's world is divided into those whose business it is to obey the law, and those whose business it is to administer and enforce it. His aristocracy, secular and sacred, is a legal, judicial one: king, knight, and clergy, are the guardians of law.

Particularly interesting here is Langland's

attempt to bind the knight to the role so agreed by insinuating into it the central chivalric virtue of faith or truth to one's pledged word. The agreement is made in what may be termed the language of chivalric good faith. Piers specifically uses the term 'covenant' at 27, and the knight 'pledges his troth' to observe the 'forward':

> 'By my power, Piers, I plighte thee my trouthe
> To fulfille this forward, though I fighte sholde;
> Als longe as I lyve I shal thee mayntene'.

(34-6)

It is by imposing covenants and forwards on Gawain, which he is then bound by the knightly truth he professes to observe, that the Green Knight/Bertilac tests that truth in *Sir Gawain and the Green Knight*. The terms 'covenant' and 'forward' are much in evidence when the two crucial agreements are made, and Gawain, too, pledges his troth to them (*SGGK*, 378-403; 1105-25). The contractual 'year and a day' he is granted recurs here in Piers's warning to the knight not to take bribes in his administration of justice on his estates, for all he takes he must "yelde ... ayein at one yeres ende In a ful perilous place - Purgatorie it hatte" (43-4). The contractual terminology that naturally suggested itself in the Romance to convey the solemn obligation of the knight to 'keep truth'[4] is pressed into service here too. As in Passus I, the effect is to absorb chivalric truth into that larger kind of moral truth with which Langland is especially concerned, and to suggest that the knight's boasted 'good faith' is owed above all to this social contract by which he is covenanted to defend truth by the pursuit of those who offend against it. Typically, Langland brings together abstract and concrete in his emphasis on this duty of hot pursuit to the end that Piers's community be rid of destructive pests:

> 'In covenaunt that thow kepe Holy Kirke and myselve
> Fro wastours and fro wikked men that this world
>   destruyeth;
> And go hunte hardiliche to hares and foxes,
> To bores and to bukkes that breken down myne hegges;
> And go affaite thi faucons wilde foweles to kille,
> For thei cometh to my croft and croppeth my whete'.

(27-32)

In thus representing hunting and hawking as beneficial to farmers in ridding them of vermin,
Langland turns the characteristic leisure-time
pursuits of the aristocracy into a more precise and
literal instance of the larger purgative role he
assigns them; and again brings together secular-
economic and moral-spiritual utility, as with the
sacks and chasubles sewn by the women.

Piers, recollecting that the knight holds a
position of responsibility with regard to the
enforcement of the law in one other respect also,
sees fit to add a rider to the covenant ("Ye, and
yet a point", 37), affecting the Knight's administration of justice in the manorial courts. He
must "mayntene Truthe" there, as well. In particular, he must never allow meed to enter into the
courts of law from which she was banished in Passus
IV. She can be a force for undue severity as well
as wrongful leniency, for the knight might be
tempted by covetousness to extort more in the way of
taxes and fines than was really due. He is thus
instructed to impose penalties only where justice
and truth require, and to be guided rather by charity
for his fellow-men than by greed in the collection
of fines:

> 'Loke ye tene no tenaunt but Truthe wole assente:
> And though ye mowe amercy hem, lat mercy be taxour'.

> (38-9)

And he is further warned never to accept bribes in
the form of "presentes and yiftes" (41). For he will
be brought to the divine accounts to pay his debts
as will all men, and be forced to "yelde it ayein at
one yeres ende In a ful perilous place - Purgatorie
it hatte". For all are equal before the law of God,
and "in charnel at chirche cherles ben yvel to
knowe, Or a knight from a knave there" (49-50).
Though a policeman and a judge, and so on earth one
of the law's aristocrats, he is himself subject to
the law of God whose prime tenet is *Redde quod debes*.

Passūs IV-V have already established that
payment of debts in the form of penalties, satisfaction, restitution, is the essential first step
in the journey to Truth. Before proceding to the
'pilgrimage at the plough' (102), therefore, Piers
makes a will testifying to the fact that he is
literally and spiritually clear of debts. It is a
will that disposes of all that is his, soul, body,

and goods, in perfect accord with that justice that
gives to all their due. His soul he commits to Him
who has 'best deserved' it (87), in anticipation of
that last great settlement of accounts that is a
recurring image of the poem:

> 'Til I come to hise accountes as my crede me telleth,
> To have a relees and a remission on that rental I
> leve'.

"Having been tenant long to a rich Lord"[5] called
Truth (V.539 ff), Piers owes dues and services as
rental to that lord, which he has done all in his
power to pay. As man is tenant to God, however,
he can never repay the debt due from original sin.
But Piers trusts, by paying all he can, to receive
through the Atonement an official "relees" from
debt and a formal remission from that part of it
not in his power to pay. Again, mercy is reconciled with justice through the strict precision of
the legal and financial vocabulary of "accountes",
"relees", "remission", "rental".

To the Church he leaves his body, for burial
and prayers are his due from the church as their
part of the tithing contract. Piers was prompt in
paying his debt to it ("I paide it hym prestly",
93), and the Church must now pay hers. All his
material goods are committed to his dependents,
those whom he has an obligation to support, his
wife and children. He has discharged his debts to
God and man, and can thus claim with the testimony
of a good conscience:

> 'For though I deye today, my dettes are quyte;
> I bar hom that I borwed er I to bedde yede'.

(98-9)

This will work on several levels of significance.
In the first place, travel being more time-con-
suming and hazardous in the Middle Ages than it is
now, intending pilgrims had to contend with the
possibility that they might not return. They
therefore often made a point of putting their
domestic and moral affairs into the same good order
as the prospect of imminent death would have
dictated. To make a will was not uncommon. And,
for the same reason, it was apparently thought
proper to take what might be the last opportunity
to pay outstanding debts, for dying in debt was to
be avoided at all costs.[6] Prior to her journey to

the Holy Land, Margery Kempe had the banns of that
intended pilgrimmage proclaimed in church, precisely
so that her debtors could come forward to claim
repayment before her departure.[7] Piers's will here
combines both these duties of an intending pilgrim;
for it is a testament cast as a payment of debts.
It represents that ideal state of conscience the
Christian ought to spend his life ensuring will be
his on his death-bed: when about to come into the
presence of Truth itself, he must leave behind him
no debts unpaid to his neighbour, and no debts to
his God of sin unatoned for.

   'Payment of debts' is also likewise the
essential pre-condition of the 'pilgrimage to
truth' envisaged also by Sloth:

> 'And yet wole I yelde ayein, yif I so muche have,
> Al that I wikkedly wan sithen I wit hadde;
> And though my liflode lakke, leten I nelle
> That ech man shal have his er I hennes wende;
> And with the residue and the remenaunt, bi the Rode
>   of Chestre,
> I shal seken truthe erst er I se Rome!'

                                        (V.456-61)

Here, too, the reference is to the settlement of
his debts incumbent on the intending pilgrim.
"Residue and remenaunt" is a testamentary expression,
and occurs also in Piers's debt-paying will (VI.
100). In both cases, the phrase refers to that
which remains after all debts have been paid as the
wherewithal to support the pilgrim on his journey.
For as with literal pilgrimages, so with this
allegorical one to Truth: it cannot possibly be
undertaken in debt, non-payment of which contravenes the very definition of *iustitia* or truth
(*reddere debitum unicuique*). And as Avarice could
not hope to pursue an honest mercantile career
henceforward on the basis of dishonestly gained
capital, so a truthful living cannot be earned
while anything remains fraudulently with-held from
its due recipient. More importantly, the course of
rightful gain is by this will preluded by an act of
rightful payment. All that is gained by truth is
destined ultimately to be truly paid out again to
meet the debts of justice. Piers's debts have
claimed all that he is and has. The "residue and
the remenaunt" with which he is to embark on the
pilgrimage at the plough, to re-enter on the cycle
of earning and paying, amounts to precisely nothing:

or rather it amounts to the very fact of having paid all debts which is the indispensible wherewithal for the service of truth. Only to the necessaries of life, food, drink, and clothing (Piers's sole residue and remanant) does one have title; the surplus that outweighs needs is not owned, but owed (I.17-57).

Piers's attempt to enforce the equitable rule that all should earn the bread they eat runs into the eternal problem of what should be done with those who refuse to work (not with those who cannot - Langland had no problem with them, the charity that sums up the law of God being perfectly explicit on that point, 136-8, 218-224). The problem had presented itself in Langland's day with a peculiar vividness, in the form of the bands of unemployed wastrels who roamed the countryside: some feigning disabilities, and cheating a living out of society by receiving in alms what they would have been quite capable of earning by labour; some little more than vagabond thugs who took what they needed by theft and assault. These are the beggars and bullies who in this Passus resist Piers's plans to impose the universal duty of labour and so ensure 'plenty among the people'. The first group are met with at 115ff; these are the false beggars, who answer his reproaches with whining pathos and hypocritical piety, offering for their food the prayers for the donor that were traditionally conceived of as constituting the pious 'labour' beggars offered in exchange for the "lyflod" granted them in alms:[8]

> Somme leide hir legges aliry, as swiche losels conneth,
> And made hir pleynt to Piers and preide hym of grace:
> 'For we have no lymes to laboure with, lord, ygraced be ye!
> Ac we preie for yow, Piers, and for youre plowgh bothe,
> That God of his grace youre greyn multiplie
> And yelde yow of youre almesse that ye yyve us here;
> For we may neither swynke ne swete, swich sicknesse us eyleth'.

>   (122-8)

The bullies are represented by Waster, who doesn't

.trouble himself to feign incapacity, but simply determines to help himself by force:

> 'Wiltow or neltow, we wol have oure wille
> Of thi flour and of thi flesshe - fecche whanne us
>   liketh,
> And maken us murye thermyde, maugree thi chekes'.

(156-8)

The two groups represent the fraud antithetical to the justice that gives all their due, under its two aspects of guile and force. They take what they have earned no rights in.

The law had in very fact attempted to meet this problem, by the Statute of Labourers, in just the way Piers attempts to meet it. That is, in responding to the combined problem of the shortage of labour caused by the plague, and of the above-mentioned bands of roaming vagabonds ("Because a great part of the people and especially of the workmen and servants, has now died in the pestilence ... And because many sound beggars do refuse to labour so long as they can live from begging alms, giving themselves up to idleness and sins, and at times to robbery and other crimes ..."),[9] it had enacted that all able-bodied men not legitimately otherwise employed should be obliged at law to work in the fields for stated rates of pay (as opposed to the "excessive wages", it claimed were being demanded), and had declared illegal the giving of alms to "such as can very well labour". Piers, too, attempts to make all who have no other legit-imate calling labour for their "mete" and "mesur-able hyre" (198); and both he and Hunger declare that no alms will be given to "wastours" (148, 212-7) - for that would be to extend a false mercy, false ἔλεος.

Piers, then, like the King before him, faces a problem of law-enforcement, not just as the duty to "labour for lyflod" is represented as a law of natural justice, of "kynde" (247); and, as, being the expressed will of him who is the ruler of this paradigm of a state, it has the force of law by virtue of the maxim *Quod principui placet legis habet vigorem*; but also as the measures proposed were in very fact, at the time in which the events are set, literally part of the law of the land (316-7), and therefore had behind them the auth-ority not only of natural but also of positive law. Enforcing that law is another matter. The Statute

itself was found to be unenforcible, and was
eventually withdrawn. Piers meets with not much
better success.

The realism with which Langland confronts the
obstinate problem of the determined Waster who
simply says, 'Shan't, and you can't make me',
becomes particularly apparent if one compares this
Passus with that passage of *Mum and the Sothsegger*
which likewise attempts an allegorical formulation
of it, at 871ff. There, the poet falls asleep,
and in his dream sees a fertile land of plenty on
which man has imposed perfect order and control
through his labour; he proceeds to a garden,
another image of order and control, where he meets
a franklin watching over a bee-hive, and squashing
the drones in it. The franklin represents, of
course, the vigilance and control of good rule, and
the drones the parasites of society eliminated by
it. To allegorize the latter as drones to be
squashed under the thumb reduces the problem to
manageable proportions, and makes the solution to
it appear simple. The Waster who threatens the
good order and consequent "plentee" of Passus VI is
a much more rudely intractable affair. His resistance to authority has a crude force not easily to
be dealt with by the latter, beautifully caught in
the vulgar defiance of, "And bad hym go pissen with
his plowgh, forpyned sherewe!" (155) - later to be
matched by the expressive "Ye? Baw!" with which his
counterpart, the Brewer, responds to Conscience's
rules of life in Passus XIX (399). That those
responsible for government should bring such men
to answer to the law is easier said than done.
Piers tries that: that is, he summons the Knight,
who has already been established as representing
the agency for law-enforcement in this mini-state.
The Knight duly delivers a stern warning to Waster,
ordering him to toe the line, "Or thow shalt abigge
by the lawe, by the ordre that I bere!" (166).
Waster's response is simple. He has never worked
before, and he is not going to begin now (167);
and he thumbs his nose at the knight and the law
("And leet light of the lawe, and lasse of the
knyghte", 168). The passage is not, I think, meant
as a criticism of the knight as representing an
obsolescent order that has outlived its usefulness
to society.[10] It is Langland's acknowledgement that
the justice Piers is attempting to impose is
ultimately unenforcible (as the Statute of Labourers
was found to be) by conventional policing methods.
There are limits to the extent to which law can

co-erce the observance of justice; and those
limits are determined, as Conscience had implied at
the end of Passus IV, by the willingness of those
subject to the law to observe it voluntarily.

The resources at Piers's disposal are not
quite exhausted, however. He is also able to call
on Providence to "awreke" him and his flouted law.
For providence was regarded as a dimension of
justice in the Middle Ages. Natural disasters -
flood, famine, plague, storms, failures of harvest -
and even unnatural ones - such as the reigns of
tyrants or the revolts of peasants - were attributed
to a God inflicting through providence the penalties for sin, once conscience and government had
revealed themselves unequal to the task of
correction. Their cause was iniquity, and their
cure repentance and amendment. Such things were
the ultimate safety devices of a moral universe
against disorder and disobedience. They came to
punish the unjust, either unbidden, or in response
to the prayers of the just.[11] And whatever more
recondite things Piers may be, he is certainly a
just man whose appeal to Providence would deserve
to be heard.

In summoning Hunger, he is also invoking the
natural penalty provided by the law of "kynde" for
refusal to labour for "lyflod", which is to go
hungry. The operation of the law can be neutralized,
as can that of all laws, by mercy: that is, the
charity of others may provide the non-labourer with
the food he would otherwise lack. But Piers, again
like the king in Passus IV, is refusing to spare
the wrongdoer the natural penalties of the law
through the intervention of his merciful "almesse".
Waster, like Wrong, must feel the full force of the
penalties the law provides for offences against
itself. The law here is the law of "kynde". And
the beauty of the natural law, left to its own
unimpeded operation, is that it is its own very
efficient policeman. Nothing could be more
impressive in its terrifying unnegotiability than
the prompt and violent assault on the miscreants
by Hunger that now occurs. He meets Waster and his
sidekick the Breton on their own terms, attacking
them with crude and unceremonious force, boxing
their ears and wringing their guts:

> Hunger in haste too hente Wastour by the mawe
> And wrong hym so by the wombe that al watrede hise
> eighen.
> He buffetted the Bretoner aboute the chekes

> That he loked like a lanterne al his lif after.
> He bette hem so bothe, he brast ner hite guttes.

(174-8)

Here is a siezure, an arrest or 'attachment', whose
force and efficacy could be matched by no human
police-force. It speaks with a logic rougher than
that of the "curteis" admonishment of the Knight
(164), and it ensures a conformity with the law
more speedy and absolute than anything that could
be achieved not only by him, but even by whole
armies of "constables and sergeaunts":

> Faitours for fere herof flowen into bernes
> And flapten on with flailes fro morwe til even,
> That hunger was noght hardy on hem for to loke
> For a potful of peses that Piers hadde ymaked.
> An heep of heremytes henten hem spades
> And kitten hir copes and courtepies hem maked,
> And wente as werkmen with spades and with shoveles,
> And dolven and dikeden to dryve awey Hunger.
> Blynde and bedreden were bootned a thousand,
> That seten to begge silver, soone were thei heeled;
> For that was bake for Bayard was boote for many
>   hungry;
> And many a beggere for benes buxum was to swynke,
> And ech a povere man wel apaied to have pesen for
>   his hyre,
> And what Piers preide hem to do as prest as a
>   sperhauk.

(183-96)

The effectiveness of the allegory here lies in the
violent temporal contraction. Hunger does indeed
shrink the stomach and hollow the cheeks; and it
might well cause beggars not beggars by necessity
to work, and hermits not hermits by vocation to
abandon their hermit's garb for the shorter working-
jacket of a labourer. But both the physical and
the social process would be essentially slow and
gradual ones. Langland's imagination has contracted
them concertina-like into one dramatic instant:
the results of one blow, one dosage of a miracle
cure, one slash of the scissors. A similar effect
is achieved in Passus XX, in the account of the
attacks of Sickness, Age, and Death, who play a
role equivalent to that of Hunger here (in both
cases, physical suffering is represented as the
most effective and persuasive ally that justice has

against recalcitrant mankind). Death

> ... al to duste passhed
> Kynges, and knyghtes, kaysers and popes.

(100-101)

Again, the essentially gradual process of the
crumbling into dust of a dead body has been dramatically reduced to an instantaneous powdering on
impact. In the same way, the gradual onset of age
that results in progressive loss of hair and teeth
is contracted to figure as the transformation
wrought by one launch of the horsed Age over the
head, one blow in the mouth from him (XX.185-92).
By such means does Langland suggest the mighty force
of the "lawe of kynde".

Hunger restores the authority of the law,
effects obedience to it, rendering the labourers
"buxum" and "meke" (205). Once again, Langland
has asserted his faith in the efficacy of penalties.
This is the language the unjust understand. If
offence does not recoil upon the offenders with a
punitive back-lash of pain (in the form of penalty,
penance, or repentance), it can never be truly felt
as an evil. Without penalties, the law is an
emasculated cypher, as ineffectual as the "curteis"
reproof offered by the Knight.

So the law of "kynde" has enforced itself
through penalties as did the law of the king in
Passus IV - penalties which Piers, like the King,
has refused by a false mercy to forbear from
inflicting. By such means he has compelled
observance to the law of "labour for lyflod", to
that primary law of "measure for measure" which
rules all levels of justice, here reflected in that
"mesurable hyre" (198) for which all must now
perforce be content to work. Piers's problem, like
the King's, is how to make people "meke", how to
"amaistren hem and make hem ... at (his) wille"
(205-11): bring to that essential obedience to
rule and authority the wills of those over whom
self-interest (meed or sloth) has at present the
only "maistrye" they acknowledge. On this question,
he takes counsel at Hunger, the harsh logic of the
law of "kynde", as the King had at Reason.

Hunger, like Reason, now proceeds to lay down
the law: quite literally in this case, since his
reply is in part to re-affirm the provisions of the
Statute of Labourers that, "because many sound
beggars do refuse to labour so long as they can live

205

from begging alms, giving themselves up to idleness
and sins, and at times to robbery and other crimes -
let no one ... presume under colour of piety or
alms to give anything to such as can very well
labour, or to cherish them in their sloth: so that
thus they may be compelled to labour for the
necessities of life". That is, he counsels Piers to
withhold food from "Bolde beggeris and bigge that
mowe hir breed biswynke" (213), to force them "go
swynke" (216). But his summing up of how the law
stands, like that conducted by Conscience in Passus
III and Reason in Passus IV, includes a *distinctio* -
between different kinds of beggars, to supplement
those already made on meed and mercy. The present
one is related to the previous ones in that it, too,
concerns meed and mercy: it bears on the question
of alms, the gifts of mercy, provision of "lyflod"
that spares those who do not or cannot labour for it
the natural penalty of hunger. When should the law
take its course, when should mercy intervene? As
before, it emerges that there are cases where mercy
is legitimate and proper, others where it is not;
cases deserving mercy, and cases undeserving of it.
Those who refuse to work should be denied it almost
totally, and allowed to go hungry; but to the
genuinely unfortunate all the mercy and charity of
the New Law is due in full measure (218-28).

Both Hunger, and Langland through him, are
anxious to emphasize that the rule of "labour for
lyflod" here invoked has the sanction not only of
positive law, but of natural and divine law as well.
Equity underlies all laws, and all laws therefore
agree in enjoining this precept. Of its being in
accord with the divine law Langland makes a special
point. For Piers shows himself a little anxious on
this issue. He knows that all men are his "blody
bretheren", and that Christ bid him "loven hem ech
one" (207-8). And having listened to Hunger's
distinctio, he plainly has misgivings that the
course recommended might be contrary to the mercy
and charity of the New Law, and specifically asks
Hunger: "Mighte I synneles do as thow seist?"
(230). To this query Hunger responds with adamant
energy in the affirmative, citing as his authority
texts taken from all three legal eras of Biblical
history. From the *Tempus Naturae* comes a quotation
from that very first Book of all, in which is
recorded the birth of mankind and the penalty he
incurred for the breach of the first law imposed on
him, "Genesis the geaunt, the engendrour of us
alle", which lays it down that

> ' "*In sudore* and swynk thow shalt thi mete tilie,
> And laboure for thi liflode", and so Oure Lord
>   highte '.

(233-4)

This is re-inforced by a citation from the *Tempus
Legis* (from the Book of Proverbs):

> ' "*Piger pro frigore* no feeld wolde tilie -
> And therfore he shal begge and bidde, and no man
>   bete his hunger" '.

(236-7)

And from the New Law, which did not subvert but
consummate the Old, Hunger takes the parable of the
talents, driving his point home with the irritable
emphasis of the uneuphonious word-play on "mnam":

> 'And bynam hym his mnam for he ne wolde werche,
> And yaf that mnam to hym that ten mnames hadde'.

(241-2)

He ends by reconciling the law of Kynde and the *Lex
Christi* itself on this point, in further illustration of Langland's conviction that the New Law
should never be thought of as dispensing with that
fundamental equity that underlies all laws; in the
present instance, the agreement between the law of
nature and the law of Christ is emphasized by
chiasmic parallelism:

> '*Kynde Wit wolde that ech a wight wroghte*,
> Or in techynge or in tellynge or travaillynge in
>   preieres -
> Contemplatif lif or Actif lif, *Crist wolde men
>   wroghte*'.

(247-9; my italics)

There is one difficulty, however, with the
divine law on this point - a difficulty deferred for
fuller recognition in the next Passus. How one is
to distinguish between false and genuine beggars is
not made clear; presumably cases of doubt should be
ruled by the precepts expressed in the lines
appended by Hunger to the second category - the
unfortunate to whom charity should be shown:

> 'Love hem and lakke hem noght - lat God take the
>   vengeaunce;
> Theigh thei doon yvele, lat thow God yworthe:
> *Michi vindictam et ego retribuam*'.

> (225-6*a*)

The texts here cited, however, suggest that the
proper response to the problem according to the
divine law may be other than the discriminatory
course proposed to Piers by Hunger. They imply
that it is not man's place to judge his neighbour,
but to love him, leaving the role of punitive
correction to God. Thus while the divine law does
indeed enjoin the earning of "lyflod" through
labour, spiritual or physical, it also appears to
deny the authority to enforce this rule against
others who break it. At this point, Langland finds
it most convenient to ignore the conflict so hinted
at, though his honesty will not allow him to ignore
it a second time when he meets it again in the
following Passus. He there finds himself at one
point firmly re-asserting Hunger's law about discrimination in the bestowing of alms:

> Caton kenneth me thus, and the Clerc of the Stories:
> *Cui des, videto* is Catons techyng;
> And in the Stories he techeth to bistowe thyn
>   almesse:
> *Sit elemosina tua in manu tua donec studes cui des.*

> (71-3)

This time, however, he specifically acknowledges
with an *Ac* ('But ...') that the divine law does not
unequivocally endorse this course of action:

> Ac Gregory was a good man, and bad us gyven alle
> That asketh for His love that us al leneth:
> *Non eligas cui miserearis, ne forte pretereas illum
>   qui meretur accipere; quia incertum est pro quo
>   Deo magis placeas.*

> (74-75*a*)

Here he recognizes more fully the prohibition
against presuming to judge hinted at in Hunger's
speech. As so often in Langland, a problem realized
as a subterranean presence in one Passus proceeds to
surface in a later one. And the narrator is
obviously pained and puzzled by this discovery that

the law of God forbids the course justice suggests
should be taken against those who defy that law.
The matter remains far from settled even in Passus
VII, though it is then acknowledged. The seeming
contradiction turns out to be, in fact, the first
of many that gradually force upon Langland the
consciousness that there is a basic conflict between
his aims as a Christian and his aims as a social
reformer: between his desire to save his soul by
observing the law of God, and his desire to reform
society by compelling others likewise to observe
the authority of that and all derivative laws.
Christianity, he is increasingly to find, will not
serve him in the latter ambition, and does not
address itself to the problems inherent in
realizing it. Not that Christianity has nothing to
say on social matters; on the subject of how one
should behave toward one's neighbour, it has, as
Langland recognized, a great deal very much to the
point to say - both in the ten commandments of the
Old Law, and in the New Law precept, "Whatsoever ye
would that men should do to you, do ye even so to
them" (Mt.7:12), both based on justice and fairness,
and used by Langland as the 'route' to Truth (V.564-
82). But it works to reform from within, not from
without. It has nothing to offer the would-be
reformer of others, bidding the just man to attend
rather to the beam in his own eye than the mote in
his neighbour's, to refrain from judging that he be
not judged, to extend love and charity to all,
leave vengeance to the Lord, and exhorting to
forbearance, suffrance, patience, in the necessary
disciplining of his own soul to meekness. It has
very little to offer those who desire to correct
others (not necessarily an unworthy aim) as well as
themselves. It lays down rules, but refuses to all
but conscience the authority to enforce them. It
is thus in the poem Conscience alone who is finally
left to enjoy this authority, such as it is: and
very helpless he finds himself to correct the
errors of those whose own consciences have ceased
to reprove them.[12] Christianity is ultimately
proved by its very nature to resist becoming the
institutional reality Langland's piously authoritative nature would like to make of it, and to
be inevitably vulnerable to infiltration and
'entrism': the friars enter through "Hende-Speche",
through that very charitable welcome Christianity
itself bids should be extended to all.

Langland's realistic assessment of the
obstinate recalcitrance to justice human nature,
ruled by self-interest, will always offer shows
itself not just in his acknowledgement that hunger
is more persuasive than precept; but also in his
realization that the salutary effects even of hunger
will last no longer than hunger itself. Piers
himself foresees that the meek obedience to his law
hunger has effected will endure only as long as
Hunger is there to police that law:

> 'For I woot wel, be thow went, thei wol werche ful
>   ille;
> Meschief it maketh thei be so make nouthe,
> And for defaute of hire foode this folk is at my
>   wille'.

> (204-6)

He proves "too true an augurer". When Hunger is
rocked to sleep at harvest time, the workers soon
allow his lesson also to fall into oblivion, and
resume their old selfish and demanding ways:

> And tho wolde Wastour noght werche, but wandren
>   aboute,
> Ne no beggere ete breed that benes inne were,
> But of coket and clermatyn or ellis of clene whete,
> Ne noon halfpeny ale in none wise drynke,
> But of the beste and the brunneste that brewesteres
>   selle.
> Laborers that have no land to lyve on but hire
>   handes
> Deyned nought to dyne aday nyght-olde wortes;
> May no peny ale hem paie, ne no pece of bacoun,
> But if it be fressh flessh outher fisshe fryed outher
>   ybake -
> And that *chaud* and *plus chaud* for chillynge of hir
>   mawe.
> And but if he be heighliche hyred, ellis wole he
>   chide.

> (302-12)

The implicit assumption here that it is unbearable
presumption in the working classes to be choosy
about their food is calculated to offend somewhat
the more democratic sensibilities of our own age.
Yet that is precisely what Langland is suggesting.
These men are mere 'beggars' and landless labourers;
and yet they, as the snatches of French suggest,
are aspiring to *haute cuisine*, affecting delicate

stomachs, and, dissatisfied with the *table d'hote*, are developing on *à la carte* choosiness most unbefitting their station. Langland's original readers would have appreciated the force of the charge. His was a society intensely conscious of hierarchy. The blurring of social distinctions struck them as an impious affront to the ordained order of the universe, conducing not only to social and political, but even to moral and spiritual chaos. The threat to the clarity of these distinctions (posed by the increasing prosperity of the lower and middle classes) they sought desperately to ward off by, for instance, passing 'sumptuary' statutes that carefully specified what kind of dress, ornamentation and food was proper to what estates.[13] If 'order' perished, confusion only could reign ("If degree is vizarded ..."). When, in the poem *Winner and Waster*, Waster asks,

> 'Woldeste þou hafe lordis to lyfe as laddes on fote?
> Prelates als prestes þat þe parishen ʒemes?
> Proude marchandes of pris, as pedders in towns?'

> (375-7)

a modern reader is tempted to reply, 'Why not?' But to Waster it is a rhetorical question only, assuming the answer 'God forbid!' And he proceeds to outline the distinctions in diet and life-style that should properly be perpetuated if the established social order is to survive:

> 'Late lordes lyfe als þam liste, laddes as þam falles, -
> þay þe bacon & beefe, þay botours & swannes,
> þay þe roughe of þe rye, þay þe rede whete,
> þay þe grewell gray, & þay þe gude sewes

> (378-81)

A society that so jealously guarded hierarchical order would readily have responded to the implications of the charge of forgetfulness of their station Langland here levels at his labourers. They would have accepted it as symptomatic of that flouting of the due moral order that Langland more generally accuses them of. In his own words, they do not "knowe (their) owene"; a fault analogous with their forgetfulness likewise of the law of fair exchange, "labour for lyflod", and of the larger justice of which it is part and which directs to 'take

211

but one's own' - the rule of "measure for measure"
now violated in their unwillingness longer to work
for "mesurable hyre": they now want to be "heigh-
liche hyred", to take more than is fair measure for
the labour given in return.
     They proceed to indulge in that sin which in
Middle English went by the distinctive term
"grucchyng", complaining about their lot in life,
and criticising their superiors:

> And that he was werkman wroght warie the tyme.
> Ayeins Catons counseil comseth he to jangle:
> *Paupertatis onus pacienter ferre memento.*
> He greveth hym ageyn God and gruccheth ageyn Reson,
> And thanne corseth he the Kyng and al his Counseil
>   after
> Swiche lawes to loke, laborers to greve.

(313-17)

Although the Marxist rhetoric of the down-trodden
proletariat had not yet developed in Langland's day,
he has here, especially at 313 and 317, anticipated
it, catching the authentic note of self-righteous
whining against the 'bosses'. Though far from
unsympathetic to the sufferings of the 'poor and
oppressed', Langland did not, like other literary
champions of the group (such as Dickens, for
instance), romanticize them. He has already shown
in the fable of the rats and mice, and shows here
again, that their misfortunes do not prove them
morally superior to the rich; given half the
chance, they would be, and are, just as greedy and
self-seeking.
     More important in the above lines is the
demonstration that what is being resisted is the
law - the law on all its three levels of natural,
positive, and divine. They resist the law of God
and the instinctive sense of right and wrong given
to man in the form of his reason (315), and the law
of the land (the Statute of Labourers) as duly
decreed by the King in Council (*Praecepta Regis sunt
nobis vincula legis?*). However, Langland has
already shown that he thinks Hunger the only
infallible guarantor of that law; and he here
repeats his faith in that ultimate providential
dimension of justice which alone seems capable of
enforcing it through penal correction. And this
time he specifically attaches a legal and judicial
role to such providential catastrophes:

> Ac whiles Hunger was hir *maister*, ther wolde noon
> of hem chide,
> Ne stryven ayeins his *statut*, so sterneliche he
> loked!
> Ac I warne yow werkmen - wynneth whil ye mowe,
> For Hunger hiderward hasteth hym faste!
> He shal awake thorugh water, wastours to *chaste*,
> Er fyve yer be fulfilled swich famyn shal aryse:
> Thorugh flodes and thorugh foule wedres, fruytes shal
> faille -
> And so seith Saturne and sent yow to warne:
> Whan ye se the mone amys and two monkes heddes,
> And a mayde have the maistrie, and multiplie by
> eighte,
> Thanne shal deeth withdrawe and derthe be *justice*,
> And Daw the Dykere deye for hunger -
> But if God of his goodnesse graunte us a trewe.

(318-330; my italics)

Again, the apocalyptic mode gives a vent to
Langland's idealism without prejudice to his realism.
It allows him to assert his faith that the insult to
law and justice will not go for ever unpunished,
that the law will find its champion in the penal
visitations of providence, if nowhere else; but,
conversely, there emerges the melancholy implication that providence is the only thing that will
and can fulfil this policing role. Like the
previous two passūs, then, this one ends on a note
of moral conviction qualified by one of practical
pessimism. For it, like them, has adduced the rule
of "measure for measure" in which Langland has
absolute faith; but whether others can be brought
to understand and observe it, whether the law can be
enforced, remains very much a moot point.

II: *Passus VII*

It is highly fitting that the *Visio* should
culminate in a Passus that centres on a problematic
pardon. The poem has from the first been concerned
to establish justice or Truth as the essential
attribute of God and good living, and to insist that
mercy itself obeys that divine principle and can
never run counter to "doom of Right". Passus IV has
identified what, in the context of human law, would
be illegitimate mercy; Passus V has set on foot a
sequence that, according to the law of Holy Church,
ought to lead to an officially authenticated

'pardon': confession → amends → pardon[14] (moral
and formal amends - reform of ways and undertaking
a pilgrimage - have been conflated by the allegory,
as the practical amends of undertaking an honest in
place of a dishonest way of life (the ploughing of
the half-acre) is accepted as doing duty also for
the formal penitence of pilgrimage). Church indulgences were available at the shrines of saints that
formed the goals of penitential pilgrimages.
Surely these pilgrims to the shrine of Truth itself
will find at the end of their journey of the true
penitential amends of reformed ways an equivalent
pardon: find, indeed, the "pleyn pardon" (102),
plenary indulgence, or "plenyr remyssyon" that the
inveterate pilgrim Margery Kempe found on offer at
some of the most important shrines of the Holy
Land.[15] This would be a mercy that Reason/Justice
itself has been heard to sanction: a mercy earned,
not bought by meed, given in consideration not of
monetary amends, but of amended ways (IV.113-144).
    The poem appears at the beginning of the Passus
to be confident that it has identified just such a
legitimate pardon, a mercy in accord with justice
and Truth. For it is a pardon said to issue from
Truth itself, and the allegorical implication that
it is therefore entirely consistent with the true
justice that "rewardeth ryht as men deserveth"
seems borne out by the facts. It is to be the
reward of those who have led with Piers the honest
and useful social life he stands for. For the Passus
begins by indicating allegorically, with a logic
most readers perfectly assent to, that truth is more
truly 'sought' and reached thus than through any
literal journey of pilgrimage, and that, for the
folk in the field of this world, such social
integrity, payment of the debt of labour owed for
"lyflod", is itself the road that leads to true or
just pardon:

> Treuthe herde telle herof, and to Piers sente
> To taken his teme and tilien the erthe,
> And purchaced hym a pardoun *a pena et a culpa*
> For hym and for hise heires for everemoore after;
> And bad hym holde hym at home and erien hise leyes,
> And alle that holpen hym to erye, to sette or to
>   sowe,
> Or any maner mestier that myghte Piers availe -
> Pardoun with Piers Plowman Truthe hath ygraunted.

(1-8)

There follows what appears to be a more particular enumeration of the types of persons
referred to in 6-8 as the recipients of this papal
indulgence, which is the allegorical documentary
form taken by the pardon (19,38,64) - a bull issued
by the Pope, the supreme authority in the Church,
the ecclesiastical 'head of law' himself. From
this, too (9-104), there emerges further confirmation of its perfect consistency with that essential
principle of justice "ensaumpled" by Reason: *nullum
malum inpunitum, nullum bonum irremuneratum*. Those
who do no good are excluded; and those who do no
evil are included. That is what this passage
asserts. Much of it is written in the universal
present ("Kynges and knyghtes ... *Han* pardon";
"Bysshopes yblessed ... *Arn* peres with the Apostles
- this pardon Piers *sheweth*"; "laborers ... *Haveth*
the same absolucion that sent was to Piers";
"Beggeres ... *beth* noght in the bulle"; "olde men
and hore ... *Han* as pleyn pardon as the Plowman
hymselve"); and thus stands half way between
narrative and interpretation. The tense is not
inconsistent with medieval narrative style, which
moved freely between the past and what may be called
the 'dramatic' narrative present tense. But the
transition to it here also suggests that the narrator
is at this point stepping in to interpret his own
allegory, to explain exactly what a pardon from
Truth to the 'heirs' of Piers, and to those who
perform "any maner mestier that myghte (him) availe",
means. It means that those who benefit society by
performing faithfully their role in it will be
acknowledged by that Truth that is the ultimate head
of the divine law; such men "knowe (their) owene",
execute their offices to the "commune profit" those
offices should serve. Those who have no claim to
be called Piers's heirs or work-mates are those who
defraud or exploit the community or otherwise abuse
their roles in it to the detriment of the common
good; such are not to be numbered among the just,
and will therefore be deleted from the *liber
viventium*, as Piers had declared (VI.75), and so do
not figure in this 'bull'.
This passage, then, spells out in detail just
what inclusion in the Bull as an heir of Piers
involves for all the different degrees of society -
beginning, significantly, with the guardians of
human and divine law, who are once more placed in
telling juxtaposition. The kings and the knighted
aristocracy, whose business it is to "kepen Holy

Chirche And rightfully in remes rulen the peple
(9-10), are followed by bishops, the aristocrats of
the ecclesiastical hierarchy, who have an equivalent
duty of guidance and correction with regard to the
divine law: should indeed by "Legistres of bothe
lawes, the lewed therwith to preche, And in as muche
as thei mowe amenden alle synfulle", 14-15). To
those who faithfully observe the duties so specified
Langland promises rewards that offer a nice definition of the relationship between the two laws.
They will be ranked in heaven with the representatives of the Old and of the New Law respectively.
The first

> Han pardon thorugh purgatorie to passen ful lightly,
> With patriarkes and prophets in paradis to be
> felawe.

(11-12)

While the bishops ("if thei ben as thei sholde", 13)

> Arn peres with the Apostles - this pardon Piers
> sheweth -
> And at the day of dome at the heighe deys to sitte.

(16-17)

Human law stands to divine law as the Old Law to the
New Law: figure to reality, imperfect foreshadowing
to perfected fulfilment.
    Merchants are the one group who are treated as
'marginal' cases: they have "manye yeres" in "the
margyne", but not full pardon *a pena et a culpa* (18-19).
Langland's objection to the profession is not to the
practice of buying and selling at a profit *per se*,
but is of a rather more technical kind: their
calling more or less requires them to disregard
"halidayes" (which should be work-free), and to use
such common asseverations as 'by my soul' and 'God
help me' to support rather exaggerated claims for
their wares in order to sell them (20-22). On the
other hand, by the criterion of "commune profit",
Langland shows that he appreciated the fact that the
money earned by private enterprise could often be
ploughed back into the community in ways immensely
beneficial to it. In fact, many of the enterprises
today funded by the Welfare State (the education of
the poor, the maintenance of roads and bridges, the
foundation of hospitals) were in his day financed
from private capital bequeathed or donated by pious
merchants. He therefore represents mercantile

activity as specifically sanctioned by Truth
himself, on the condition that the profits be
invested in such works of public charity; they
must

> ... save the wynnyng,
> And amende mesondieux thermyd and myseise folk
>   helpe;
> And wikkede weyes wightly amende,
> And do boote to brugges that tobroke were;
> Marien maydenes or maken hem nonnes;
> Povere peple and prisons fynden hem hir foode,
> And sette scolers to scole or to some othere
>   craftes;
> Releve Religion and renten hem bettre.

>   (25-32)

The curative effects of such injections of private
capital are emphasized by the verbs "amende" and
"do boote to": physical structures, roads, bridges,
buildings, are as effectually restored to health by
them as are the sick and the needy. And justice is
effectively satisfied by such acts of 'amends': at
their death, such merchants are promised the protection of St. Michael himself (33). That is, the
very scales of justice, "seinte Mihales weie",[16]
will favour them, as is implied in the personal
sanction granted their activities by Truth. Such
tangible evidence of benefit to the commonalty
must establish them as the work-mates of Piers,
whose aim it is to ensure that all contribute to
"commune profit" and do nought to hinder "plentee
among the peple".
    Langland nicely manipulates the allegory at
this point to provide a legal analogy for the
justification of mercantile activity despite the
rather minor offences against Truth it involves.
Pope Truth obviously cannot openly countenance such
clear infraction of His laws as breaking His church's
regulations and lying evidently constitute; but He
does give the merchants a dispensation 'under his
secret seal' nevertheless to proceed without
misgiving:

> Ac under his secret seel Truthe sente hem a lettre,
> And bad hem buggen boldely what hem best best
>   liked, *etc*

>   (23-4)

The allegory is here borrowing an analogy from the

famous 'dispensing' power of the King and the Pope, as heads of their respective laws. Where, in peculiar and anomolous circumstances, laws were thought to operate against the interests of the justice they were designed to serve, a dispensation under the privy or secret seal could be granted, by the King (in secular matters) or the Pope (in ecclesiastical). This is the logic employed here. Pope Truth can dispense under privy seal (*dispensare in secreto*), where for some reason the truth His laws are designed to serve are more honoured in the breach than in the observance. Though technically infringing it, the merchants may actually in the process most effectually further the interests of truth, by conducing to social justice: hence they require a dispensation under the secret seal.

Langland, then, raises no objection to trade as in itself a morally questionable career; indeed, mercantile abilities are later included in the list of talents bestowed on men by Grace to enable them to earn an honest living (XIX.235-6). Other moralists had come to the same conclusion. Commerce was in theory a perfectly legitimate activity, provided that even measure as between labour and gain, and consumption and need, was observed: that is, so long as profits were commensurate with efforts, and surplus over needs was distributed in alms and public works to satisfy the needs of others.[17] They did, however, like Langland, show themselves concerned at the perjuries merchants inevitably committed in crying up their wares, and with their frequent (and often necessary) breaches of the prohibition against Sunday trading.[18] Langland's reservations are specifically on these counts, but he grants them a dispensation on the grounds, apparently, of these being almost inevitable evils attendant on activity which nevertheless benefitted the community if carried on by men of integrity. For it was "necessity, utility, or just cause" that was held properly to justify the exercise of the papal dispensing power.[19]

Excluded from the Bull are the two prime representatives of the occupational vices of venality and idleness discerned in the Prologue: "the Men of lawe ... that pleteden for mede" (39-59), who sell justice and law itself; and the "Beggeres and bidderes" (64-97) who refuse to pay the debt of labour for "lyflod", and live on eternal social credit, "borwen everemo" (80). The contrast the two groups had presented in the Prologue with those who "putten hem to the plough ... swonken ful harde", is repeated here. For between them are placed the

honest labourers (60-3), who have "the same
absolucion" as the Ploughman himself, and whose true
and equitable taking thus contrasts with the
iniquitous receipts of those who precede and follow
them. For the "laborers" who "treweliche taken and
treweliche wynnen, And lyven in love and in law",
and are of "lowe herte", epitomize all that
Langland has striven to establish as truth, or
iustitia: they are the law-abiding, the meek, the
debt-free. They have incurred no debts to society
through taking what is not truly due them.

With the lawyers, Langland adds something to
the arguments he has already advanced (III.230-58)
on the distinction between the unlawful receipt of
'meed' by the clerks of God's law and man's, and
the lawful 'hire' taken by other labourers. Why is
it that only hire taken by them amounts to a meed
that precludes the meed of heaven? For Langland
here condemns not only lawyers who take bribes,
munera super innocentem (41), as before, but also
any who take "any mede of mene men for hit motyng"
(58) - who demand fees from those who cannot afford
them. He here reveals that it is, in fact, any kind
of system that makes justice inaccessible to "the
povere That is innocent and nedy and no man
apeireth" (46-7) that he objects to, whether the
meed prejudicial to their interests takes the form
of bribes from the rich, or fees beyond the reach
of slender means. His first solution is implicitly
to define free pleading for the poor as a kind of
verbal alms, assuring the meed of heaven to him
"that spendeth his speche and speketh for the
povere" (46), in the same way that the givers of
coin to the needy are later promised repayment with
interest in heaven (80-81*a*). But he then advances
a more radical thesis which would make it quite
illegitimate for clergy, the "lered", secular or
sacred, ever to take remuneration for their
services:

> Ac to bugge water, ne wynd, ne wit, ne fir the
>   ferthe -
> This foure the Fader of Hevene made to this foold in
>   commune:
> Thise ben Truthes tresores trewe folk to helpe,
> That nevere shul wex ne wanye withouten God hymselve.

(52-5

'Wit' is thus added to the list of those things God
gave "in commune" to all, and which all are therefore

entitled to have access to. No-one can have
property in the truth which knowledge - moral,
rational, or natural - discerns.[20] The "lered" are
therefore but the treasurers of Truth; the coin is
not theirs to trade with, but to distribute among
their lord's "meynee" (for whom it was a lord's
duty to provide), the "trewe". The thesis further
equates lawyers and clergy, for the bishop has
likewise been compared with the steward-treasurer of
'our Lord', charged with distributing His wealth
among that lord's people, and due to render accounts
of "what he *lerned* yow in Lente ... And what he
lente yow of Oure Lordes good" (V.295-6). Each
profession has special understanding of the laws
designed to guide men on the way to truth. The very
purpose of law is thus frustrated if their learning
is not freely distributed among all.

In denying law to the poor, lawyers thus
defraud the needy of their rights in Truth's
'treasure'. And it is in this that the two vices
of venality and idleness come together:

> For he that beggeth or bit, but if he have nede,
> He is fals with the feend and defraudeth the nedy,
> And also gileth the gyvere ageynes his wille.

(66-8)

Guile, the most insidious form of the fraud contrary
to justice, is later defined as the one things
Justice must fear (XIX.301). This group 'defraud
the needy' by taking the alms intended for them,
and thus upsetting the equitable distribution of
the totality of resources available to meet the sum
of human needs. They live in gluttony and in sloth
(Prol.43-5); VI.143); and, as Gluttony and Sloth
had done, they remove from circulation what should
be available to serve the needs of others (V.374,
439). The obstacles thus thrown in the way of
Piers in his efforts to bring "plentee among the
peple" cause Langland now sternly to re-iterate the
substance of Hunger's counsel to Piers: *Cui des,
videto* (72).[21] But, as already indicated, he now
faces squarely the conflict between this directive
of the social reformer and the Christian prohibition
on presuming to judge one's bretheren. Gregory, he
suddenly recalls, was 'a good man', and forbade such
discrimination: *Non eligas cui miserearis, ne forte
pretereas illum qui meretur accipere; quia incertum
est pro quo Deo magis placeas* (75a). This results
in a long passage of uncertain direction, in which

Langland struggles manfully to reconcile himself to
this the revealed but inexplicable will of his Lord,
only to find his anger breaking out the more
violently from his attempt to restrain it. Obediently retracting his warning *Cui des, videto*, he
attempts to console himself for the possible
miscarriage of justice that might follow on indiscriminate alms-giving by reflections based on what
for him is the guiding logic of credit and debt.
He who gives is paying in to his moral account,
building up credit in heaven, where the interest
rate to depositors is a good one. For God acts as
"borgh", or surety, for what is lent to all
beggars, good or bad, and so the lender need not
fear loss of his moral investment through backing
the wrong horse. It is those who take who stand
to incur literal and moral debt:

> For wite ye nevere who is worthi - ac God woot
>   who hath nede.
> In hym that taketh is the trecherie, if any treson
>   walke -
> For he that yeveth, yeldeth, and yarketh hym to
>   reste,
> And he that biddeth, borweth, and bryngeth hymself
>   in dette.
> For beggeres borwen everemo, and hir borgh is God
>   Almyghty -
> To yelden hem that yeveth hem, and yet usure moor.

> (76-81)

But the image back-fires, as the thought of men not
constrained to do so living on eternal credit,
fraudulently obtaining advances on the basis of
God's suretyship of need, makes Langland's anger
break out anew, and the intended consolation to
deceived donors ends in stern warning to donees:

> Forthi biddeth noght, ye beggeres, but if ye have
>   gret nede.

> (82)

With righteous severity he tells them that, have
they but bread enough to put in their mouths, they
have no business to ask for more, and should 'solace'
themselves with recalling the lives of voluntary
need led by the saints (83-5). There follows what
would amount to the most radical condemnation of *all*
forms of begging he has yet offered. No matter what
Gregory said, the life of a debtor the beggar lives

221

is actually cursed by a just God ("The Book banneth
beggarie", 86), he claims. This would be difficult
to substantiate, but Langland has lost his temper,
and offers as his authority only a decidedly forced
interpretation of the text, "I have been young, and
now am old; yet I have not seen the just forsaken,
nor his seed begging bread" (Ps.36:25). To interpret this assertion of faith in God's loyalty to
His own as an implicit curse on beggary, as an
activity the 'just' man, the true seed of a just
God, simply would not by definition engage in, is
perverse.[22] But Langland is beyond caring, and now
launches into the most vitriolic denunciation yet
of the life of the pseudo-beggars:

> For thei lyve in no love, ne no lawe holde:
> Thei ne wedde no womman that thei with deele,
> But as wilde bestes with 'wehee' worthen uppe and
>   werchen,
> And bryngen forth barnes that bastardes men calleth.
> Or the bak or som boon thei breketh in his youthe,
> And goon and faiten with hire fauntes for everemoore
>   after.
> Ther is moore mysshapen amonges thise beggeres
> Than of alle othere manere men that on this moolde
>   walketh.
> Tho that lyve thus hir lif mowe lothe the tyme
> That evere he was man wroght, when he shal hennes
>   fare.
>
> (88-97)

The brutal and bestial habits here attributed to
this brotherhood of beggars are obviously intended
to carry moral as well as literal significance.
Unlike the true labourers who live "in lawe" (62),
these hold "no lawe", refuse to observe the human
and divine laws that enjoin justice and payment of
debts. As so often in Langland, this lawlessness
expresses itself most vividly in sexual licence,
the disregard for the 'lawful wedlock' within whose
bounds sexual activity should be contained. The
beggars respect no lawful limits in their relations
with women, and the fruit of their actions is
illegitimacy itself. Likewise, the deliberate
maiming and distorting of the human form is clearly
meant to express a larger kind of misshapen
crookedness. Having mutilated that form, they may
indeed come to curse the time they were given it in
more ways than one. For their habits are a
distortion of the true nature of man (made in the

image of God) morally as well as physically.

Langland's tone undergoes an almost comically radical alteration as he remembers to reassure those genuinely incapable of work (98-104) that his strictures do not extend to them. And here we meet the first instance of the converse of the principle of singularity of meed: singularity of punishment. If the scales of justice preclude two rewards for one deserving, they also preclude double *pena*. If heavenly meed is forestalled by earthly meed, so is the divine "pane" for sin by the willing acceptance of an earthly life of "pane" imposed by providence:

> That taken this myschief mekeliche, as mesels and
> othere,
> Han as pleyn pardon as the Plowman hymselve.
> For love of hir lowe hertes Oure Lord hath hem
> graunted
> Hir penaunce and hir Purgatorie upon this pure erthe.

> (101-4)

Single *pena* was, in fact, an important principle of justice in the Middle Ages, being yet another aspect of that devout faith in exact balance between desert and its (punitive or remunerative) hire. It was laid down in the *Decretals* that "God does not judge twice in the same matter" (cf Nahum I:9), and, on the basis of this text, it was held that "the rule always prevails that there ought not to be double punishment".[23] And, in accord with this principle, and with the general commitment to the rule of "measure for measure", the worldly sufferings of the just and innocent were often regarded, as here in Langland, as decreasing by just that amount the purgatorial *pena* due them in the afterlife. Thus Margery Kempe thanks God for her various tribulations, seeing in them "pane in þis world in remissyon of (her) synnys".[24] So here, too, the meek in misfortune are seen as undergoing a vicarious "pane", which will purchase them remission of their sins ("pleyn pardon") and exemption from penalties in the afterlife.

A pardon the application of which could be interpreted as the narrative voice has here intervened to expound it would indeed by a pardon utterly in accord with Reason's justice, leaving *nullum bonum irremuneratum* and *nullum malum impunitum*. And had the *Visio* ended here, it would have described an arc of perfect logic: the first dream sequence would have explored mercy in the context of human law and

justice, and established that a mercy contrary to
justice was false mercy; the second would have
explored mercy in the context of divine justice,
and established the just mercy of God. But this is
not the end of the *Visio*, let alone the end of the
poem, which has another thirteen Passūs to run. All
at once it emerges that the narrator has been
speculating, interpreting his own dream before it
was ended, expounding his own allegory before it
was quite played out. In this, he suffers the fate
of many another interpretative critic of his poem:
he finds that events suddenly slide out from under
the firm grasp of his thesis.

For the above exposition was apparently not
offered with a knowledge of the actual text of the
pardon, which the dreamer has not yet seen, but
which he now presses close to witness, over the
shoulder of an officious priest - who at this point
offers the assembled "lewed" the advantage of his
"lered" ability to read and construe Latin texts
(105-6). For everybody's peace of mind, he had
been much better not to intrude where he was not
invited, and to recall the medieval adage that
office uncommitted stinketh.25 For his "clergial"
intervention serves only to plunge into sudden
confusion the minds of poet, characters, and readers
alike, just as we had all apparently reached such
firm ground.

For the text of the pardon turns out to consist
simply in a two-line quotation from the Athanasian
Creed:

> *Et qui bona egerunt ibunt in vitam eternam;*
> *Qui vero mala, in ignem eternum.*

This the priest accurately and pithily Englishes
thus, declaring it at the same time to constitute
'no pardon':

> 'Peter!' quod the preest tho, 'I kan no pardon
> fynde
> But "Do wel ahd have wel, and God shal have thi
> soule",
> And "Do yvel and have yvel, and hope thow noon oother
> That after thi deeth day the devel shal have thi
> soule!"'

> (111-14)

Whatever we may think of him, his 'construing'
cannot be faulted. Unfortunately, it is limited to

the letter which kills, for as to the spirit that
saves the priest is dumb, and what 'construction' is
to be put on this pardon, in a larger and more
important sense, we are left to decide without his
help. The task is a formidable one, and has claimed
much critical ink.[26] Part of the problem lies in
the fact that two questions are really raised
simultaneously:

(1)   Does the text amount to a pardon, or does it
       refute the whole concept of pardon, by
       asserting that the meed of heaven, *vita
       eterna*, is gained through desert, doing well,
       and not through pardon?

(2)   Are the recipients of the Bull doing well,
       or not? That is, how does the text relate
       to the description of the scope of the Bull
       the narrator has just offered us? Does the
       first stand to the latter as summary to
       exposition, "teme" to "sermoun", principle
       to application? - If so, the text would
       merely epitomize the principle upon which
       the narrator has proceeded in extending or
       denying to the various members of society
       the salvation the Bull promises. Or does
       the text act as a conditional rider to the
       narrator's statements? - If so, those
       the narrator has specified will achieve the
       salvation he promises only *if* they now
       proceed to 'do well'. What, in short, is
       'doing well', and are the folk in the field
       doing it, or is something more than good
       faith in the performance of one's social
       role required?

The first question is really of an intellectual
nature; the second is of immediate practical relevance. Piers goes straight to the second, seeming by
"kyndely knowynge" to understand what he must now
do to 'do well'. The dreamer addresses himself to
the first, comes down in favour of Do Wel, and only
then sets off on his long search through the *Vita*
to identify that character, not noticing that Piers
has shown him the way.
     As to the first, it is sometimes claimed that
the priest is showing a typically narrow "clergial"
pedantry in declaring himself unable to discern any
pardon in the words before him. It *is* a pardon, the
argument runs, only the priest in his blinkered
"leredness" cannot see it.[27] Such a position can be

maintained only by assuming in the reward promised to Do-Wel an implicit pardon of either (a) *original* sin, or (b) such ill as he must inevitably commit as an inherently sinful man. But this is to gloss the text by importing considerations that are not invoked hereabouts in the poem, and to ignore the fundamental conflict between the text of this 'pardon' as it stands and the normal, basic sense of the word (forgiveness of the penalty to wrong-doing). For the words when read appear to leave no scope for the forgiveness of evil, which is what a pardon essentially is: "do yvel" meets only its due penalties of "have yvel" and unremitting fire, *ignis eternus*. The priest seems, therefore, quite correct in saying that the document before him is worded so as to exclude the possibility of pardon, remission of penalties.

In short, we must be careful not to solve the problem by evading it, and by failing to recognize that the text acts in context to explode all the poet's attempts to reconcile mercy (or pardon) with justice. In its assertion of rigorously absolute equity, it throws open once again the whole question of the compatibility of truth and pardon. Can a 'pardon' *ever* emanate from 'Truth'? Can a God who is Justice itself ever send to man a promise other than that embodied in the scales of justice, in which doom is exactly proportioned to deed and desert? If salvation is in the gift of Truth, then this document clearly announces on what principle Truth or Justice will grant or withhold it. The text, at first perhaps so surprising, actually follows with a grim inevitability from the line that introduces it, where the narrator recalls that it comes from Truth: it was "iwriten right thus in witnesse of truthe" (110). An authentic pardon from a God called Truth can be expressed no otherwise than so as to bear witness to His unalterable justice or truth in giving like for like: well for well, and ill for ill. And if Truth speaks thus, then one were better advised to seek Do-Wel than pardon for Do-Yvel. And this the dreamer, after carefully weighing the evidence in favour of the two courses (pardon v do well), closes the *Visio* by asserting to be indeed the case. When you come before that Truth in whose edict remission of penalties cannot figure, your request to 'have well' had better be made on the grounds of 'do well' than on the basis of a 'pokeful of pardon', the concept of which Truth has apparently been revealed by his own non-pardon not to acknowledge.

It is to the theoretical question of whether
salvation should be sought from the mercy that
pardons, or from the justice that gives well in
return for well, that the dreamer addresses himself.
For he realizes that he has been assuming all along a
God of perfect justice, and that he can assume no
other. Langland's God can be nothing other than the
Truth which gives well for well and ill for ill with
unremitting consistency, and "never doth from doom
of right depart".

But to the reader it is the second question
that inevitably presents itself when the 'pardon' is
read. Strict justice is all that is apparently
available from Truth: all that can be 'purchased'
from Him (3,38). Very well. If the poet wants to
point to the fact that He cannot therefore logically
provide a pardon, let him. But we are following a
narrative, and we want to know whether the addressees
of this document have got their pardon - or their
'well' that is the due return for doing well,
whichever the author wants - or not. As story-
readers, we do not particularly care what he chooses
to call it, and what bothers us is probably primarily
the unnervingly general and provisional nature of
the text. What does it mean by refusing to back the
poet in specifying what the *bona* are that merit
vita eterna, and by subtly implying that it has yet
to be established whether the folk in the half-acre
are doing well or ill? The text in context manages
to combine categoric plainness with sphinx-like
impenetrability. We are permitted to know without
a shadow of a doubt that God is just; but we are
forbidden to know more specifically whom He will
save and for what, and whom He will not save.

Besides this inevitable general doubt, a more
particular one arises. In the allegory, the
'pardon' is the reward of a penitential pilgrimage
to Truth. The question of whether Piers's work-
mates are those *qui bona egerunt* to whom it promises
salvation is therefore closely related to this one:
is their work in the half-acre (their faithful
performance of whatever part in society providence
has cast them to play) equivalent to that journey,
or is it not? The poem had decided, at the
beginning of Passus VII, that it was: Truth
specifically commands Piers to stop where he is.
Well, we take the point: more progress toward truth
is made through getting on with one's job than
through going off on those disguised holidays from

work the Prologue has revealed literal pilgrimages often were (46-52). The device is quite in accord with Langland's practice of confronting what most offends him in the world by providing a 'truer' metaphorical version of it: the 'pilgrimage' of labour; the 'meed' of heaven; the 'treasure' of truth; the 'minstrel music' of the poor and disabled, etc.

But it had originally been seen by Piers not as the journey but as preliminary to it:

> "I have an half acre to erie by the heighe weye;
> Hadde I eryed this half acre and sowen it after,
> I wolde wende with yow and the wey teche".

> (VI.4-6)

This is the first we hear about the half-acre. The lines suggest that in Piers's mind there is a progress to be made beyond the honest labour it represents if these folk are to arrive at truth, but that that labour is an essential pre-requisite. The folk must plough the half-acre before they go, because no-one who has not even learned to do an honest day's work in the field of the world can hope to come to any profounder knowledge of the truth that pays all its debts. Moreover, it would be a contradiction in terms if the latter were sought as a beggar, on credit, in the manner of those who "borwen everemo"; one must ensure that one can, in the medieval phrase, 'live of one's own' in the process. No man can pursue truth in debt, or raise the works of justice on a basis of injustice and falsehood. However, there occurs fifty lines on a passage in which the relationship of the labour to the journey seems to have altered somewhat, and to have become in fact ambiguous. At the conclusion of his 'covenant' with the Knight, Piers declares:

> 'And I shal apparaille me', quod Perkyn, 'in
> pilgrymes wise
> And wende with yow I wile til we fynde Truthe'.
> He caste on hise clothes, yclouted and hole,
> His cokeres and hise coffes for cold of hise nailes,
> And heng his hoper at his hals in stede of a
> scryppe:
> 'A busshel of bred corn brynge me therinne,
> For I wol sowe it myself, and sithenes wol I wende
> To pilgrymage as palmeres doon, pardon for to have.

228

> And whoso helpeth me to erie or sowen here er I
> wende', *etc.*

(VI.57-65)

Here, the labour seems both to be and not to be
the pilgrimage itself. The pilgrim's clothes in
which Piers promises to apparel himself are interpreted by the *narrative* to refer merely to the
ordinary working clothes he dons to attend to the
immediate task of ploughing the half-acre, which
implies that that honest 'swink' is itself the
'pilgrimage' to truth. But in Piers's *own* mind,
the journey is still something subsequent upon the
labour, and the 'pardon' consequent upon a pilgrimage undertaken after it: he will plough, and
"*sithenes* wende To pilgrimage"; sowing and earing
are something to be done "er" he goes. One could
regard the ambiguity here merely as evidence of a
transitionary stage in the allegory, anticipating
the equivalence of labour and journey to be stated
at the beginning of Passus VII. But in context,
the significance appears otherwise: if the labour
is part of the journey, it is only the first leg;
it is to be succeeded by some purely religious act,
some activity done for God's sake alone and not
for the world, and it is on this that the ultimate
goal of the 'pardon' depends. Piers is to set his
own house in order, his own private peasant-holding
of the half-acre, but is then to proceed to pay the
debt of labour he owes on the estate of the lord
whose tenant he is - the estate he has described at
V.539ff and had promised to guide the penitents to.
He is to labour for himself, and then for his lord.
    This would accord with the medieval conception
of the lesser and the greater perfection constituted
by the active and the contemplative life respectively (the two kinds of 'work' which Hunger in the
same Passus declares Christ to have enjoined on
man, 249): honest secular employment in the service
of the world, and the labour of the spirit in
prayer, penance, and meditation in the service of
God and in renunciation of the world. This
bipartite view of virtue is reflected in the actual
practices of the time: the pious would often end
their days in a monastery, on the principle that,
once their 'active' life was over, their declining
days should be dedicated to God alone. The younger
years belong to the service of the world and society
and "commune profit", to one's neighbour; the older
to God.[28]

229

This is precisely the reasoning Piers employs
at the opening of his will (VI.83-104). Now that he
is "old and hoor", the time has come for him to pass
from secular to religious labour, as other old men
do:

> 'For now I am old and hoor and have of myn owene,
> To penaunce and to pilgrimage I wol passe with thise
>   othere;
> Forthi I wole er I wende do write my bequeste'.

There are, however, two elements in the temporal
clause of 83. Langland's view of the moral relationship between the active and the contemplative,
secular and religious labour, has a practical as
well as an evaluative dimension. The religious
succeeds the secular, not just as age youth, and
better well, but also because the latter gives one
the means to pursue the former at one's own expense,
and not at other people's, as a borrowing beggar. -
Hence the field must be ploughed before the pilgrimage can begin. As a result of his active life of
secular labour, Piers now 'has of his own', and can
pay all his debts and still have, as Sloth had
hoped to have, a "residue and a remenaunt" on which
to subsist now that he intends to do something more
than simply pay his own way in the world. With the
'residue and the remnant' of what he has saved from
his life of labour, then, Piers is now to 'pass' to
pilgrimage. But we may ask in what the transition
consists, since his new life appears to be indistinguishable from his old:

> "And with the residue and the remenaunt, by the Rode
>   of Lukes!
> I wol worshipe therwith Truthe by my lyve,
> And ben His pilgrym atte plow for povere mennes sake.
> My plowpote shal be my pikstaf, and picche atwo the
>   rotes,
> And helpe my cultour to kerve and clense the furwes".
>   Now is Perkyn and thise pilgrimes to the plow
>   faren.

(VI.100-5)

While the words "worshipe therwith Truthe" and "ben
His pilgrym" imply a new dedication of his energies
to purely religious ends, there is to be no change
in the physical nature of Piers's activities. There
is, however, to be a change in their aim and
intention. He is henceforth to plough, not simply

in honest labour for his own "lyflod", but "for
povere mennes sake". It is in this that the transition from secular to religious implied in the
pilgrimage to succeed the plough lies. It is not a
physical but a spiritual change, in motivation and
disposition. Piers is to use his achieved indep-
endence, not to renouce his work for a higher
activity, but to continue it for the profit of
others and not simply for himself, purely out of
love of God and his neighbour in Him - out of
charity, in fact.

For what Piers has done is to move from truth,
in the sense of honest fairness, to charity: the
movement described by Holy Church's discourse in
Passus I (which begins with an emphasis on truth,
but ends with one on the love that gives freely,
which is both essential to, and yet greater than
truth); and by the poem as a whole, which begins
in the *Visio* with a God of Truth, but finds the
search develops into one for charity. It is the
vis transitionis: the power of the pass-over from
the Old to the New Law, which is both a fulfilment
of the Old and greater than it.[29] Piers is now
doing more than the man who 'truly takes and truly
wins'; he is doing something *ex gratia*, something
not required by simple truth. What he is giving
"for povere mennes sake" is not just his labour and
the fruits of his labour (which he promises free to
the disabled and to religious in "almesse", 137,146);
but also the free gift of his 'wit' in becoming an
'overseer' to guide, instruct, and control - giving
freely that law the men of law will be damned for
selling - from pure love of Truth. He is thus in
many ways already an anticipatory model for Do-Best,
as it is later to be cumulatively defined: in the
charity that gives freely; in the exercise of
moral authority; and in 'being bold to blame the
guilty', obtaining the right to do so from having
always himself obeyed the law they infringe.[30]

Both Piers and the folk are 'pilgrims' then;
but in different ways. They are pilgrims as the
image is being used generally and negatively by the
narrative to indicate a 'course of life' rather than
a physical progression, and as literal pilgrimage
is due to be expressly ruled out by Truth. But
Piers is a pilgrim according to his own more
specific and positive use of the image, by which it
represents not "labour for lyflod" itself, but something that labour is a preliminary to. When, there-
for, the narrator cancels the entire notion of a
pilgrimage yet to take place, and grants the pardon

originally seen as consequent upon the pilgrimage ("pilgrymage ... pardon for to have") to the labour that was in fact to have been preliminary to it, he is considerably relaxing what Piers had originally seen as the pre-condition of the pardon. He is treating the intended pilgrimage as if it had been a literal one, which, in fact, it had never been: the journey Piers is to take them on is a moral one (V.566ff), and Piers's own 'passage to pilgrimage' involves no literal scrip or pikestaff. And he is thereby allowing less than Piers had originally envisaged as the purchase price of the pardon, which was at first seen as the reward of some *allegorical* pilgrimage, some disinterested act performed for the love of Truth alone, to suceed the labour, which was to have been a mere preliminary to it.

When the pardon is read, the question of whether the allegorical pilgrimage it was to be the reward of has or has not taken place recurs. The dreamer himself appears to revert to Piers's logic, when he proceeds in Passus VIII to set off on his own pilgrimage to seek the Do Wel that merits *vita eterna*, from which one deduces he does not after all assume himself to have located it in the honest labour of the half-acre. Once more, he seems to have been right first time, and wrong second (or rather, Piers was right, and he was wrong): what merits *vita eterna* is, after all, something more than "labour for lyflod", as he had originally implied; the pilgrimage is subsequent, and not simultaneous. As with Mede and Wrong, Langland has allowed us to moderate a hard line only to re-assert it and show us how imperceptibly we have been beguiled into relaxing it.

So Piers was apparently right in seeing 'pardon' as the reward of some figurative pilgrimage for which labour was but a pre-requisite, some activity beyond honest labour, and the poem wrong in equating the two. This is perhaps scarcely surprising in view of the fact that Piers knows he has "kynde knowynge" of Truth (V.538), where the dreamer knows he has none (I.138).

There is one other factor to be taken into account in determining whether or not the folk of the half-acre qualify for the 'meed' of heaven the Bull promises to Do Wel. This is Conscience's speech on meed, and on the distinction between meed and 'measurable hire', at III.230ff. From that it had emerged that 'meed' was the term given to the

payment or reward of the works of justice (commonly
defined as doing one's duty, what one owes and
ought, *debet*, giving all men their due). Justice
and hire are, as it was often pointed out, anti-
pathetic, for no-one ought to take hire for what he
owes it to Truth and to his neighbour to do anyway.
Any extra *ex gratia* reward cannot therefore be
called hire, since justice merely gives what is
already due, and is therefore 'owed' no payment.
Its reward is therefore termed meed, and is received
justly from God in the afterlife, or iniquitously
on earth. All other works may take such payment as
constitute "mesurable hire" on the principle of
"*Dignus est operarius* his hire to have". The payment taken by providers of various goods and
services, therefore, constitute 'hire', and does not
disqualify the recipients from the 'meed' of
heaven. Payment for the works of justice, however,
is meed, and is taken by those concerned at their
peril, for it pre-empts the meed of heaven. Legal
officials and priests are therefore forbidden to
sell what it is everyone's right to have access to:
'wit', knowledge of the law, divine and human.
Similarly, every man *qui operatur iustitiam* will
receive the 'meed' of heaven, providing he has
received no other 'meed', that is, payment for
doing what he owes it to Truth to do anyway:

> 'Tho that entren of o colour and of one wille,
> And han ywroght werkes with right and with reson,
> And he that useth noght the lyf of usurie
> And enformeth povere men and pursueth truthe ...
> And alle that helpen the innocent and holden with
> the rightfulle,
> *Withouten mede* doth hem good and the truthe
> helpeth -
> Swich manere men, my lord, shul have this firste
> mede
> Of God at a gret nede, whan thei gon hennes'.

> (238-45)

Hence Piers will take no payment for 'informing
poor men' of the way to truth (V.557-9). And he
knows that the 'pardon' that gives the meed of
heaven will follow not on his life of honest labour
for "mesurable hire", but on a 'pilgrimage' out of
that life in which he will labour freely "for povere
mennes sake", out of disinterested love of Truth
alone. For the meed of heaven is given to those
works of Christian truth and justice which are done

without the incentive of earthly hire or meed,
"withouten mede".

Now, his co-labourers are not in the same
position. They are working for "mesurable hire".
This they are perfectly entitled to ask, as
Conscience had made clear; and this in itself
constitutes an essential first step on the road to
Truth: they thereby avoid the offence of injustice
constituted by defrauding society by taking from it
more than is a 'commensurate' return for what they
put in. But they have yet to progress to those
disinterested works freely performed for love of
Truth for which the payment is not hire but meed -
which, in short, will receive their reward in
heaven. At present they are merely out of debt, not
in credit for 'meed'. Piers, however, is modelled
of the same clay as Chaucer's Ploughman, who
laboured not only for himself, but also "For Cristes
sake, for every povere wight, *Withouten hire*, if it
lay in his myght" (*CT*.I.537-8).

It is only now that the logic of the pilgrimage
to follow, and the freely-given *iusticia* that earns
meed, becomes apparent in all its rigour. Salvation
is a much tougher proposition than had at first
appeared. The hard-working community we have come
to regard as the essence of truth itself proves
after all not yet even to have set foot on the road,
or done a single act deserving of 'meed' as opposed
to "mesurable hire".

Previous problems, then, over what it is that
merits the heavenly meed of pardon, and whether
labour for 'measurable hire' is or is not the
pilgrimage at the end of which that pardon lies, may
be said to prepare us somewhat for the question-mark
the pardon leaves over the salvation of the workers
of the half-acre. But in its absolute justice ("Do
wel and have wel", "Do yvel and have yvel") there is
a grim inevitability that arises out of the whole
structure and development of the *Visio*. For
despite apparently arbitrary discontinuities in the
surface narrative, not inappropriate to the fiction
of a dream, there lies in fact a fairly strict
method beneath the *Visio's* madness. The organization is, in its own way, quite as severely logical
as that produced by the *quaestiones*, divisions, and
sub-divisions, and elaborate categorizations
beloved of medieval scholastics. The Prologue, in
its survey of *sacerdotium* and *imperium*, introduces
the theme, by focusing on the problematic relation
of mercy to justice within the sphere of each of

these *regimina*. How does the clerical power of the
keys, the power to grant or withhold absolution,
square with the assumption that in justice it is
the 'cardinal' virtues that the gates of heaven
respond to? How does the angelic injunction to
mercy square with the King's responsibility to
ensure that rules and laws are enforced? - While
the Prologue concentrates mainly on the secular
state, and the authority of its lord, Passus I
proceeds to the Church and the authority of the
divine lord. The Prologue further identifies two
types of offence against social justice at large
in the world: venality and sloth. Taking money
for what should not be sold, or taking what is
unearned by labour, are two ways of defrauding
society and preventing the equitable distribution
of its collective resources.

Having thus, in the Prologue and Passus I,
identified human and divine law, salvation on earth
and in heaven under the aegis of state and church
respectively, as its subject, the poem proceeds to
devote one dream-sequence of three Passūs apiece to
each member of its twin theme. The Mede sequence
takes up Passūs II, III and IV, which explore law
and justice in the state, culminate in the question
of whether the King should give justice or mercy to
Wrong, and contrast the vice of venality with the
Truth of which Holy Church was the exponent. The
second dream, following the sequence confession-
pilgrimage-pardon, takes up Passūs V, VI and VII,
which are concerned with mercy and justice according to divine law, culminate in the question of
whether the King of Heaven grants salvation through
the mercy of pardons or through the just reward of
Do Wel, and contrast the vice of sloth (epitomised
in the beggars and wasters) with the true and
honest labour of the ploughman. The second
sequence is to a certain extent dependent on the
pattern set in the first, whose findings are being
re-applied. In the closing Passus of the latter,
Reason was discovered to preclude any mercy that
violated the essential principle of justice
epitomized in his maxim *nullum malum inpunitum,*
nullum bonum irremuneratum. No less can be true of
heavenly justice, therefore, whose ruling principle
is discovered, in the closing Passus of the second
sequence, to be the precise equivalent of Reason's:
do well and have well, do evil and have evil. Any
'pardon' that comes from Him will bear the imprint
of this principle, for it cannot violate the
justice it expresses. It is the principle that

dictates the conduct of justice on earth by the King, who must be above all just, and also that of God, who is nothing if not Truth. In each case, the scope for mercy is severely delimited by the tags quoted. *Quid pro quo*, measure for measure, as you sow so shall you reap, the inviolable principle on which all law and justice rest, is not to be overriden by pardon; for even where He pardons, Truth will observe it.

The 'construing' Reason had asserted his Latin maxim to require is repeated here in the Priest's translation of the words in the Bull ("I shal construe ech clause and kenne it thee on English"). For what both 'mean' in plain English, their implic- ations, need to be very thoroughly got by heart: justice is inviolable, and does not write off debts.

When the dreamer awakes to do his own bit of construing, to muse upon "this metels" (144), it is to both dreams he is referring, for the message of both is the same: mercy and pardon can operate only within the limits of the justice that dictates "measure for measure": *nullum malum impunitum, nullum bonum irremuneratum*: do well and have well, do ill and have ill. Whether, so constrained, they can then operate at all is still problematic. He therefore decides, not surprisingly, on the evidence of both dreams, that the prudent plaintiff will base the case he is preparing to put before the great court of Doomsday on justice rather than on mercy, since the latter has apparently so small room for manoeuvre: that is, that the Do Wel who can claim "have wel" from justice is rather more reliable (morc "siker for the soule", 181) than pardons which claim it from mercy (174-201). He is circumspect in expression. The writer of this poem is not one to impugn the authority of Church or State, and since it is the official teaching of his Church ("a leef of oure bileve", 176) that the Pope has "power pardon to graunte The peple, withouten penaunce to passen into joye", and that "pardon and penaunce and preieres doon save Soules that have synned seven sithes dedly" (174-9), he will practise the meek obedience to authority he has preached and "leelly" abstain from asserting what is contrary to faith. But he is quite convinced in his own mind that to *rely* on these pardons ("to *trust* on thise triennals", 180) is dangerous; for both his dreams have shown him that mercy and pardon subserve justice, God is Truth, and that both Wrong in Passus IV, and the folk in Passus VII, in different ways, had found a looked-for pardon

harden into justice when it came to the point. So
it would be imprudent to trust in pardons that may
be ruled out of court, where justice to Do Wel is
certain. With due respect, therefore, he is
prepared to stand by the 'construction' he has just
put upon the 'pardon' and the priest's own construing of it (168-73). The text demonstrated, he
considers, that God's words when scrutinized
assured, promised salvation only to Do Wel; they
did not promise 'pardon' to Do Yvel. The 'pardon' had
figured in the allegory as a papal Bull authorized
by Truth; and when read, it had proved only that
the one kind of pardon the Church could grant that
Truth would sanction was one which observed strict
justice: do well and have well, do ill and have
ill. He therefore construes the incident as demon-
strating that Do Wel is the prior principle, and
pardons only valid as they are guaranteed by it.
The rehearsal and translation of the text by the
priest proved, he feels, that 'pardons' cannot
compare with Do-Wel in efficacy; and that justice
at Judgment will recognize his claim before any
Church pardon to Do Yvel:

> Al this maketh me on metels to thynke -
> And how the preest preved no pardon to Dowel,
> And demed that Dowel indulgences passed,
> Biennals and triennals and bisshopes lettres,
> And how Dowel at the Day of Dome is digneliche
>   underfongen,
> And passeth al the pardon of Seint Petres cherche.

(168-73) [31]

The two dreams with their parallel subordination of mercy to justice come together in the
reflections that close the *Visio*. Here, the
presumption against the legitimacy of pardons at
divine justice (the conclusion of the second dream)
is phrased in the legal and court-room terminology
of the first:

> Forthi I rede yow renkes that riche ben on this
>   erthe,
> Upon trust of youre tresor triennals to have,
> Be ye never the bolder to *breke* the ten *hestes*;
> And namely ye maistres, meires and jugges,
> That have the welthe of this world and wise men ben
>   holden,
> To purchace yow pardon and the Popes bulles.
> At the dredful *dome* whan dede shulle arise

237

> And comen alle bifore Crist accountes to yelde -
> How thow laddest thi lif here and hise *lawes*
>   keptest,
> And how thow didest day by day the *doom* wole reherce.
> A pokeful of pardon there, ne provincials lettres,
> Theigh ye be founde in the fraternite of alle the
>   foure ordres
> And have indulgences doublefold - but Dowel yow
>   helpe,
> I sette youre patentes and youre pardon at one pies
>   hele!
>   Forthi I counselle alle Cristene to crie God
>   mercy,
> And Marie his moder be oure meene bitwene,
> That God gyve us grace here, er we go hennes,
> Swiche werkes to werche, while we ben here,
> That after oure deth day, Dowel *reherce*
> At the day of *dome*, we dide as he highte.

(182-201; my italics)

The triple reference to "doom" above all makes the message clear: Wrong will be judged, as in Passus IV, by a court that will "deme (him) as (he has) deserved". (IV.178). There, he will answer to another King for breaches of the 'law', the recorded "hestes" of the King of kings. He will need to produce corroborative evidence in his own behalf, and will find that there, too, the court will accept only the evidence of a reliable witness ("And as moost folk witnesseth wel, Wrong shal be demed", IV.181), who may testify ("reherce") to his obedience to the law, and is likely to disallow the flimsy documentary claim (purchased by Mede) on its 'pardon'. The closing words of the *Visio* are formed by Do Wel's testimony that "we dide as he highte": we did as we were told; obeyed the law of God's "hestes", as Holy Church had said we ought (Truth "wolde that ye wroughte as his word techeth"), and as Piers had ("I do what Truthe hoteth"). In fact, we had better trust in acquittal from the justice of the court through the evidence of our works of observance of the law, than in leniency from its mercy on the evidence of pardons for breaking it.
    Mercy is not entirely absent from the closing prayer. God's "mercy" and "grace" has a role to play, but one subservient to justice. The narrator asks for it only to aid him in satisfying justice. It is a very deliberate adaptation of the conventional

closing appeal to the mercy of those supreme inter-
cessors, Christ and the Virgin Mary. And it accords
with the view Langland later gives of the Passion.
The mercy it constituted was such as to make it
possible for us to satisfy justice, by paying for
us the penalty of original sin; thenceforth the
just could deserve heaven. And if Christ did not
come to call the just but the sinners, He did not
come to pardon sinners into heaven; He came to
call them to repentance and to payment of their
debts.

The insistant *traductio* on "werke" in 199
introduces what is to become a new emphasis in the
poem henceforward. It is derived from the verbal
"do" in Dowel's name. It is deeds, "werkes", facts
that earn heaven: "feith withouten feet is feblere
than nought", Holy Church had said, and her "feet"
was the love that "lenes". The new more general
sense of "werke" replaces the narrower sense of
'toil' it has borne hitherto. Literal, physical
work, "swynke", labour, has been discredited as in
itself constituting the "wel-dedes", the works of
Dowel, that merit the meed of heaven, implicitly by
the pardon, and explicitly by Piers, who, on hearing
it, at once vows to "swynke noght so harde". But
the new broader sense bears ever after much of the
logic in justice that has been established for the
narrower. As it is right that man should "werche"
for his "lyflod" and his "hire", so it is "werkes"
that earn the Christian *operarius* his hire of
eternal life from God. But the dreamer is now
rather uncertain what those "werkes" are, if they
are not literally "werke", and proceeds in the
following section to embark on a long search to
identify Dowel. Piers has pointed the way, but he
has not noticed.

Piers's own re-action to the revelation of the
contents of the Bull deserves especial attention.
For the poem has established him as a figure of
some authority, a fathful servant of Truth with
"kynde knowynge" of Him. Yet it is ignored, not
only by the priest, who merely scoffs at his "lewed"
pretensions to knowledge of Scripture, without
addressing his own "lered" mind to the substance of
what Piers says; but also by the poem and the
dreamer - no comment on it is offered by either, and
both proceed in their search for Dowel entirely as
if his words here were an utter irrelevance to it.
But it is precisely the 'construction' put upon the
problematic text by Piers, already established as

the poem's 'hero', that ought to be decisive. It
is in fact one that further discredits any theory
that the priest is wrong, the folk *are* doing well,
the document before us *is* a pardon, and the "lered"
minister is simply sewing sophistic cockle in the
clean wheat of the simple piety of the "lewed".
Whatever we may think of the priest (and he is not
a pleasant character), Piers does not take the text,
when it is read and translated to him, as sanctioning the assumption we have all been working on:
that the meed of heaven is earned by honest labour.
He takes it rather as an admonishment to him to
renounce that life of labour henceforth.

Piers's reaction (like the pardon itself) is
a strange mixture of the clear and the enigmatic.[32]
His feelings and the course of life he resolves
upon are easily evident; though the explanation
for them is not. His immediate response is
recorded in these words:

> And Piers for pure tene pulled it atweyne
> And seide, *'Si ambulavero in medio umbre mortis*
> *Non timebo mala, quoniam tu mecum es'.*

(115-7)

Quite what the "pure tene" is directed at is not
clear. At the priest? At himself, for having
mistaken the road to salvation? At the pardon,
which has in effect tricked him, and turned out to
be no pardon? Or at all, or at none of these
things? He is at any rate clearly angry and
mortified, and feels the shadows gathering round
him to the extent that he needs to remind himself
that God is ever present even through the darkest
night of the soul. He is falling back upon simple
faith, trust, and hope in God, as his following
words also testify (since he follows up this
quotation from the Psalms with a resolution to
trust more in God henceforth to provide for his
"lyflod"). For he is prompted by the pardon into
a resolve radically to alter his way of life;
what he resolves upon is clear, though why is not:

> 'I shal cessen of my sowyng', quod Piers, 'and
>   swynke noght so harde,
> Ne aboute my bely joye so bisy be na moore;
> Of preieres and of penaunce my plough shal ben
>   herafter,
> And wepen whan I sholde slepe, though whete breed me
>   faille.

> 'The prophete his payn eet in penaunce and in
> sorwe,
> By that the Sauter seith - so dide othere manye.
> That loveth God lelly, his liflode is ful esy:
> *Fuerunt mihi lacrime mee panes die ac nocte.*
> 'And but if Luc lye, he lereth us by foweles
> We sholde noght be to bisy aboute the worldes blisse:
> *Ne soliciti sitis*, he seith in the Gospel
> And sheweth us by ensamples us selve to wisse.
> The foweles in the feld, who fynt hem mete at
> wynter?
> Have thei no gerner to go to, but God fynt hem alle'.

(118-130)

In one way, his words merely confirm his own original conception of how the 'pardon' was to be won. In positing a 'pilgrimage' to follow the ploughing, he had implied some necessary transition from secular to religious, from active to contemplative, from physical to spiritual labour. He had in a sense made that transition himself, but he is now to make it in an even more decided and radical form. The poem had overruled him, but he was right, and is now even more convinced that there is some activity beyond honest labour requisite for the Christian life of Dowel. It has already been pointed out that Langland's characteristic way of indicating stylistically the inferiority of one course to another is to reduce the former to metaphorical status. He had so indicated the superiority of honest labour to literal pilgrimage:

> And heng his hoper at his hals in stede of a
> scryppe.

(VI.61)

> 'My plowpote shal be my pikstaf, and picche atwo
> the rotes'.

(VI.103)

> Now is Perkyn and this pilgrimes to the plow faren.

(VI.105)

But now the plough and the all-important "lyflod" it earns are themselves reduced to the figurative status that implies their inferiority as vehicle to the tenor they convey: "Of preieres and of

penaunce my plough shal ben herafter"; *Fuerunt mihi
lacrime mee panes die ac nocte*. Hitherto, we have
been asked to see labour only in relation to those
things to which it is morally superior: irresponsible idleness, and the empty piety of literal
pilgrimages that ignores the pilgrimage of this
life. Now, suddenly and disconcertingly, we are
asked to see it in relation to something to which
it is inferior, something in comparison with which
it looks, not laudably hard-working, but "bisy"
(119,126). It is difficult to convey the precise
shade of derogatory meaning that word could carry
in Middle English. "Bisynesse" was often used to
translate the Latin *solicitudo* (*cf* 127), which
connoted an over-anxious involvement in affairs of
this world, an enemy to that spiritual sense of
proportion that subordinates the temporal to the
external. In this sense, it could, interestingly
enough, be collocated with "ydel" (futile); the
apparent oxymoron 'idle business' is found for
instance in both Hoccleve and Gower.[33]
    In this, we have the clue to the inadequacy
Piers, and through him Langland, is discovering
in the vision of Dowel   the *Visio* has offered
us: a hard-working community, honestly earning
its "lyflod", each taking no more than his due,
and performing assiduously the role in society he
has been cast to play. There is something carnal
and worldly about such a view, Piers suggests;
it centres on "bely joye". Langland implies that
in his search for Christian truth, he has over-
identified moral with economic well-being. In one
sense, he never really separates the two; he wants
no religion that has nothing to do with the elim-
ination of social inequities and frauds, and,
over and over again he stresses, the relief of the
worldly distress of the poor. But in his social
pre-occupation, he has assumed that spiritual
truth is nothing more than the social integrity
conducive to "plentee among the peple", than
"Werchynge and wandrynge as *the world* asketh".
But Christianity is ultimately directed towards
another and better world, and those who live "in
longynge to ben hennes" (XIX.249), who selflessly
abdicate all concern with their own "lyflod" in
perfect trust in God, who devote their labour not
in the flesh but in the spirit to that next world,
must therefore have "chosen the better part". That
he has lost sight of spiritual labour is evidenced
by the total omission from the Bull of those who
had committed themselves to just such a life as

Piers here resolves on: the "ancres and heremites",
who "In preieres and penaunce putten hem", and "Al
for the love of Oure Lord lyveden ful streyte",
referred to with approval in the Prologue and in
Passus VI as the contemplative equivalents of the
ploughman. Their absence is significant: had they
been included, the 'impugning' of the pardon and
Piers's consequent decision would lose much of its
point. To earn one's "lyflod" honestly by labour
is truth; to renounce all concern with it in
faith and hope in and love for God (117,123,130) is
to move from the cardinal to the theological
virtues, from Martha's to Mary's part.[34]

Nevertheless, Piers's words here constitute
so drastic and unheralded a revision of the whole
system of values established over Passūs VI-VII
as to give us the sensation that the poem's ground
is collapsing beneath our feet. Not only is Piers
to renounce the "swynke" which has become the
touchstone of his moral worth; worse, he is to
become very nearly indistinguishable from that type
of person branded as an unpardonable offender
against social equity, the eternal debtor who
'borrows evermore', and waster of what has been won
through the labour of others: the beggar. In fact,
Piers's expressed trust that the Lord will provide
for His own ("That loveth God lelly, his liflode is
ful esy") is uttered in the true spirit of the text
the narrator had earlier perverted into a curse on
beggary: "I have been young, and now am old: and
I have not seen the just forsaken, nor his seed
begging bread". His own distortion of the Christian
message the dream is now forcing the poet to
acknowledge.

Langland has already had some warning that it
is on the question of beggars that he is likely to
encounter the most serious discrepancy between his
social and his Christian aspirations. The logic of
social justice counsels discrimination between the
idle and the unfortunate; Christianity appears to
forbid it (*Mihi vindictam et ego retribuo; Non
eligas cui miserearis*). And it is on the subject
of beggary that the discrepancy is now most
dramatically revealed. The same state social
justice condemns as irresponsible may actually
(undertaken from different motives, of course) be
more acceptable to God than a life of conscientiously fulfilled social duties. Not only may
Christianity diverge from social utility: it may
actually run directly counter to it. Piers weeping
and bede-muttering is likely to be a lot less

tangibly beneficial to the community than was Piers
ploughing. The notion that his religion can flout
all the basic rules of social fairness and duty is
at present too appalling a one for the dreamer to
register, except obliquely through this speech of
Piers, which glances quite off his conscious mind.
Yet Holy Church had in a sense warned him that he
might not find perfect congruence between the
social ideal of "plentee among the peple" and the
Christian ideal of spiritual health and well-being:

> 'Al is noght good to the goost that the gut asketh,
> Ne liflode to the likame that leef is to the soule'.

(I.36-7)

Piers's speech is also the most vivid example
of the receding point of perfection the poem
represents the Christian as always chasing. We and
the poet have aimed at social equity and integrity;
now that it is attained, it is suddenly revealed to
be lesser than a higher ideal that the very attain-
ment of it suddenly brings into view. This is a
recurrent feature of the poem's mode of proceeding.
Holy Church begins by emphasizing the supremacy of
truth; once the point is established, she reveals,
disconcertingly, that it is, after all, worthless
without love. The triumph of justice in Passus IV
only reveals more work to be done (the conversion
of the commons), without which the victory is
pointless. The search for Dowel constantly
reveals a Dobet and a Dobest. The patience the
dreamer comes to see as the essential soil for grace
and the solution to all ills disappears as soon as
he materializes, to be replaced as the object of
search and inquiry by charity. The Christian life
is a perpetual journey, because the goal can never
be regarded as attained. As soon as it is, complacency is born, and from it the pride, which, as
Piers had warned, will cast you from the very
temple of truth itself, and undo all you may have
achieved (V.609-617).[35] You must progress, if only
to avoid regressing. "It takes", as the red queen
said, "all the running you can do to stay in the
same place". The notion is epitomized in an
exchange between the dreamer and Scripture in
Passus X. The dreamer claims that it is baptism
that saves. Scripture corrects him: baptism will
save only those who are not yet baptized:

> 'Ac Cristene men withoute moore maye noght come
> to hevene'.

(X.349)

Once you are baptized, you cannot regard the goal
of salvation as reached: you must aspire to something more. Dowel is only Dowel until it is
reached, when it is replaced by the obligation to
Do Bet. To do well is to be always aiming to do
better than you are.

Piers here in effect takes a great leap forward
into the poem, to a point not reached by the dreamer
until Passus XIV 29ff, which passage really requires
to be read in conjunction with the present one.
For Piers with his "kynde knowynge" has arrived in
an instant at an instinctive understanding of
Dowel. The dreamer, with his own confessed lack of
it, does not notice, and sets out on his much
slower and more laborious path through thought,
wit, learning, study and imagination, to identify
this entity. And it takes him a further seven
Passūs to arrive by painful trial and error at
precisely the truth Piers had in his dream immediately perceived. That is, his conscious mind only
slowly catches up with his subconscious: until
finally, in the confrontation between Patience and
Haukyn, he finds himself giving full and elaborate
confirmation to that earlier uncomprehended but
intuitive perception. The parallel between Piers's
speech at VII.118ff and Patience's at XIV.29ff is
similar to that between Holy Church's at II.20ff
and Conscience's at III.230ff, before discussed.
In both cases, the poem gradually wins its way
through to a detailed statement of a truth glimpsed
in advance, but not consciously comprehended. The
poem had moved away from Holy Church's position on
Mede: that she was illegitimate and antithetical
to mercy, a claim supported by a cryptic allusion
to Psalm 14. But that position is later fully
endorsed by Conscience. The poem similarly ignores
Piers's speech here, which likewise turns out to
be an anticipatory summary of a conclusion to be
reached, not this time one, but seven passūs later.
It is in Haukyn that the dreamer comes to see
the point of Piers's renunciation of the active
life of labour the *Visio* had until then celebrated.
Haukyn is in many ways a character from the *Visio*
world, and seems at first to have much in common
with what had at that time formed the basis of the

245

poem's conception of the ideal man (Piers): the
ploughman, type of those who "swonken ful harde",
antitype of the beggarly idleness that refuses to
"labour for lyflod", and engaged in work essential
to the sustenance of society. Haukyn in fact
identifies himself with the *Visio* Piers, an identification to which his own 'active' aversion to
idleness lends support:

> 'What the preest preieth the peple hir Paternoster
>   to bidde
> For Piers the Plowman and that hym profit waiten -
> And that am I, Actif, that ydelnesse hatie;
> For alle trewe travaillours and tiliers of the erthe,
> Fro Mighelmesse to Mighelmesse I fynde hem with
>   wafres'.

> (XIII.236-40)

239 is pure *Visio* in spirit, and 239-40 in fact
recalls the Piers of Passus VI:

> 'And alle manere of men that by mete and drynke
>   libbeth,
> Helpeth hym to werche wightliche that weynneth
>   youre foode'.

> (19-20)

> 'And alle kynne crafty men that konne lyven in
>   truthe,
> I shal fynden hem fode that feithfulliche libbeth'.

> (68-9)

For Haukyn, too, is in the business of purveying
bread for the community ("A wafrer, wol ye wite",
226), "breed" which all require, and which he
"swinks" hard for:

> 'Beggeris and bidderis of my breed craven,
> Faitours and freres and folk with brode crounes.
> I fynde payn for the Pope and provendre for his
>   palfrey'.

> (241-3)

> 'For er I have breed of mele, ofte moot I swete,
> And er the commune have corn ynough many a cold
>   morwenyng;
> So, er my wafres be ywroght, muche wo I tholye'.

> (260-2)

He contrasts his honest and useful labour with the
wastrel idleness of those who get money for
scurrilous 'minstrelsy', as the Prologue had done,
and as Piers had done (in his derogatory references
to "Jakke the Jogelour" and "Robin the Ribaudour,
for hise rusty wordes", VI.70,73). He himself is
a 'minstrel' of a different sort. 'Waferers' were
actually on occasion classed with minstrels, since
they often formed part of the troupe (to which
musicians and singers also belonged) that magnates
would maintain for their personal comfort.[36] They
sweetened his leisure hours with delicacies, as
the minstrels did with indelicacies. In claiming,
then, that he is a minstrel, and, two lines later,
a 'waferer', Haukyn is not contradicting himself,
but defining more specifically his place within a
broader general category. Haukyn contrasts his
useful activity with the empty idleness of other
kinds of minstrels, and complains that his substance
meets with less reward than their inanity (a
contrast and a complaint both thoroughly in the
Visio spirit, with its respect for useful labour,
and its angry contempt for wastrels):

> 'I am a mynstral', quod that man, 'my name is
> *Activa Vita*.
> Al ydel ich hatie, for of Actif is my name,
> A wafrer, wol ye wite, and serve many lordes -
> And fewe robes I fonge or furrede gownes.
> Couthe I lye and do men laughe, thanne lacchen I
> sholde
> Outher mantel or moneie amonges lordes mynstrels'.

>   (224-9)

But this useful life of productive labour is no
longer seen in the favourable perspective put on it
by the *Visio*, and by Haukyn himself: as the
antithesis to irresponsible idleness:

> 'Al ydel ich hatie, for of Actif is my name'.

>   (225)

> 'And that am I, Actif, that ydelnesse hatie'.

>   (238)

This was the dialectic adopted by the *Visio*, but
Piers had substituted a binary opposition in which
"actif" figures not as 'not idle', but as a "bisy"
solicitude inferior to spiritual, or contemplative,

labour. And, though to Haukyn his name of *Activa Vita* suggests the vice he avoids -

> 'I am a mynstrel', quod that man, 'my name is *Activa Vita*.
> Al ydel ich hatie, for of Actif is my name'

- the term would inevitably rather suggest to a medieval reader the other half of another antithesis ("Contemplatif lif or Actif lif, Crist wolde men wroghte", VI.249), in which it was not the superior but the inferior member.[37] Moreover, it is not by confronting him with a Waster that the poem now defines this Winner, as in Passus VI, when it had seen the perfection represented by Piers largely in these terms. Again, though Haukyn himself in his opening words interprets the word *Activa* in his name according to a winner-waster polarity, the poem contrasts him with Patience, in whose company he is encountered, and who preaches to him just that passive acceptance, that trusting openness to fortune, that Piers had placed above "bisy swynke". So the redefinition Piers had offered is being re-enacted. The "labour for lyflod" the *Visio* had defined favourably according to a winner-waster, toil-sloth dialectic, he had suddenly redefined as an anxious "bisinesse" inferior to the serene indifference to "lyflod" born of implicit faith and trust in God. So, too, behind Haukyn's own "Actif-ydel" antithesis, the poem suggests two others that force a less favourable view of his 'activity': his is the physical and secular toil of the *Activa Vita*, inferior to the spiritual labour of the *Contemplativa*; and the embittered and self-righteous fretfulness engendered by his 'active' life is contrasted with the serene resignation of the more 'passive' Patience - occupationally passive, but energetic indeed in the ardour of his faith and hope. - For Haukyn is a terrible moaner: his first speech is one long, accusing grumble about how under-rewarded such honest workmen as he are, what a hard time he has of it, and what shirkers and rascals everyone else is - though take away the wine, and it all sounds not at all unlike the *Visio* line on "trewe travaillours and tiliers of the erthe".

And the dreamer is surprised to discover how 'stained' this "trewe travaillour" he had idolized in the *Visio* now, on closer inspection, appears. One by one he discerns on Haukyn's coat, and hears confessed from his own lips, all seven of the

deadly sins (XIII.271-408). Of course, there is an
element of obsessive exaggeration, both in this
discovery of the spiritual bankruptcy that pre-
occupation with "labour for lyflod" can produce,
and in Patience's subsequent eulogy of the blessings
of poverty (XIV.103-319), which, though it may be
conceded to keep one out of the more expensive
kinds of trouble, is rather inimical to charity than
otherwise. But Langland is doing penance for
having got it wrong on labour and beggary before,
and, as Pandarus remarks, there is no ardour so
immoderate as that of the convert.[38] He is also,
at this stage of the poem, in a particularly
heightened state of humility and submissiveness
(having been rebuked by Ymagynatyf for constantly
finding fault with the clergy instead of trying
to profit from the wisdom they could impart), and
ready temporarily to attend to the beam in his own
eye and not the mote in his neighbour's. And the
transition from external to internal correction
was another of the many shifts of emphasis implied
in Piers's speech at VIII.118ff. One's first duty
is to reform oneself, not society.

And as the dreamer's criticism has been turned
inward, so is Haukyn's - he passes from social
complaint to confession and penance. And the particular attention given to self-righteousness and
fault-finding in the catalogue of Haukyn's sins
(the faults of pride (271-312) that the dreamer
discerns and describes for himself, as opposed to
hearing from Haukyn, as with the subsequent sins)
suggests that Langland has also heard in Haukyn's
opening speech a mortifying echo of the tone he had
himself adopted in the *Visio* (and through much of
the Dowel section), when Haukyn and his like had
formed his positives: angrily denunciatory and
resentful of those whose greed or sloth harmed the
common interest, without asking himself whether
the stones he cast came from a hand itself free of
fault. At least, if such expressions as the
following are not a transferred confession, they
ought to be:

> And inobedient to ben undernome of any lif lyvynge;
> And so singuler by himself as to sighte of the peple
> Was noon swich as hymself, ne noon so pope holy;
> Yhabited as an heremyte, an ordre by hymselve -
> Religion saunz rule and resonable obedience;
> Lakkynge lettrede men and lewed men bothe, *etc*

> (281-6)

Who was it who had dressed himself up as a hermit
at the beginning of the poem, rather than submitting
to the rule of some regular order, to confer upon
himself not the duty of self-correction, but the
right of castigating clergy and laiety alike, and
shown himself in Passus X recalcitrant to instruction, and obsessed with the faults of others to a
degree that only too justly earns him Reason's
reprimand (XI.386), "And er thow lakke eny lif,
loke if thow be to preise"?

Patience recommends to Haukyn precisely the
course Piers had counselled: a moderation of
"bisy" preoccupation with the cares of active life,
and "labour for lyflod"; and he cites in his
support precisely the text *Ne soliciti sitis*, and
the example of the "foweles in the feld", that
Piers had argued from:

> 'We sholde noght be to bisy abouten oure liflode:
> *Ne soliciti sitis &c; Volucres celi Deus pascit*
>   *&c; Pacientes vincunt &c'.*

(XIV.33-4)

And as Piers had felt that in labouring to nourish
his body he was starving his soul, and had substituted a metaphorical plough productive of metaphorical *panes*, so Patience introduces Haukyn to a
more vital kind of sustenance than the literal
bread produced by his physical "swynk":

> 'And I shal purveie thee paast', quod Pacience,
> 'though no plough erye,
> And flour to fede folk with as best be for the
> soul'.

(XIV.29-30)

Langland has come to see the spiritual feeding of
the community represented by the teaching and
example of Patience as superior to that aim of
ensuring "plentee among the peple" through the
teaching and example of a ploughman-governor. When
Haukyn expresses derisive incredulity, Patience
proceeds to produce the "Vitailles of grete vertucs"
he has promised, and repeats the assurance of Piers
that he "that loveth God lelly, his liflode is ful
esy":

> And seide, 'Lo! here liflode ynogh, if oure bileve
>   be trewe.
> For lent nevere was lif but liflode were sharpen,
> Wherof or wherfore or wherby to libbe.
>   'First the wilde worm under weet erthe,
> Fissh to lyve in the flood, and in the fir the
>   criket,
> The corlew by kynde of the eyr, moost clenneth
>   flessh of briddes,
> And bestes by gras and by greyn and by grene rootes,
> In menynge that alle men myghte the same
> Lyve thorugh leel bileve and love, as God witnesseth'.

> (XIV.39-47)

Again, the focus is on the theological virtues of
faith, hope, and love, the loving faith that trusts
in God to provide for His faithful. He will not
let them starve, and what anyway will 'sustain'
them through all sufferings is that peculiar sacred
passivity, that willingness to suffer all that
Providence may see fit to visit upon one, that is
the very opposite of Haukyn's activity and "bisy"
anxiety to provide for the morrow:

> But I lokede what liflode it was that Pacience
>   so preisede;
> And thanne was it a pece of the Paternoster -
>   *Fiat voluntas tua.*

> (48-9)

Haukyn is further urgently counselled to embrace
the life of willing poverty Piers had enjoined upon
himself, and ends in just those tears of penance
the ploughman had also sworn would be his daily
bread henceforth, perceiving with him that his
active life, though shunning the vice of selfish
idleness, had actually debarred him from more
important aspects of 'doing well', from the humility
and faith that puts God above 'good':

> 'Allas', quod Haukyn the Actif Man tho, 'That
>   after my cristendom
> I ne hadde be deed and dolven for Dowelis sake!
> So hard it is', quod Haukyn, 'to lyve and to do
>   synne.
> Synne seweth us evere', quod he, and sory gan wexe,
> And wepte water with hise eighen and weyled the tyme
> That evere he dide dede that deere God displesed -
> Swouned and sobbed and siked ful ofte.
>
> (XIV.320-6)

One cannot help feeling a little sorry for Haukyn surnamed *Activa Vita*. It was really rather unfortunate for him that he chanced to meet Patience and Will Langland that day. He meets them a normal, unhealthy member of the working population: feeling over-worked and underpaid, well on the way to a peptic ulcer, jaundiced and irascible, but sustained by an aggrieved sense of his own worth and importance. He leaves them a broken man, ruined for wafering - and society has lost one bread-provider the more, for he, like Piers, is now presumably to become a poorer, idler, hungrier, but better man.

His tears awake the dreamer, who, though acknowledging at once that he still had far to go before he could claim to "kyndely knowe what was Dowel" (XV.2), has at least reached the point Piers had attained at the very start of his journey. He has reached the beginning, if not the end. And he now understands what his subconscious had heard back in Passus VII, for in Haukyn he has perceived the limitation of the active life, and the narrowing and souring effect both of single-minded "labour for lyflod" and of his own earlier fretful preoccupation with the social iniquities that impede "plentee among the peple".

It is a singularly honest and committed poet who can say, as Langland says at the end of Passus VII, that he has got it all wrong, and will have to start again: labour is not Dowel after all. And it is one with a singular mixture of intuition and dogged perseverance in reasoning who can imagine a character who knows better than he, one capable of such striking anticipation by "kynde knowynge" of the truths he will only slowly and painfully reason through to.

NOTES

1. See J.W. Baldwin, i.57,125,271,310; ii.44.
2. *CT*.VII.287-8; *Mum and the Sothsegger*, ed. M. Day and R. Steele, E.E.T.S. O.S. 199 (1936), III.267.
3. See no.44 to ch.II *supra*.
4. *cf*: "Knights ought be true, and truth is one in all" (*FQ*.V.xi.56).
5. The first line of a sonnet by George Herbert based on the same conceit as Langland employs here. For the comparison Piers draws between the *debita* of sins and 'rental' owed to the Lord, *cf* Skelton's *Magnificence*,1.2294

6. See pp.7-8 *supra*.
7. *The Book of Margery Kempe*, p.60; *cf*.p.105.
8. *cf*: "Beggeres for hir biddynge bidden men mede" (III. 219); and *cf*. *Libro de Buen Amor*, sts.1727-8); J.W. Baldwin ii.182.
9. *Statutes of the Realm*, Vol.i.pp.307-8.
10. As is suggested by D. Aers, *Chaucer, Langland, and the Creative Imagination* (London, 1980), p.18.
11. *cf*. Robertson, p.9; for the attribution of calamities of various kinds to providential justice, see Abelard's *Ethics*, p.109; *The Book of Margery Kempe*, p.119; *Policraticus* VI.xvii (p.230); for their occurence specifically at the request of the just or innocent, *cf*. *Policraticum* VI.xxix (p.277); C text III.90ff.
12. Anna Baldwin likewise emphasizes that "Conscience is the least authoritative ruler in *Piers Plowman*" (p.80).
13. On the statutes that attempted to regulate apparel and diet in order to preserve social distinctions, see Scattergood, *Politics*, p.344; Brewer, p.14; R.D. French, *A Chaucer Handbook* (2nd ed., New York, 1955), pp.27-8.
14. See further J.A. Burrow, 'The Action of Langland's Second Vision', *Essays in Criticism* xv (1965), 247-68.
15. *The Book of Margery Kempe*, p.72.
16. St. Michael was often represented as weighing souls in the balance (see Bennett, n. to VII.33; *Ancrene Wisse*, *ed.cit.*, p.20); for the psychostasis (the weighing of the soul at judgment), see R. Woolf, 'The Tearing of the Pardon', in Hussey, *Critical Approaches*, pp.50-75 (pp. 59,69).
17. See Aquinas, *ST*. II-II.lxxvii.4; J.W. Baldwin, i.263-4; O'Brien, p.144ff.
18. J.W. Baldwin, i.262-3, 265-6.
19. *Ibid*.i.335; for other references to the dispensing power, see, eg. *ibid*.ii.230; *Libro de Buen Amor*, sts. 143-7; C text, IX.138, where the concept is most movingly employed to pardon the sins of lunatics, "For vnder godes secret seal here synnes ben kevered".
20. Langland is here applying to advocates a principle by no means uncommon in itself, since other theologians had also banned the sale of knowledge and understanding, "the fruits of the mind", on the grounds that, as gifts of grace, they represented spiritual commodities the sale of which thus constituted simony. (J.W. Baldwin, i.122,126).
21. "Take heed whom you give to". For condemnation of those who show no discretion in their alms, giving to the needless rather than the needy, see *Lay Folks' Catechism*, 11.665-6, 1091-2 (Wycliffite version).
22. *cf*. Bennett (n. to VII.87), who points out that Langland himself later interprets the text differently (at XI. 274-9).

23. See J.W. Baldwin, i.146; *Policraticus* VIII.xviii (p.357).
24. p.251; *cf. Hoccleve's Complaint*, ll.344-50.
25. See Robinson's note to *Parliament of Fowls*, 1.518.
26. For discussion of and references to the critical liter-
     ature on this problematic pardon, see Frank, p.25;
     Pearsall, n. to C text IX.291; Woolf, 'Tearing' (see
     n.16 *supra*).
27. See Schmidt's note to VII.110-4, and Pearsall's to C.IX.
     291.
28. See, for instance, the proper characteristics of old age
     as described in Dante's *Convivio*, IV.xxviii (ed. G.
     Busnelli and G. Vandelli, 2 vols (Florence, 1964), ii.
     350ff).
29. For fuller treatment of this subject, see the Epilogue,
     infra.
30. See VIII.96-99; IX.202ff; X.256-7; XIII.138.
31. Schmidt glosses ll.169-70 "(belonged) to Do Well, And
     (I) judged that D. excelled ..." But 169 should surely
     be interpreted (in the light of the next line) "*in
     comparison to* Do-Wel", and there is no need to posit an
     awkward ellipsis of 'I' in 170 (as Bennett and Pearsall
     also do). The dreamer is stating what he considers the
     priest's intervention to have established: that, when
     properly 'construed', one's passport into heaven turns
     out to be not a pardon, but good deeds. The editors
     are perhaps understandably reluctant to give any credit
     for this important revelation to so nasty a piece of work
     as the priest here obviously is. But his learning has
     been the means whereby both Piers and the dreamer are
     prompted to take crucial decisions. In fact, the
     incident leads into the whole question of the value, if
     any, of "clergye" (learning), how and whether it is
     devalued by imperfect cler*ics*, which is to be explored
     in some depth in the coming Do-Wel section of the poem
     (VIII-XIV), concluding in Ymaginatyf's warning that we
     should not despise "cler*gye*" because many cler*ics* are
     vicious, "Ne sette short by hir science, whatso thei don
     hemeselve. Take we hir wordes at worth, for hire
     witnesses be trewe" (XII.122-3). It would be unwise,
     therefore, to assume that the priest's words can have
     contributed nothing useful to the lessons the dreamer
     says he has learned, simply because he himself is an
     objectionable person; this would be to ignore the whole
     problem of valuable knowledge in the hands of worthless
     men that is due shortly to become so important an issue.
32. Both the tearing of the pardon by Piers and his subsequent
     speech are omitted from the C text, which shows a general
     tendency to rationalize at the expense of dramatic and
     poetic effect (*cf*. p. 176 *supra*). But the deletion of
     the speech in the later revision does suggest that it was
     found problematic as it stood.

33. *How to Learn to Die*,1.278; *The Complete Works of John Gower*, ed. G.C. Macaulay, 4 vols (Oxford, 1901), *Confessio Amantis* IV.1151-2; see also V.J. Scattergood, 'A Note on the Moral Framework of Donne's *The Sunne Rising*', *Neuphilologische Mitteilungen* lxxxxii (1981), 307-14 (p.311). *cf* also Hilton's comment that it is difficult for those in the active life, "occupied in worldly bisynys", to cultivate the more perfect spiritual understanding achieved in the contemplative experience, the labour of the spirit *(Scale of Perfection* II, p.58).

34. Martha and Mary (see Luke 10) were held to typify the active and contemplative life respectively, and Christ's assertion that Mary had 'chosen the better part' was taken as affirming the superiority of the latter over the former. (See, for instance, *The Cloud of Unknowing*, ed. P. Hodgson, E.E.T.S. O.S. 218 (1944), pp.47-58).

35. For the notion that pride and wrath constitute the especial threats to a state of achieved spiritual grace (V.609-17), *cf. Scale of Perfection* II,pp.80-82).

36. See C. Bullock-Davies, *Menstrellorum Multitudo* (Cardiff, 1978), pp.25,44ff.

37. In the C text some of the lines given to Haukyn in B are transferred to the *Visio* and attributed to a character called Actif who is answered by one called Contemplacioun (VII.292ff). The transposition provides further evidence that the Haukyn episode is meant to be seen as importantly relevant to the *Visio* and its preoccupation with honest labour, and that the contrast between him and Patience is intended to recall that between secular and spiritual labour.

38. *T&C*.I.998-1008.

EPILOGUE: THE VITA

EX VI TRANSITIONIS: THE PASSOVER FROM THE OLD TO THE
NEW LAW

The lengthy continuation of the poem (Passūs
VIII - XX in the B text) that follows on the *Visio*
is often distinguished from the latter by the term
Vita - an appellation first applied to it by early
scribes, who evidently saw this second part of the
poem as consisting chiefly of an account of the life
of the poet (physically and spiritually), largely
spent in searching for a satisfactory definition of
the good life: that is, in attempting to define who
or what is *Do-Wel*. And since the poem has a cons-
picuous tendency to organize its thinking about
spiritual truth according to trinitarian schemes (in
imitation of the image of Truth or God Himself),
many of these early scribes further subdivided the
Vita into three parts (Passūs VIII-XIV; XV-XVIII;
XIX-XX), which they entitled - after the trio most
frequently used by the poem itself in its recurrent
tripartite definitions of modes of virtuous living -
the *Vita de Do-Wel, Do-Bet,* and *Do-Best* respectively[1].
    Justice and law remain central pre-occupations
throughout all three sections. It is, in fact,
highly significant that the A text breaks off at a
point in the narrative where the dreamer's doubt and
confusion have become extreme enough to call into
question even the fairness and logic of God's
justice. Having applied for illumination to Clergie
(those learned in God's law) and Scripture (the
written evidence of God's law, chiefly the Bible),
Will is suddenly filled with doubts as to their
value, and the consultation culminates in a long and
angry tirade by him (B.X.369-472), shortly after
which the A text comes to an abrupt halt. His
outburst raises many fundamental issues, but chief
among them is an apparent inequity in the distribution of divine rewards.
    Will's objections are at first unproblematic

enough: it is not learning or wisdom *per se* that
merits salvation; praxis not theory, works not
words, however wise, are what count. But as he proceeds, he finds his argument developing in a more
disturbing fashion. His examples start to suggest
that *works* themselves are not decisive. Mary
Magdalen and the penitent thief gained heaven "Tho
that *wroughte* wikkedlokest in world tho thei were"
(424)[2]. It is not only the wise who do not practise
what they preach whose fate is unsure; there are
'witty *and wel libbynge*' whose future destiny is
"yhudde In the hondes of almyghty God" (428-9).
That the simple faith of "povere commune laborers ...
swiche lewed juttes" should "Percen with a Pater-
noster the paleys of hevene" (457-9), where the more
subtle learning of divines cannot, is not a position
likely to precipitate a crisis of faith in Will or
anyone else. But, on *Visio* logic, it is worrying
that it is apparently some much more incalculable
quantity than good *works* which is the determining
factor; for salvation is granted them despite the
fact that they "inparfitly here knewe *and ek lyvede*"
(462).

Here is an apparent disproportion between
'works' and 'hire', doing well/ill and having well/
ill, a God not working on the equitable principles
laid down in Passus VI and VII. Is simple faith
more worthy than wisdom *and works*? It was on that
principle, after all, that God damned those who knew
not the true Faith of Christ (the pagans and the
pre-Christian just), whatever their words or their
works - one of the thorniest problems for medieval
apologists for God's justice[3], and one that is
raised here as a problem related to that of the
supreme efficacy of the "pure bileve" (461) of those
whose knowledge and works are impure. For, as Will
points out to Scripture, one of the most respected
of the authors of her precious "bokes" was Aristotle,
whom orthodox Christianity holds damned as lacking
the true Faith; and there were others like him,
who, whatever their '*werkes* and wit" now "wonyeth
in pyne" (385).

Langland plainly felt the concept of a God who
could give ill for well, and well for ill, damning
"witty and wel libbynge" pagans, and saving a thief
with a lifetime of law-breaking behind him, to be so
appalling he could not continue. In the B version,
he represents the above interview as having precip-
itated in him so severe a crisis as to cause him to
abandon all concern with Do-Wel - and presumably
therefore the poem as well - until his forty-fifth

year[4] (XI. 46-51). And even then he can only
proceed after he has provided himself with some
answer to these apparent inequities: by recalling
the legend of Trajan (Passus XI), a just pagan who
was saved; and by settling it in his imagination
(Passus XII)[5] that the penitent thief was not *very*
saved, but had a low and *un*safe position in heaven
(196-209). And Ymagynatyf's last words purport to
prove God's justice from His very name, explained as
an acrostic: *Deus dicitur quasi dans vitam eternam
suis* (XII. 285-92).

God's primal attribute of justice, and the
poem's first premise (God = Truth), is thus
re-affirmed. It can proceed on no other basis.
How, then, can he also be merciful? Does mercy not
remit penalties, and thus violate "the equilibrium
of justice"? It is with the reconciliation of
divine mercy with divine justice that much of the
rest of the poem is concerned: one cannot sin with
impunity, relying on God's mercy as a court of
appeal from His justice, and hope to get heaven
without paying the debts of sin. So included in all
three sections of the *Vita* is some representation
of the nature of the transition from the Old to the
New Law and the relationship between the two. It
is this that provides a focus for the problems
raised in the *Visio* about the apparently contradictory claims of justice and mercy, and the related
question of whether merit consists in perfect
'truth' or 'love' (Holy Church had begun by asserting
truth as the deciding factor in salvation, but
ended by saying it was useless without love, which
seemed to replace truth as the 'key' virtue that
'unlocks' grace, I. 202). Both questions are
reducible to one concerning the Passover[6] from the
Old to the New Law. What happened when the God of
justice of the Old Testament, where the chief
measure of merit was *iustitia*, truth to His *ius* as
laid down in the Ten Commandments, became the New
Testament God of mercy, who translated the whole law
into the single injunction to love ("Thou shalt love
the Lord thy God with all thy heart ... Thou shalt
love thy neighbour as thyself. On these two commandments hang all the law and the prophets," Mt.
22: 37-40)?
Of the modes of defining the relationship
between the Old and the New Law current in his day,
Langland finds most fruitful that view of the
matter in which the New Law was seen not as superseding the Old, but as standing to it as the 'spirit'

to the 'letter', as being not the overthrow but the
revelation and fulfilment of the true meaning of the
Old ("I am come not to destroy the law but to
fulfil," Mt.5:17).   The Old Law is not discarded
but perfected in the New. The New Law of love was
not a 'new law', but a revelation of the spirit of
the Old, a new emphasis on the inner disposition or
spirit necessary for voluntary or willing obedience
to God's Commandments. As Anima says, this New Law
is not something other than but the perfection of
the Old Law which the Jews still espouse:

> 'And Jewes lyven in lele lawe - Oure Lord wroot it
> hymselve
> In stoon, for it stedefast was, and stonde sholde evere-
> *Dilige Deum et proximum*, is *parfit* Jewen lawe.'

> (XV.580-2)

For the Ten Commandments are merely a codification
of the behaviour that would be the natural result of
love of God and one's neighbour. They spell out in
letters what is dictated by the spirit of love or
charity that is implicit in them, and which was
revealed in Christ's New Law. In this sense, the
New Law is that "kynde" knowledge of the law that
Will seeks from the start: obedience that comes
from the natural prompting of the will, not from
conscious adherence to an acquired set of precepts.
     This view of the relationship between the Old Law
and the New is already evident in Langland's treatment of the subject on the two occasions in the
Visio where the transition from the one to the
other is alluded to. Holy Church's discourse in
Passus I (moving as it does from the primacy of
truth to the primacy of love via an account of the
Incarnation and Redemption) describes such a transition. But love is represented by her not as superseding or replacing truth, but as being the heart
or spirit and the "kynde knowynge" of truth; for
the commandment of love which Christ had asserted as
the New Law that contained the Old is quoted by her
in answer to Will's request for "kynde knowynge" of
truth:

> 'It is a *kynde knowynge* that kenneth in thyn *herte*
> For to loven thi Lord levere than thiselve.'

> (142-3)

Submission to the New Law consists in an inner
disposition or state of will which leads one
"kyndely" to be true and obedient to the commandments of God as spelled out in the Old Law,

spontaneously to do "as his word techeth" (I. 13).
Later on, it will be recalled, Holy Church asserts
that love stands to truth as "dedes" to "feith" (186-
7): it makes a reality of, realizes and fulfills the
faith professed as it were only by the letter of the
Old Law until willingly put into act - by the good
will to God and one's neighbour that is love.

The journey to Truth as described by Piers in
Passus V is the second occasion on which the passage
from Old to New Law is obliquely represented in the
Visio. As I have already pointed out, that journey
proceeds from the Ten Commandments of the Old Law,
through the "wiket" of the Incarnation and Redemption, to the love or charity that is the single
command of the New:

> 'Thou shalt see in thiselve Truthe sitte *in thyn herte*
> In a cheyne of charite, as thow a child were,
> To suffren hym and segge noght ayein thi sires wille.'

> (606-8)

Again, the New Law of love is revealed as the perfection and the realization of truth, not as superseding
it; it is truth written on the heart, not on tablets
of stone - the spirit and not the letter of the law,
obedience to written precept having been replaced by
obedience to the absolute authority of love in the
heart. Love is truth, obedience to the law, willed
and internalized - "kynde knowynge".[7]

In the *Do Wel* section of the *Vita*, it is the
figure of Patience who provides a medium through
which Langland traces a similar though more complex
spiritual progression, again expressed in terms of a
passage from the Old to the New Law. When Conscience
in Passus XIII leaves Clergie behind to walk the
world with Patience, he is represented as progressing
from one form of Christian knowledge to another: from
knowledge of the letter of the law, the sort of formal knowledge of Christian doctrine and precept impart-
ed by books and clerics, to the more inward and perfect appreciation of those truths gained from living
them through in love and patience. This pass-over
the poem defines as a kind of private and inner counterpart to the necessary historical transition from
the Old to the New Law that played so crucial a
part in God's plan of salvation for mankind as a
whole. For in the departure scene, Clergie is quite
distinctly associated with the Old Law[8]. Urging
Conscience to stay on solid ground with him, rather

than be seduced away into directionless wandering by
the rhapsodies of Patience (in whose brand of
Christianity Clergie plainly finds something 'soft'),
he says:

> 'I shal brynge yow a Bible, a book of the olde lawe,
> And lere yow, if yow like, the leeste point to knowe,
> That Pacience the pilgrym parfitly knew nevere.'

> (185-7)

Patience, for his part, is associated with the
transition to the New Law. His riddle (the exact
interpretation of which is a subject of some disagreement) apparently concerns the Passover (it
includes the phrase *Ex vi transicionis*) and the
transition to the new age of grace it prefigured
("In a signe of the Saterday that sette first the
kalendar" - presumably a reference to Easter
Saturday, the first day of the new age of grace,
when, following the Harrowing of Hell, the Old
Testament just crossed from the darkness of Limbo
into the eternal day of heaven). More importantly,
Patience is represented as a fervent evangelist of
the New Law of love, which he indicates as the
source of such Christian knowledge as he possesses:

> '*Dilge*, and Dobest - do thus taughte me ones
> A lemman that I lovede - Love was hir name,' etc.

> (138ff)

And his teaching speaks to the heart or the will
and not to the head. No-one can understand his
riddle, but Conscience finds himself moved (literally and metaphorically) by his fervour:

> 'Ac the wil of the wye and the wil of folk here
> Hath meved my mood to moorne for my synnes.
> The goode wil of a wight was nevere bought to the
> fulle:
> For ther nys no tresour therto to a trewe wille.'

> (190-3)

His is the spirit, not the letter of Clergie's
"bookes." Where Christian doctrine informs the
rational and moral understanding, Patience completes the process of conversion to truth thus begun
by directing the heart and the will toward it. And
in this Langland sees the spiritual process his
allegory depicts as accomplishing a consummation
similar to the perfecting and fulfilling of the Old
Law in the New.

For "parfit" is one of the triad of linked words (the other two are "pilgrym" and "preve") that by virtue of alliterative association come as the Passus proceeds to attach themselves to the figure of Patience as his defining attributes[9]. Patience puts to the test (*probat*), lives out the Christian doctrine learned from Clergie. He makes 'fact' of 'faith'. In willing passivity to all God may see fit to send him, he abandons the security of house and regular income for the uncertainties of the travelling pilgrim's life, with perfect faith in God to provide ("soothfast bileve" and *"Fiat voluntas tua"* (XIII. 217; XIV.49) are his victuals). His love, faith, and hope (the theological virtues rather than the cardinal virtues of the natural and the old or written law[10]) perfect the Christian education of the soul, by making felt realities of the Christian truths received from Clergie. Love, faith, and hope are virtues of the heart or will, not of the head. He turns formal knowledge into "kynde" knowledge, felt conviction. He stands to Clergie as experiential understanding to knowledge gained through written authority. It is in these terms that Conscience contrasts his pilgrim's knowledge with that of Clergie. It is gained from first-hand experience of the world, and may thus contain what no clerk can get from a book:

> 'Patience hath be in many place, and paraunter knoweth
> That no clerk ne kan.'
>
> (133-4)

All three key words are found together at the actual moment of transition itself, when it is made clear that the more formal knowledge transmitted by Clergie is not made obsolete or redundant by the deeper understanding that comes through patience:

> 'I shall dwelle as I do, my devoir to shewe,
> And confermen fauntekyns oother folk ylered
> Til Pacience have preved thee and parfit thee maked.'
> Conscience tho with Pacience passed, pilgrymes
> as it were.
>
> (212-5)

Just as it is the Church which formally baptizes and confirms in Christianity, so it also provides the necessary initiation in the process of Christian understanding. The formal knowledge it imparts in dogma and precept is not dispensible. Moral and intellectual obedience or truth to its teachings

can, however, only be completed, perfected, by more
private, inward means. There comes a point when one
can learn no more from Clergie, but must start to
feel and experience its truths for oneself, in a
process akin to that whereby the New Law perfected
and revealed the spirit underlying the letter of
the Old.

In fact, what Langland has done is to use the
concept of the historical progression of mankind
from one kind of God-given law to another as a
schema[11] for representing a transition from one kind
of understanding to another. In this respect, the
Passus is a logical development from the preceding
one, in which Ymagynatyf had similarly given an
analysis of different kinds of understanding based
on the scheme of the three eras or laws of Biblical
history: to wit, *tempus naturae* (when men were
guided only by their own natural or "kynde"-given
knowledge of right and wrong); *tempus legis* (when
they had the fuller and more precise regulation of
the written law of the Ten Commandments); *tempus
gratiae* (when, after the Redemption, the grace of
the Holy Ghost was made available in the New
Dispensation of mercy). Ymagynatyf applies this
triad to modes of understanding Christian truth (XII.
55-274): "kynde wit", the moral and rational
intelligence all men possess by nature; "clergie",
which supplements the natural intelligence with
the more specific and systematic doctrine taught by
the Church, and which he associates with 'law' and
'writing' (72, 97); and "grace", a more immediate
and perfect kind of illumination, inspiration by the
Holy Ghost, for which a soul is made fit chiefly by
humility - "*Patience* and poverte the place is ther
it groweth" (61). When, therefore, Conscience is
seen in the next Passus passing from Clergie to
Patience, the suggestion of a spiritual transition
analogous with that from the Old to the New Law is
in accord with the analysis of ways of knowing
already offered by Ymagynatyf [12].

In Passūs XIII-XIV, then, Langland has used
the concept of the three successive laws of Biblical
history, and in particular the transition from the
Old to the New Law, as a *schema* through which to
explore more profound and complicated spiritual
processes and relationships. The same procedure -
that of using the historical process whereby mankind
was guided to salvation as a key to analysing the
development toward spiritual perfection in the
individual soul - can be discerned in the *Do-Bet*

section of the *Vita* (XV - XVIII). Here, the tripartite division of Biblical history deriving from
the concept of the three distinctive laws to be
observed in it is clearly alluded to in the three
figures successively encountered by Will in Passūs
XVI - XVII - Abraham, Moses, and the Good Samaritan:
a rehearsal of Biblical history thus forming a
prelude to and preparation for the great account of
the Crucifixion and Harrowing of Hell in Passus
XVIII, events which marked the all-important and
final transition from the Old to the New Law, and
which form the climax of the section. The meetings
take place after Will has woken from his inner
dream of the Tree of Charity, and the figures are
clearly intended to represent the three eras/laws
of Biblical history: Abraham was the most important
of the patriarchs of the *tempus naturae*; Moses
brings with him the Ten Commandments he had received
on Mount Sinai (XVII. 2), which formed the written
law of the *tempus legis*; and the Good Samaritan
was the figure whose actions Christ Himself held up
in parable as the epitome of the New Law of charity,
the *Lex Christi* to which he takes the wounded man
(XVII.73).

Yet these characters are also identified as
the three theological virtues Faith (XVI. 176),
Hope (XVII. 1), and Charity. So that here, too,
Langland is correlating the notion of the three
laws that guided mankind toward salvation with the
means whereby an individual fits himself for salvation. Historical and private disciplines are again
brought together as comparable guiding aids in the
process of spiritual illumination and improvement,
collective and personal [13].

An incident representing the importance of the
transition from the Old to the New Law, and the
relationship between them, again follows as the
climax of the sequence: the parable of the Good
Samaritan. In Langland's version, the parable
becomes, through the identification of the priest,
Levite, and Samaritan with the three laws and the
three virtues, a demonstration of the difference
between the older laws and the New Law, and the
superior power of the latter to save/salve. It is
the only law which enjoins positive aid to fellow-
creatures in need (the other two are mainly negative
in force, and only prohibit injury to others).
Similarly, it is the only one which brings salvation
with it. For neither of the laws represented by
Abraham and Moses could, according to the common
interpretation of Biblical history, offer more than

provisional salvation, safe-keeping in Limbo
pending man's redemption by Christ, which alone
could justify and sanctify his obedience to such law
as was available to him at the time when he lived
(XVI.261-9; XVII.19-24). So it is from the
Samaritan, and not from Abraham or Moses and his
"maundement", that the injured man, representative
of sin-sick humanity, receives salve. In the same
way, an individual, in order to merit salvation
from his sins, must supplement faith and hope, and
adherence to the laws of "kynde" and to the written
law of the Bible, with love or charity. In sum,
only through the grace and mercy made available in
the New Dispensation established by Him who gave the
New Law of Love can one get true 'salve' for one's
sins - because it is the only law which commands
you to offer salve to the wounds of others. In this
there is a justice of the most compassionate kind,
an ideal mixture of the Old and the New.

And here again, in fact, Langland stresses the
New Law not as a break with the past, but as the
fulfilment of the spirit underlying its letter; its
perfection, not its overthrow. For Moses's law is
referred to by its New Testament summary in the
double command of love, the New Law to which Christ
declared the whole of the Old to be reducible:

> He plukkede forth a patente, a pece of an hard roche,
> Whereon was writen two wordes on this wise yglosed:
> *Dilige Deum et proximum tuum* -
> This was the tixte trewely - I took ful good yeme.
> The glose was gloriously writen with a gilt penne:
> *In hiis duobus mandatis tota lex pendet et prophete.*

(XVII.10-15)

This is to insist on the interconnection between
the Old and the New Law[14]. Charity does not supersede, or dispense with obedience to, God's law as
written in the Ten Commandments. Love of God and
one's neighbour is the unstated principle they
imply. In one way, this reference to the Old Law
via its New Law summary could be said to confuse
matters. Why is it Moses and his "maundement" have
it not within them to help the wounded man, if the
law in question enjoins the same duty of love as
the *Lex Christi* represented by the Samaritan? But
in another way the device importantly establishes
the Samaritan and his New Law as not in fact a 'new'
law, but simply adherence to the whole spirit of the
Old and a fulfilment of it. By none of the Ten
Commandments read according to the letter would

Moses be bound to help an injured fellow man. Only
according to the whole underlying spirit of their
text, as revealed in its New Law gloss, would he be
compelled to do so. So the Samaritan's New Law is
simply the perfect realization of the spirit of the
Old, Moses's law in action. That action is in
response to the inner compulsion of love, not the
outer constraint of written precept. Love is the
Old Law written on the will rather than on stone.

The remainder of Passus XVII is taken up with
an explanation of the importance in Christian theology of love or charity - given by the Samaritan,
its exponent in word and deed. Through taut and
pointed word-play on the term "kynde" (see in particular 272-6), he argues that to be unkind/uncharit-
able is to be unkind/unnatural, and to commit an
offence against the very heart or spirit of Christianity, against the very Spirit and nature of God
("Goddes owene kynde"). Want of charity, an
offence that strikes against the whole spirit and
not merely the letter of the Christian law, he thus
identifies with the sin against the Holy Ghost or
Spirit, which the Bible declares to be unforgive-
able[15]; for grace is attributed to God in His Third
Person, His Spirit, to offend whom is thus "wil-
fulliche" to 'quench' any possibility of mercy or
grace (288). It is a perversity of the will or
spirit -

> 'For ther nys sik ne sory, ne noon so much wrecche
> That he ne may lovye, and hym like, and lene of his
>   herte
> Good wille, good word'
>
> (347-9)

- which offends God in *His* essential spirit of mercy
and grace[16].

The Samaritan thus establishes that mercy
itself obeys the principle of equity John of Salis-
buty saw as underlying all law ('do as you would be
done by')[17]-as had the Angel ("*Qualia vis metere,
talia grana sere ... Si seritur pietas, de pietate
metas*", Prol. 136-8), and Holy Church ("haveth
ruthe ... For the same mesure that ye mete, amys
outher ellis, Ye shulle ben weyen therwith whan ye
wenden hennes," I.175-8). God is a God "withoute
mercy" (XVII.217) to all who show none. Love and
mercy in man kindle into life the flame of the Holy
Ghost, and "melteth (God's) myght into mercy - to
merciable and to noon othere" (233). To be
"*ingratus* to thi kynde" (256) is 'willfully' to

renounce grace, and so deserves none. It is the
same principle as underlies the pardon's 'Do well
and have well, do ill and have ill'; God's loving
kindness is shown only to the loving and the "kynde".
The mercy of the New Dispensation and the love of
the New Law work toward the fulfilment of the Old
Law of justice, and accoring to the Old Testament
precept of "an eye for an eye, a tooth for a tooth".
And, as had been established in the *Visio* with
regard to human law, the penalties required by
justice must be paid. God cannot be merciful in
defiance of His primal attribute of justice. The
Samaritan is insistent on this point. The heavenly
king must, like the earthly, exact vengeance and
satisfaction for wrongs and injuries done others.
As an earthly judge cannot parden an offender until
"equite" is satisfied (307), so it is with the
eternal judge. There must be some *pena* undergone in
satisfaction for the offence: "er his rightwisnesse
to ruthe torne, som restitucion bihoveth" (316).
Where other means of amends are not open to the
wrong doer, "for swich that may not paie", the self-
imposed *pena* of repentance may be accepted as
"satisfaccion"(317) - but satisfaction there must be.
In fact, this climax to the Faith-Hope-Charity
sequence unfolded in Passūs XVI- XVII, designed to
emphasize the supreme importance of charity, contains within itself perhaps the most impassioned
and dramatic plea for justice to be found in the
whole poem, issuing as a resouding imperative from
mindfulness of the wrongs done the innocent:

> ' Innocence is next God, and nyght and day it crieth
> "Vengeaunce! Vengeaunce! Forgyve be it nevere
> That shente as and shedde oure blood - forshapte
>   us, as it seemed:
> *Vindica sanguinem iustorum*!"
> Thus "Vengeaunce, vengeaunce!" verrey charite
>   asketh.'

> (289-92)

Charity itself must champion the cause of justice.
The guilty cannot be held more dear than the innocent, true compassion for whom must call aloud in
righteous wrath for the wrongs suffered by them to
be avenged: their blood must move not only justice
but charity itself to vengeance.
So even in the midst of this exposition of the
supreme importance of the New Law of Love, the
inviolability of the Old is asserted. The same is

true of the culminating passus of the *Do-Bet*
section, the famous account of the Crucifixion and
Harrowing of Hell (Passus XVIII). These were the
very events that inaugurated and sealed the New
Dispensation. Through them, man was redeemed from
the penalty he had incurred in the Fall. The justice of the Old Dispensation became the mercy of the
New at precisely this point of time. It is appropriate, therefore, that this, the very moment of the
transition between the two, should constitute the
most memorable passus of the poem, since the relationship between them bears so centrally on Langland's
need to reconcile justice and mercy, the Old and the
New Law - or, more precisely, to preserve the Old in
the New, to establish God as still just, and the
assumption that His justice can be evaded by
reliance on His mercy as a delusion (a heresy that
the friars as false prophets are encouraging at the
end of the poem, in giving absolution without atonement, without satisfaction for justice).

For the most striking aspect of Langland's
account of the Crucifixion and Harrowing is the way
in which these events, traditionally associated so
centrally with the mercy of God, are represented
consistently and insistently as a triumph for and a
vindication of His justice. In the first place, the
popular conception of the crucifixion as a battle is
here used to depict a joust with a judicial function
- this is a trial by combat, intended to determine
legal title to disputed property: Pier's fruit.[18]
This has been made clear in the anticipatory allusion
to the forthcoming joust found in Passus XVI:

> And thanne sholde Jesus juste therfore, bi juggement
>   of armes,
> Wheither sholde fonge the fruyt - the fend or hymselve.

(95-6)

Pilate sits as referee and judge to "deme hir
botheres right" (XVIII. 37). Christ paradoxically
wins the joust by being slain in it; for it is the
giver (Longinus) and not the receiver of the mortal
spear-thrust who acknowledges defeat and "Yilt hym
recreaunt rennyng, right at Jesus wille" (100)[19].

When Christ arrives before the gates of Hell,
physical 'debate' gives way to verbal, but His
object remains unchanged: to vindicate the justice
of His title to the comdemned souls, and thus of His
action in re-possessing Himself of them. For this
is His principal concern in His lengthy speech

addressed to Hell and its inhabitants: to prove
that this present act of mercy toward mankind,
remission of the penalty incurred at the Fall, is
perfectly in accord with justice.   And in case we
should miss the chief point He and Langland are
making, the entire episode is framed by an account
of the dispute and reconciliation of the four
daughters of God - Righteousness, Truth, Mercy, and
Peace - in an expanded narrative version of Psalm
84:11 ("Mercy and truth are met together, righteousness and peace have kissed each other").   Before His
speech, Truth and Righteousness claim that justice
can admit of no remission of the death-sentence
passed on mankind;   Peace and Mercy, however,
declare that such a pardon is at hand.   After it,
all four kiss in reconcilement.   The incident is a
way of pointing to the significance Langland intends
Christ's speech to have: we are to see Him as
having justified His mercy, as having fulfilled the
Old Law in establishing the New.   God did not and
does not extend mercy in violation of justice.[20]
     In the first place, Christ establishes that the
devil is not being cheated of his due, but has got
his exactly just deserts.   As Lucifer disguised
himself as a serpent to take the fruit from God's
territory ("For in my paleys, Paradis, in persone
of an addre, Falsliche thou fettest there thyng that
I lovede," 336-7), so Christ has disguised His
divinity in manhood (357) to fetch it from his.
Guile for guile is in strict accord with the Old Law
principle of *quid pro quo*:

> "the Olde Lawe graunteth
> That gilours be bigiled - and that is good reson:
> *Dentem pro dente et oculum pro oculo*."
>
> (339-40)

Christ claims man by the Old Law, then, not by a new
one.   And His mercy to man is just punishment for
Satan: Do-evil has got evil.   He sowed in guile
and theft, and has reaped what he sowed.   And
justice being the virtue which pays debts, gives to
all what is due or owing them,   that God who is
justice itself gives even the devil his due: He
has, He points out, paid the exact price, given
precise "amendes",   His life for the forfeit life of
mankind, the gallows-tree of the cross for the tree
that caused the Fall;   He as a man has paid the debt
of death man owed;   and Langland exults in the
steady beat of balanced antitheses and parallels
that drum out the very rhythms of justice itself:

> "*Ergo* soul shal soule quyte and synne to synne wende,
> And al that man hath mysdo, I, man, wole amende it.
> Membre for membre was amendes by the Olde Lawe,
> And lif for lif also - and by that lawe I clayme
> Adam and al his issue at my wille herafter.
> And that deeth in hem fordide, my deeth shal rileve."
>
> (341-6)

This memorable passage ends by drawing attention once more to the fact that Christ is exercising His mercy through the law and not in defiance of it, "by right and by reson" (a phrase used at the time to refer to justice[21]), and by citing the all-important New Testament text in which Christ asserted that He came to fulfil, not to destroy the law:

> 'So leve it noght, Lucifer, ayein the lawe I fecche hem,
> But by right and by reson raunsone here my liges:
> *Non veni solvere legem set adimplere.*'
>
> (349-50)

So in the very announcement of the New Dispensation of merciful redemption from Hell is found an assertion of the Old Law of equity and its key texts, followed by a reminder that Christ came to fulfil and perfect the law. His mercy was a supreme manifestation of His justice.[22] Having proved that His redemption of man gives Satan his due, He has now to establish that it does not deny man his: that no penalty really due their sin, no debt, is being remitted. Though their crime had incurred the death-penalty attached to it, they had not been condemned to *eternal* death ("I bihighte hem noght here helle *for evere*," so they "Shul nought be dampned to *the deeth that is withouten ende*," 333, 379). They have done time/death enough. Moreover, to visit an offence with the legal penalty affixed to it twice over is inequitable[23]:

> 'It is not used on erthe to hangen a feloun
> Ofter than ones, though he were a tretour.'
>
> (380-1)

Two death-penalties is a harshness denied even the most tyrannical of earthly kings. The death of the body is visited upon man as a due penalty for his original felony. The death of the soul (its eternal severance from God in Hell), often referred to as "the deeth secounde"[24], and here as "the deeth that is withouten ende", is not therefore due him. The Old Law does not require two eyes for an eye.

Justice demands that the punishment fit the crime, and a penalty of eternal death of the soul over and above death of the body would not therefore be consonant with "right and reson." Every man perishes physically in atonement for the felony of Adam (original sin). If he dies with any unatoned actual sin (sin committed in his own person) to his account, then he will do time, not in the death-cell of Hell, but in the ordinary prison of Purgatory:

> 'And though Holy Writ wole that I be wroke of hem that diden ille -
> *Nullum malum impunitum &c* -
> Thei shul be clensed clerliche and clene wasshen of hir synnes
> In my prisone Purgatorie, til *parce* it hote.'
>
> (391-3)

Purgatory is thus seen as God's merciful administration of His justice. It punishes without destroying. Justice, then, is not being relaxed in extending mercy to man. He continues to suffer the death-penalty pronounced on all mankind commonly for original sin, and he does time in Purgatory for actual sin. In fact, the Redemption restores "the equilibrium of justice", by alleviating a penalty that overbalanced the offence.

Christ's mercy is thus seen as a vindication of divine justice delayed since the Fall. It perfects justice in correcting injustice, and restoring the rule of 'do well and have well, do ill and have ill', the operation of which had been in suspense while the devils ill went unrequited, and man's well unrewarded in an over-severe penalty for his original ill. God's mercy, then, is born out of His justice and is conditioned by it.

    Do-Best consists of only two passūs, which represent Christ's gaining of His spiritual kingdom, His establishment of His spiritual rule (founded on merciful justice) in the New Law of love under the New Dispensation of mercy, His arrangements for its consolidation and administration by the church; and the attempts of Antichrist to pervert the ideal equilibrium by evading justice and distorting mercy. It it an account of the founding of a spiritual empire that parallels the founding of the institution of earthly kingship which had been described in the Prologue; a spiritual commonalty governed by a regime administering a law which is both just and merciful, the ideal which the angel had urged on the king (*iustus es, esto pius*, 134).

    So the interest in government that had been

apparent in the Prologue and the *Visio*, centring on
the person of the king, the administration of the
law, and fair systems of rewards and penalties, is
now once again in evidence. Christianity is an
institution that claims the right to govern the
conduct of its adherents. It must therefore have a
king who has earned the right to govern, laws that
are both fair and humane, machinery for administering them (the church), and it must justly protect
and reward those who obey them (*nullum malum* must
be *impunitum*), and visit those who offend against
them with penalties, to ensure that crime does not
pay (*nullum bonum* must be *irremuneratum*). It is
with an account of this Christian commonwealth and
its founder and emperor that the section begins.
   In the first place, Christ is described as
rising through the ranks of knight, king, conqueror
- the degrees of leadership - successively earning
the right to govern by winning a kingdom (heaven)
for His people, establishing laws that guide men on
the way of truth toward a great reward, exalting
and remunerating the good, and degrading the false,
fighting for His nation, protecting it against their
enemies, helping them towards health and livelihood,
and establishing a machinery of government to dispense pardons in accord with justice (26-199). As
a child, He is honoured as the future 'king of kings'
by the three kings who brought with them gifts that
betokened that ideal mixture of justice and mercy
with which all kings should administer their law:
"Reson and Rightwisness and Ruthe thei offrede"
(83). It is a king's duty to rule and defend His
people (42-3) - and so did Jesus. He "justified
(governed by law and justice[25]) and taughte hem The
lawe of lif" (44-5); and He perfected the defective
law they had inherited ("And lawe lakkede tho, for
men lovede noght hir enemys", 112) by revealing the
spirit of love for God and all men underlying its
letter. And he defended them by His actions and by
His teaching from physical and moral evil (from
"foule yveles, feveres and fluxes" and "from fendes
that in hem was, and false bileve," 46-7). To be a
conqueror requires in the highest degree the virtues
of generosity, nobility, and courage ("of hardynesse
of herte and of hendeness," 31) that characterize a
great ruler. This highest title Christ won by doing
battle for a kingdom, with which to enfeoff and
ennoble the true in reward for obedience to His laws
("To make lordes of laddes, of lond that he wynneth
... To maken alle folk free that folwen his lawe ...
he yeveth largely al his lele liges Places in

Paradis at hir partynge hennes," 32, 59-61). He delivered His nation from enslavement by their foes, liberating and ennobling, making "frankeleyns, free men" (39) of those who had been "Luciferis cherles" (55), and making - literally - a 'bondman' of their arch-enemy ("And bond hym as he is bounde, with bondes of yrene," 57). In short, He gained by courage a kingdom whose wealth He justly uses to exalt and enrich those who obey His law, but denies to those who "folwen noght his lawes", who thus become "foule thralles ... tikes and cherles" (33-7). It is an ideal state, whose political economy and judicial and legal system are mutually re-inforcing: the wealth of the nation is used to reward adherence to the law, and denied to disobedience - a spiritual version of the mini-state Piers had attempted to establish in Passus VI, granting or withholding the fruits of his land accordingly as his followers obey or disobey the rule of "labour for lyflod"[26].

Christ's life is further triply divided into the familiar categories of Do-Wel, Do-Bet and Do-Best. The moment at which He is said to Do Best is when He endows the Church with the power to dispense and administer the pardon and mercy He made available to all men through the Redemption: that is, when He institutionalizes the New Dispensation. Here, then, is another representation of the significance of the transition from the Old to the New Law. The New Dispensation differs from the Old in making mercy available to sinners: pardon from the penalty of original sin through the Redemption, and pardon from actual sin through the sacrament of shrift administered by the Church He founded. This latter is the Church's 'binding and loosing power' (the authority to absolve from sin), which in the poem is given by Christ to Piers, who here becomes conflated with St. Peter, the first head of the Church, and so representative of the original and ideal nature of its authority. The lines recording the conferring of this authority stress the *mercy* that is the essential characteristic of the New Dispensation as distinct from the Old:

> 'And whan this dede was doon, Dobest he thoughte,
> And yaf Piers power, and *pardon* he grauntede:
> To alle maner men, *mercy* and *foryifnesse*;
> To hym, myghte men to *assoille* of alle manere synnes'.

(183-6)

Yet here again one finds the continuing validity of

the Old Law of justice asserted, even at the moment
of its transformation into the New Dispensation of
mercy. The pardon Christ authorized the church to
grant has a condition attached:

> 'In covenaunt that thei come and kneweliche to paye
> To Piers pardon the Plowman - *Redde quod debes*.
>   'Thus hath Piers power, be his pardon paied,
> To bynde and unbynde bothe here and ellis,
> And assoille men of alle synnes save of dette one.'

(187-91)

The importance of these lines has already been
stressed,   and I can now only end as I began, by
re-emphasizing the significance both of them and of
the final events of the poem. The injunction 'Pay
what you owe' (Mt.18:28)   is of the essence of the
virtue of justice or truth, defined as it was as
'giving to all that which is due (*debetur*) or owing
them', payment of debts. In context, it refers to
the payment of literal money-debts; to justice in
one's general dealings with one's fellow men (that
aspect of the *spiritus justicie* that Brewer, who
wishes to go on cheating the public, finds unaccept-
able);   and to payment of the *debitum* of sin by
"amendes" - penance, repentance, restitution. The
double meaning of 'pay' (appease, satisfy; pay)
insists on the centrality of the concept of debt;
to satisfy justice, and the condition of the pardon,
debts must be paid. Twice the word is used, giving
the impression that this pardon, like its lesser
imitations, must be bought. It must be 'purchased'
(a word regularly used for the obtaining of pardons,
whether or not for money [27]): it is a pardon that
must be paid for, grace that does not come *gratis*,
a *quid pro quo* - a contradiction in terms, in fact.
Like its predecessor in Passus VII, its promised
mercy articulates itself in the uncompromising
'letters' of justice. To forgive or absolve from
all except debt - what else but a literal or metaphorical debt *can* be forgiven? The verb *solvere*
was used in medieval Latin to refer to the settling
of a debt [28]; here, such *solutio* is made a pre-
condition of *absolutio*.
  So the New Law of mercy is again revealed as
conditioned and governed by the prior law of
justice. God is first and foremost just, and can
give no mercy that does not satisfy or "paye"
justice. Sinners, then, cannot expect redemption
of their debts by evading the atonement demanded by

justice, just as God did not allow even Himself to
redeem mankind except by the Atonement, paying the
life due as "amendes." But no sooner is Piers's
back turned than Antichrist starts to undermine the
true foundation of mercy conditioned by justice that
could have made the church a really effective force
in keeping society on the road to truth. His forces
at once predict that they will succeed in disguising
and perverting the true and original nature of the
Christian faith and of confession and contrition:

> 'Confession and Contricion, and youre carte the
>   Bileeve
> Shal be coloured so queyntely and covered under oure
>   sophistrie ...'
>
> (348-9)

This is precisely what happens: the sacrament of
confession becomes so distorted as it is administered by the friars that its true function is quite
forgotten. Mercy is then not given in exchange for
atonement by penance, repentance, and restitution,
but sold. And when mercy can be bought for cash,
as Reason had realized in Passus IV, justice becomes
the slave of Mede.
    And it is offences against the Old Law of
justice, which as he has represented it was not
superseded but perfected and enshrined in the New,
that Langland discerns as the root cause of the
moral and spiritual degeneration from the original
Christian ideal that he now proceeds to describe.
Basically, everyone wants the New Law on easy terms,
not on terms of the Old: Piers's pardon without
the condition attached. This becomes apparent when
Conscience summons his community to the Easter
sacrament. Anyone taking the sacrament had to be
confessed first, as it was mortal sin to receive
it in other than a state of grace. Conscience
therefore offers it only to those who have satisfied the conditions already stated as attached to
valid absolution: to such as have "ypaied To Piers
pardon the Plowman, *redde quod debes*" (392-3). And
as it now becomes clear what the satisfaction of
justice through payment of debts involves, there is
a marked waning of enthusiasm.

> 'How?' quod al the comune. 'Thou conseillest us to
>   yelde
> Al that we owen any wight er we go to housel?'
>
> (394-5)

They must in justice pay any monetary or moral debts outstanding. Conscience, in reply, confirms this; and adds that they must, furthermore, forgive others their debts to them if they want their own debt of sin forgiven, since mercy operates, as we have seen, on the 'reap as you have sewn' principle of equity - as the Lord's prayer itself states:

> 'That is my conseil,' quod Conscience, ' and
>   Cardinale Vertues;
> That ech man foryyve oother, and that wole the Pater-
>   noster -
> *Et dimitte nobis debita nostra &c* -
> And so to ben assoilled, and siththen ben houseled.'

> (396-8)

Most importantly, the condition of justice attached to absolution requires men such as the brewer to stop cheating the public of their due by selling them watered-down ale. This hits where it hurts most - in the purse. And Brewer is quite adamant that justice is too high a cost for him to pay for peace of conscience:

> 'Ye? Baw!' quod a brewere, 'I wol noght be ruled
> By Jesu! for al youre janglynge, with *Spiritus
>   Iusticie*,
> Ne after Conscience, by Crist! '

> (399-401)

In Conscience's reply can be heard the anger born of dawning desperation. Justice is the staple of the New Law, the chief seed from which its mercy of salvation can be harvested:

> 'Caytif!' quod Conscience, 'cursede wrecche!
> Unblessed artow, brewere, but if God thee helpe.
> But thow lyve by loore of *Spiritus Iusticie*,
> The chief seed that Piers sew, ysaved worstow nevere.'

> (406-9)

But the seed has fallen on stony ground. Self-interest and greed make all willfully deaf to his insistence that mercy requires men to be just. And by the end of the Passus, justice has been replaced by its opposites, fraud and guile[29], in both the rulers and the ruled, in the common greed for "mede", the arch-enemy of truth and justice: there is "gyle ... among the peple" (458); extortion among the land-owners (462-7); and abuse by the king for his own

enrichment of his position as "heed of lawe" (471-2).
And by the beginning of the final Passus, the whole
crop of 'truth' or justice has been destroyed by
the choking growth of "fals" and "gile" (53-7) -
that cheating of one's livelihood out of others
that is the very opposite of giving to all their due,
and of which the friars, abusing the sacrament of
penance for their own material advantage and to the
spiritual detriment of their clients, are prime
examples. The friars are from the first associated
with this use of guile and "fals" to "spede mennes
nedes" (55) inspired by Antichrist ("Freres folwede
that fend, for he gaf hem copes," 58), and which is
the perversion of those abilities granted by the
Holy Ghost in the previous Passus (226-56) specifically to enable men to earn an honest livelihood,
to satisfy their material needs justly ("And lyve
by that labour a lele lif and a trewe", 233, 238).

The perversion of both earthly and divine law
and justice follows with a terrible inevitability.
Mede's florins overpower them with appalling ease.
First comes the corruption of law as it is administered in the literal courts, secular -

> (Coveitise) boldeliche bar adoun with many a bright
>   noble
> Much of the wit and wisdom of Westmynstre Halle.
> He jogged til a justice and justed in his eere,
> And overtilte al his truthe with 'Tak this up amende-
>   ment.'
>
> (132-5)

and ecclesiastical -

> And to the Arches in haste he yede anoon after,
> And tornede Cyvyle into Symonye, and siththe he took
>   the Official:
> For a menever mantel he made lele matrymonye
> Departen er deeth cam, and a devors shapte.
>
> (136-9)[30]

The law of the *forum penitentiale* follows suit, as
the friar "gooth and gadereth, and gloseth there he
shryveth" (369), selling absolution for a "pryvee
paiement". The friars are ready for their own
purposes to pander to and exploit the popular disinclination to receive pardon on the regular terms
from the regular priesthood; that is, to have payment of their debt of sin enjoined on them in the
form of penance and restitution. They find lawful,
regular mercy conditioned by justice too harsh a

277

cure, and so go to the irregulars, the friars, who have usurped a false status as "curatours" (326-7), and offer only a deceptive 'charm' for the sickness of sin. They give an acquittance bought for money that only makes the commonalty the more "bolde" to break the laws of heaven and earth, as the *Visio* had stated must always be the case where pardon is for sale. "Lope he so lightly, laughen he wolde, And eft the bolder be to bete myne hewen" (IV. 106-7) - a statement that had its counterpart in the warning to those who trust in their ability to "purchace yow pardon and the Popes bulles" not to be "the bolder to breke the ten hestes" (VII. 184-7).

Society is only in good order when the rules and the laws it professes are realities and really enforced. Once it has found a way of buying itself off penalties, exchanging justice for meed, it becomes lawless and falls into moral anarchy. In such circumstances, a theology of indiscriminate mercy, a Christianity in which the justice of the Old Law is no longer insisted on, and the mercy of the New promiscuously dispensed for money, is no cure, but simply a drug to lull the conscience: a real 'opiate of the people':

> 'He lith and dremeth,' seide Pees, 'and so do manye
> othere;
> The frere with his phisyk this folk hath enchaunted,
> And plastred hem so esily that hii drede no synne!'
>
> (378-80) [31]

NOTES

1. For a detailed study of the trinitarian principle governing the structure of the *Vita*, see Frank, *op.cit.*
2. Here and in the following pages all italics within quotations from the poem (except those used for Latin) are my own.
3. A useful account of medieval thinking on this subject is given by A.J. Minnis, *Chaucer and Pagan Antiquity* (Cambridge; Totowa, New Jersey, 1982), pp.31-60.
4. On the significance of the forty-fifth year (often conceived of as marking the transition from middle to old age) see J.A. Burrow, 'Langland *Nel Mezzo Del Cammin*', in Heyworth, pp.21-41.
5. 'Imagination' was the faculty capable of forming represent-

ations of or conjectures upon what was not immediately present to the senses; see A.J. Minnis, 'Langland's Ymaginatif and Late-Medieval Theories of Imagination', in *Comparative Criticism: A Year Book (3)*, ed. E.S. Shaffer (Cambridge, 1981), pp.71-103.

6.   The Christian festival of Easter (Pasch) coincided with the Jewish Passover, after which it was named and with which it remained closely associated; Easter marked the transition to the New Law and the *Tempus Gratiae*, inaugurated by the crucifixion and resurrection of Christ.

7.   The contrast between the tables of stone and the tables of the heart derives from 2 Cor.3:3, and was commonly employed, sometimes with reference to the difference between the Old Law of the Ten Commandments and the New Law of Charity (see Goldsmith, p.100, n.16), sometimes to distinguish between formal knowledge of and heartfelt commitment to God's law (see *Policraticus*, IV.vi (p.24)). That the love of the New Law represents the perfect fulfilment of the Old was also an idea Biblical in origin: see, in particular, Mt.22:37-40 and Rom.13:10˙ ('Plenitudo ergo legis est dilecto'). The latter text was widely repeated and paraphrased: see, for instance, Dunning, p.157 (quoting Augustine): Abelard, *Ethics*, p.72; *Ancrene Wisse*, p.20.

R.M. Ames, 'The Pardon Impugned by the Priest' (in *The Alliterative Tradition in the Fourteenth Century*, ed. B.S. Levy and P.E. Szarmach (Kent, Ohio, 1981),pp.47-68), also stresses the importance of the relationship between the two Laws, and the doctrine of 'letter' and 'spirit' that underlies Langland's representation of it. G. Mathew similarly comments on the intimate connection discernible in the poem between the charity of the New Law and the justice or truth of the Old: charity is "the motive force of justice ... For it is fired with the desire to give each man that which is his due (*art.cit.*, p.363).

8.   *cf* Ames, pp.55-6.

9.   In associating the words "preve", "parfit" (and later also "poverte") with patience, Langland is bringing together related conventional pairings. For all three words were, separately, often collocated with that virtue. Eg: (1) "*patientia ... probando* et manifestando omnes virtutes" (Peter the Chanter, quoted by Frank, p.73); "... *prevyng* her feith and her *pacyens*" (Margery Kempe, p.229); "*prove* men of theyr *pacyens*" (Skelton's *Magnificence*, 11.1917,2371); (2) "Quia vera *perfectio* de *patientia* nascitur" (Gregory, *Moralia*, quoted by Goldsmith, p.109, n.29); "*perfite paciens*" (*Friar Daw's Reply*, 1.225; *Minor Poems of John Lydgate*, Part I, ed. H.N. MacCraken, E.E.T.S. E.S.107 (1911), *Legend of St.*

Petronilla, 1.16);   (3) on the common association between
poverty and patience, see Frank, p.73. On the importance of the concept of 'perfection' in Langland, see
Bloomfield, *passim*, esp.pp.44ff; on poverty, see G.
Shepherd, 'Poverty in *Piers Plowman*', in *Social Relations
and Ideas: Essays in Honour of R.H. Hilton*, ed. T. Aston,
(Cambridge, 1983), pp.169-89; on the virtue of patience
generally, see the collection of essays in *The Triumph of
Patience*, ed. G. Schiffhorst (Orlando, Florida, 1978).

10.   See n.14 to ch.II *supra*.

11.   The term is borrowed from E.H. Gombrich, *Art and illusion*
(London, 1960), who uses it to refer to the received
models that form the necessary starting-point for any
artistic exercise. The artist may develop and modify
the *schema* almost out of recognition, but he cannot work
in a void without one. The terms seems to me applicable
to Langland's use of both the Trinity and the passage
from Old to New Law in the *Vita*.

12.   The contrast drawn by Langland between the knowledge of
Clergy and that of Patience is actually his own version
of a conception of two degrees of gnosis (*knowledge* and
understanding) that seems to have been quite common, and
which took various forms. In monastic philosophy and
elsewhere, it emerged as the contrast between the knowledge gained through books and the understanding acquired
through personal experience (*experientia*) and through
love (*per amorem*) - as is Patience's - which was rather a
'relish' than a 'science'; such inward comprehension
was gained from reading "in the book of experience, in
the heart, rather than a manuscript"; to write and to
read came first, to understand and "to prove" followed
(see Leclercq, pp.16,26,41,217,256). A similar contrast
between formal knowledge and felt understanding is to be
found in Hilton's *Scale of Perfection* II, where it is
used to distinguish the knowledge of Christian truth
possessed by those in the active life from the more
'perfect' understanding of the contemplative; throughout
the treatise, virtuous members of the active life are
referred to as "reformyd in faith" (that is, taking the
truths taught them by the church - by Clergy - on
trust, in faith), whereas the contemplatives are
reformed also in "felynge"; they feel those truths for
themselves. With the latter type of knowledge there
is again associated 'relish' ("savour"), and also
meekness, and the 'perfection' of love and charity that
results from inspiration of grace by the Holy Ghost
(which are also attributes of Patience); he who is thus
'reformed in feeling' knows God "not blyndely and nakedly
and unsavourly, as doþ a clerke þat seeþ Him bi his
clergi only þurgh miȝt of his naked resoun, but he seeþ
Him in vdirstandynge þat is confortid and liȝted bi þe

gift of þe Holy Gost" (pp.14-16,67,98,137). The
inferiority of knowledge gained through authority to
that acquired through experience was axiomatic enough
to allow Chaucer to play ironically on the principle in
The Wife of Bath's Prologue and *The Friar's Tale* (*CT*.
III.1-3; 1515-20; 1636-8).

13. It was not, of course, uncommon to interpret Biblical
events as spiritual allegories: in this, Langland was
the beneficiary of a rich and complex tradition. Nor
was he the first to use the concept of the Old and New
Laws figuratively (see Goldsmith, p.24).

14. *cf* Ames, p.53. Goldsmith notes that Christ's double
injunction to love is actually a quotation from the
Old Law (see Deut. 6:5; Levit. 19:18), and that this
had been pointed out by Gregory (pp.48-9).

15. The sin against the Holy Ghost was variously interpreted (for examples, see Frank, p.91; *Lay Folks'
Catechism* (Wycliffite version), ll.156-9), though
there appears to be no precedent for Langland's
definition of it. But since Abelard felt free to offer
an explanation of it at variance with that which he
represents to be the common one (*Ethics*, pp.94-6),
there was evidently sufficient lack of unanimity to
enable Langland to invent (or perhaps choose) the
one that best suited his poetic and dialectic
purposes.

16. Langland's argument here rests on a fairly complex
manipulation of several different established colloc-
ations: (1) between the Holy Ghost and love or
charity (*Lay Folks' Catechism* (Wycliffite version),
l.99); (2) between the will and charity, the latter
being rightly directed will, or 'good will'; (3) between
right will and the Holy Ghost: "þe power of þe Fadir
... þe wisdom of þe Sone ... þe good lasting wille of
þe Holi Goost" (*Jack Upland*, p.54).

17. See p.1 *supra*.

18. Trial by combat was based on the theory that the
disputants thereby submitted their cause to the
judgment of God, which would announce itself in whatever
outcome His providence ordained (see Robertson, p.9;
Policraticus, VIII.xxiii.p.402). It could legally
be resorted to in cases where misappropriation of
property (land or chattels) by force or fraud was
alleged (*Potter's Outlines*, p.121; Jenks, pp.47,57):
in the poem, Christ accuses Satan of theft by guile.
For a detailed analysis of the judicial duel and the
part it plays in the allegory here, see A. Baldwin,
pp.68ff.

19. "Recreant" means (1) "yielding or giving up one's cause";
(2) "craven, dishonoured". It related both to the *legal*

allegory of a trial by combat (which ended when one of
the parties was brought to cry craven; see *Potter's
Outlines*, p.121); and to the *theological* significance
of the scene (Longinus recants his erroneous belief that
Christ was not the Son of God (91), so yielding up his
Jewish for the Christian faith).

20. The debate of the four daughters of God was a popular
topos, but was not usually associated with the Harrowing
(see Frank, p.93). On the significance of its introduction into Passus XVIII, *cf* A. Baldwin, p.67.

21. *cf* A. Baldwin, p.42; *Potter's Outlines*, p.24.

22. Ames likewise stresses that Christ "does not appeal to
a New Law of mercy, but to the Old Law of justice"
(p.58).

23. See p.223 *supra*.

24. See *Pearl*, 1.652.

25. For "justifie" in this sense, *cf St. Erkenwald*, 1.229;
Hoccleve's *Regement of Princes*, ed. F.J. Furnivall,
E.E.T.S. E.S. 72 (1899), 1.2786.

26. In characterizing Christ chiefly as a lawgiver and
warrior defender and liberator, Langland is emphasizing
him as a mirror of kings, for it was precisely in the
dual conduct of wars and laws (*cf* 42-3) that the function
of kingship was often said to consist: "he mynestrith
to his reaume defence and justice" (*Governance*, p.127);
"the office of a King is to fight the battles of his
people and judge them rightfully" (*De Laudibus*, p.3);
he should "Keepe and deffende hem from adversitee ...
Governeth hem in lawe and equitee" (Hoccleve, *Balade
to Henry V on his Accession*, 11.18-20); a model ruler
"subjects to the law those whom he frees from the yoke
of slavery" (*Policraticus*, VIII.xxii, p.395) - as does
Christ here. 'Conquest' carried no derogatory overtones,
and was carefully distinguished from oppression and
tyranny (*cf ibid*, VIII.xxi, p.390). More importantly,
to conquer a land was to establish valid title to it by
'right of conquest' (*cf* Gower's *Vox Clamantis*, 11.332-6);
the chivalric concept of Christ as gaining for Himself
the realm of Christendom by hard-won title of conquest
is found also in a very elided form in the *Lay Folks'
Catechism*, (Wycliffite version),11.92-3: "... þat nobyl
man þat com down into erthe to gete him a Reme".

27. *cf* VII.3,38; Margery Kempe, pp.75,79.

28. See, for instance, *De Laudibus*, pp.80,86.

29. Guile (falseness) constitutes the chief threat to the
spiritus justicie (XIX.299-303); *cf* Spenser's Legend of
Justice, where references to it, personified (*FQ* V.vi.
32ff; ix.5ff) or otherwise, are frequent.

30. The Arches was the provincial court of the Archbishop of
Canterbury; the 'official' was the bishop's delegate
in the consistory court; 'Civil' refers to the Roman

Law on which much of Canon Law was based (see Pearsall,
C Text. n. to II.61; Bennett, n. to II.173; B. Gilbert,
art.cit).

31. At 378, the MSs vary as between "adreynt" and "and
dremeth"; Schmidt prints the former.

SELECT BIBLIOGRAPHY

The list is confined to works referred to in the course
of the book.

A   EDITIONS OF *PIERS PLOWMAN* *(listed chronologically):*

The Vision of William Concerning Piers the Plowman
    (Prologue and Passūs I-VII), ed. W.W. Skeat (Oxford,
    1869).
The Vision of William Concerning Piers the Plowman in
    Three Parallel Texts, ed. W.W. Skeat, 2 vols (Oxford,
    1886).
Langland: Piers Plowman: The Prologue and Passūs I-VII,
    ed. J.A.W. Bennett (Oxford, 1972).
The Vision of Piers Plowman: A Complete Edition of the
    B Text, ed. A.V.C. Schmidt (London, 1978).
Piers Plowman by William Langland: An Edition of the
    C Text, ed. D. Pearsall (London, 1978).
Piers Plowman: The Z Version, ed. A.G. Rigg and C. Brewer
    (Toronto, 1983).

Translation:
Piers the Plowman, tr. J.F. Goodridge (Harmondsworth,
    1966).

B   OTHER TEXTS *(listed alphabetically by author or title):*

Peter Abelard's Ethics, ed. with facing tr. D.E. Luscombe
    (Oxford, 1971).
Ancrene Wisse, Parts Six and Seven, ed. G. Shepherd
    (Manchester, 1972).
Aquinas Ethicus: A Translation of the Principal Portions
    of the Second Part of the Summa Theologica, J. Rickaby,
    2 vols (London, 1896).
The Works of Geoffrey Chaucer, ed. F.N. Robinson (2nd ed,
    London, 1957).
The Cloud of Unknowing, ed. P. Hodgson, E.E.T.S. O.S. 218
    (1944).
Dante: The Divine Comedy (Italian text with facing tr.),
    tr. J.D. Sinclair (Oxford, 1971).
———— *Convivio*, **ed.** G. Busnelli and G. Vandelli, 2 vols
    (Florence, 1964).
———— *Latin Works of Dante Alighieri Translated into*
    English, tr. P.H. Wicksteed (Temple Classics, London,
    1904).
The Poems of William Dunbar, ed. J. Kinsley (Oxford, 1979).
St. Erkenwald, ed. H.L. Savage (New Haven, Connecticut,
    1926).
The Works of Sir John Fortescue, collected and arranged
    T. (Fortescue) Lord Clermont, 2 vols (London, 1869).

Fortescue on the Governance of England, ed. C. Plummer
(Oxford, 1885).

Sir John Fortescue: De Laudibus Legum Anglie, ed. and
tr. S.B. Chrimes (Cambridge, 1942).

Sir Gawain and the Green Knight, ed. J.R.R. Tolkien and
E.V. Gordon (2nd ed, revised N. Davis, Oxford, 1967).

The Complete Works of John Gower, ed. G.C. Macaulay, 4
vols (Oxford, 1901).

*An Edition from the Manuscripts of Book II of Walter
Hilton's Scale of Perfection*, ed. S.S. Hussey (Ph.D.
thesis, University of London, 1962).

Hoccleve's Works: The Minor Poems, ed. F.J. Furnivall
and I. Gollancz, E.E.T.S. E.S. 61,73 (1892, 1897).
Regement of Princes, ed.F.J. Furnivall,E.E.T.S. E.S.
72 (1899).

Jack Upland, Friar Daw's Reply and Upland's Rejoinder,
ed. P.L. Heyworth (Oxford, 1968).

The Statesman's Book of John of Salisbury (the Fourth,
Fifth and Sixth Books, and Selections from the Seventh
and Eighth Books, of *The Policraticus*), tr. J. Dickinson (New York, 1927).

The Book of Margery Kempe, ed. S.B. Meech and H.E. Allen,
E.E.T.S. O.S. 212 (1939).

The Lay Folks' Catechism, ed. T.F. Simmons and H.E.
Nolloth, E.E.T.S. O.S. 118 (1901).

Minor Poems of John Lydgate, Part I, ed. H.N. MacCracken,
E.E.T.S. E.S. 107 (1911).

Medieval English Lyrics, ed. R.T. Davies (London, 1963).

Mirk's Festial, ed. T. Erbe, E.E.T.S. E.S. 96 (1905).

Mum and the Sothsegger, ed. M. Day and R. Steele, E.E.T.S.
O.S. 199 (1936).

Pearl, ed. E.V. Gordon (Oxford, 1953).

Juan Ruiz: Libro de Buen Amor, ed. with facing tr. R.S.
Willis (Princeton, New Jersey, 1972).

John Skelton: The Complete English Poems, ed.
J. Scattergood (Harmondsworth, 1983).

Spenser: Poetical Works, ed. J.C. Smith and E. de
Selincourt (Oxford, 1912).

Three Medieval Rhetorical Arts, ed. J.J. Murphy (Berkeley,
Los Angeles, 1971).

Twenty-six Political and Other Poems, ed. J.Kail, E.E.T.S.
O.S. 124 (1904).

The Wakefield Pageants in the Towneley Cycle, ed. A.C.
Cawley (Manchester, 1958).

Winner and Waster, ed. I. Gollancz (Oxford, 1921;
reissued Cambridge, 1974).

C   STUDIES:

D. Aers, *Chaucer, Langland, and the Creative Imagination*
(London, 1980).

T. Aston, *Social Relations and Ideas: Essays in Honour of*
R.H. Hilton (Cambridge, 1983).

A. Baldwin, *The Theme of Government in Piers Plowman*
(Cambridge, 1981).

J.W. Baldwin, *Masters, Princes, and Merchants: The Social*
Views of Peter the Chanter and his Circle, 2 vols
(Princeton, New Jersey, 1970).

N.F. Blake, *The English Language in Medieval Literature*
(London, 1977).

M.W. Bloomfield, *Piers Plowman as a Fourteenth-Century*
Apocalypse (New Brunswick, New Jersey, 1961).

W.F. Bolton, *Alcuin and Beowulf* (London, 1979).

D.S. Brewer, *Chaucer in his Time* (London, 1963).

C. Bullock-Davies, *Menstrellorum Multitudo* (Cardiff, 1978).

G.G. Coulton, *Medieval Panorama* (Cambridge, 1938).

E.T. Donaldson, *Piers Plowman: The C Text and its Poet*
(New Haven, Connecticut, 1949).

T.P. Dunning, *Piers Plowman: An Interpretation of the*
A Text (Dublin, 1937).

R.W. Frank, *Piers Plowman and the Scheme of Salvation*
(New Haven, Connecticut, 1957).

R.D. French, *A Chaucer Handbook* (2nd ed, New York, 1955).

M.E. Goldsmith, *The Figure of Piers Plowman* (Cambridge,
1981).

E.H. Gombrich, *Art and Illusion* (London, 1960).

P.L. Heyworth, ed. *Medieval Studies for J.A.W. Bennett*
(Oxford, 1981).

S.S. Hussey, ed. *Piers Plowman: Critical Approaches*
(London, 1969).

E. Jenks, *A Short History of English Law* (5th ed, London,
1938).

P.M. Kean, *The Pearl: An Interpretation* (London, 1967).

A. Keiser, *The Influence of Christianity on Old English*
Poetry (University of Illinois Studies in Language and
Literature, V, 1919).

A.K.R. Kiralfy, *Potter's Outlines of English Legal*
History (5th ed, London, 1958).

D. Lawton, ed. *Middle English Alliterative Poetry and its*
Background (Cambridge, 1982).

J. Leclercq, *The Love of Learning and the Desire for God*,
tr. C. Misrahi (New York, 1961).

B.S. Levy and P.E. Szarmach, edd. *The Alliterative Trad-*
ition in the Fourteenth Century (Kent, Ohio, 1981).

A.J. Minnis, *Chaucer and Pagan Antiquity* (Cambridge;
Totowa, New Jersey, 1982).

G. O'Brien, *Medieval Economic Teaching* (London, 1920).

G.R. Owst, *Literature and Pulpit in Medieval England* (Cambridge, 1933).

I.A. Richards, *The Philosophy of Rhetoric* (London, 1936).

D.W. Robertson, *Chaucer's London* (New York, 1968).

V.J. Scattergood, *Politics and Poetry in the Fifteenth Century* (London, 1971).

G. Schiffhorst, ed. *The Triumph of Patience* (Orlando, Florida, 1978).

F.M. Stenton, *Anglo-Saxon England* (Oxford, 1943).

S. Wenzel, *The Sin of Sloth: Acedia in Medieval Thought and Literature* (Chapel Hill, North Carolina, 1967).

J.A. Yunck, *The Lineage of Lady Meed: The Development of Medieval Venality Sarire* (Notre Dame, 1963).

Articles:

J.A. Burrow, 'The Action of Langland's Second Vision', *Essays in Criticism* XV (1965), 247-68.

B. Gilbert,''Civil' and the Notaries in *Piers Plowman*', *Medium Aevum* l (1981), 49-63.

P.M. Kean, 'Love, Law, and *Lewte* in *Piers Plowman*', *RES* n.s. xv (1964), 241-61.

R. Kirk, 'References to the Law in *Piers Plowman*', *PMLA* lxviii (1933), 322-7.

G. Mathew, 'Justice and Charity in The Vision of Piers the Plowman', *Dominican Studies* i (1948), 360-6.

A.J. Minnis, 'Langland's Ymaginatif and Late-Medieval Theories of Imagination', *Comparative Criticism: A Year Book* iii (1981), 71-103.

D.R. Pichaske and L. Sweetland, 'Chaucer and the Medieval Monarchy: Harry Bailey in the *Canterbury Tales*', *Chaucer Review* xi (1976-7), 179-200.